15 14 13 12 11 10 09 08   8 7 6 5 4 3 2 1

Coloring Book For All Ages
150 Drawings of Relaxing Inspiration
Original designs by Reverend Bonnie McPhail
Copyright © 2018

Bonnie McPhail

Creatspace Publishers

1

Dear Friends,

This beautifully illustrated coloring book includes 150 drawings of original designs including butterflies, dragonflies, cats, mice and beautiful floral and woodland designs. It will take you into a magical world for hours and hours of relaxation and enjoyment. Some of the designs include uplifting scripture verses to bring life, hope, and encouragement. These are all original drawings and my hope is that they will be a fun adventure as you work on them. You will find some of them very detailed and will provide hours' worth of enjoyment and others that are simple and take only a few minutes. There is something for everyone! Blessings to all!

From my heart to yours…

Pastor Bonnie

Coloring Book For All Ages

150 Drawings of Relaxing Inspiration

By

Reverend Bonnie McPhail

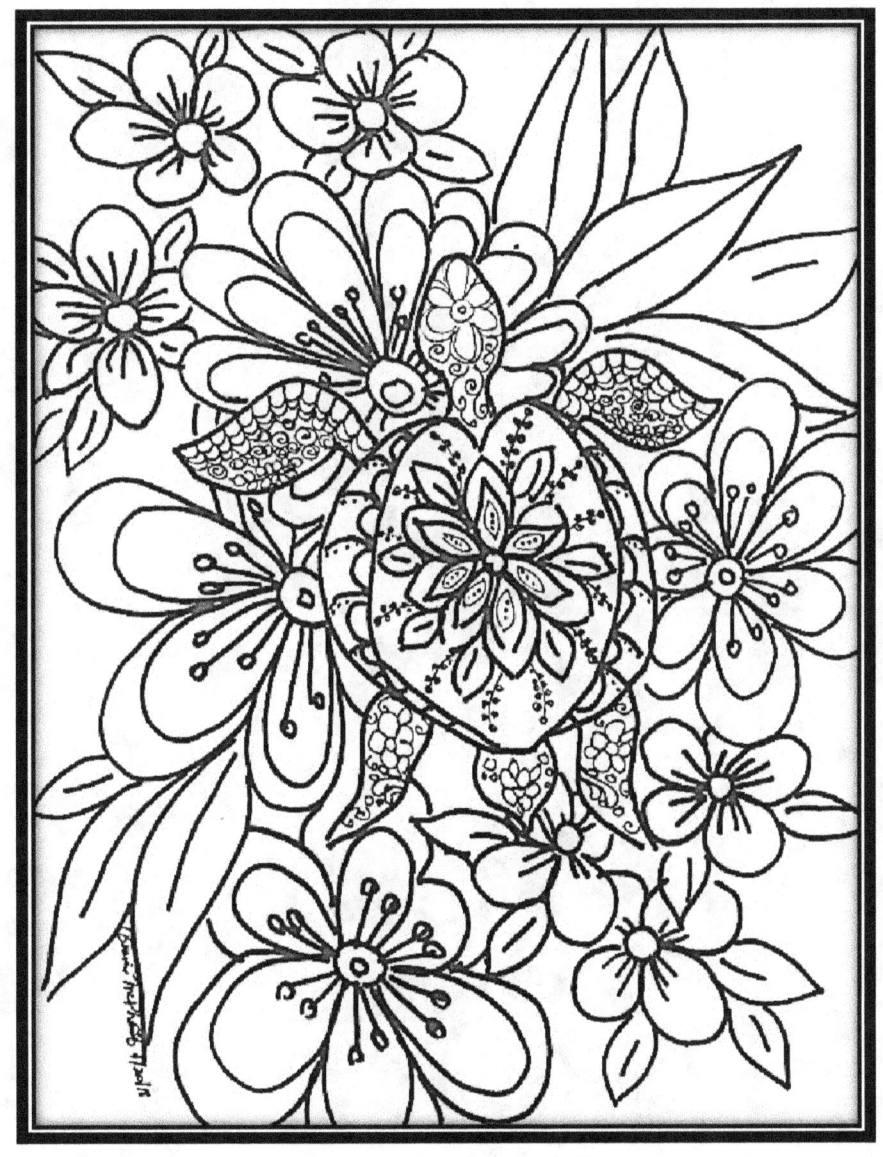

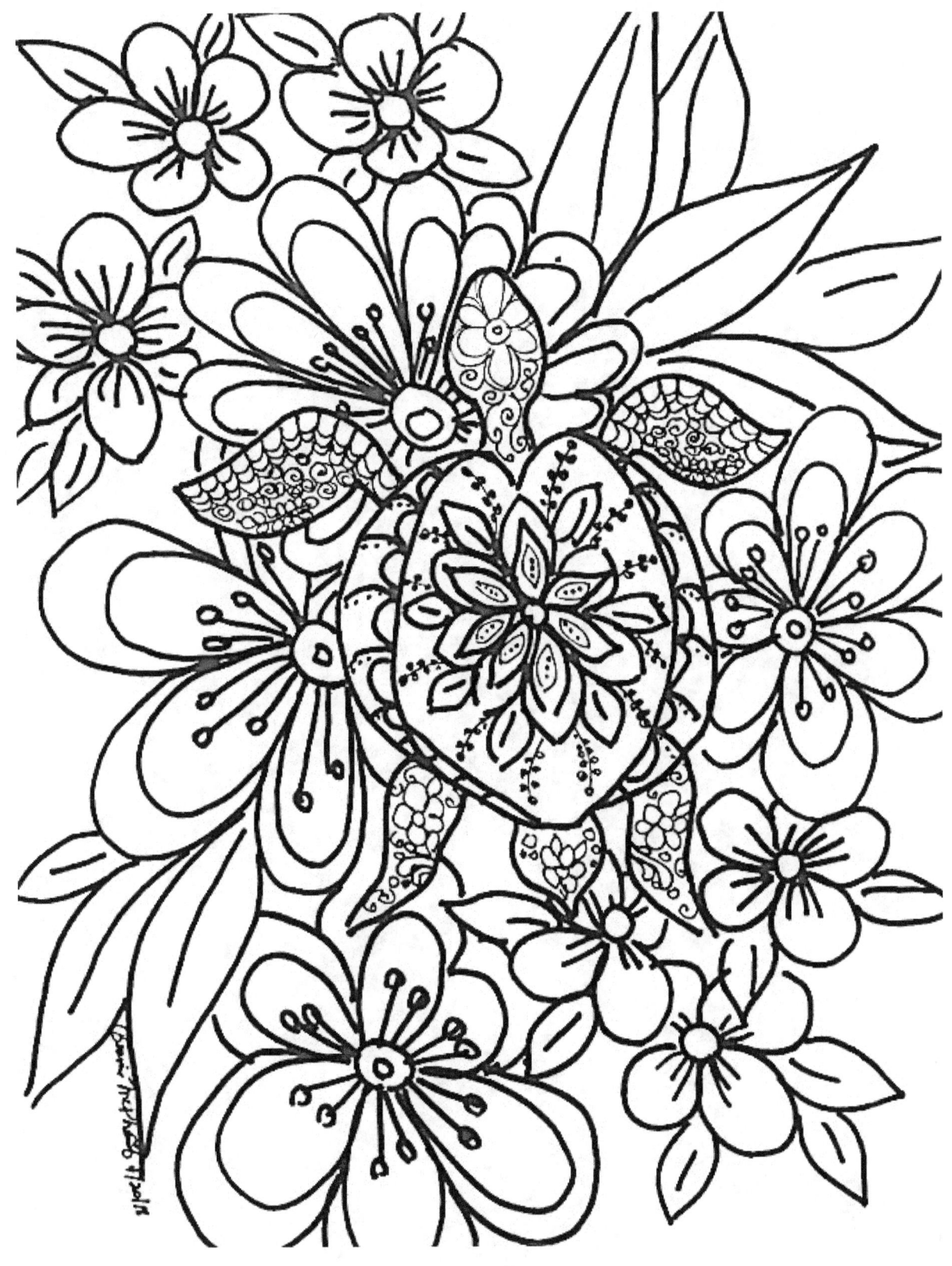

"For I can do everything through Christ, who gives me strength."
Philipians 4:13

8

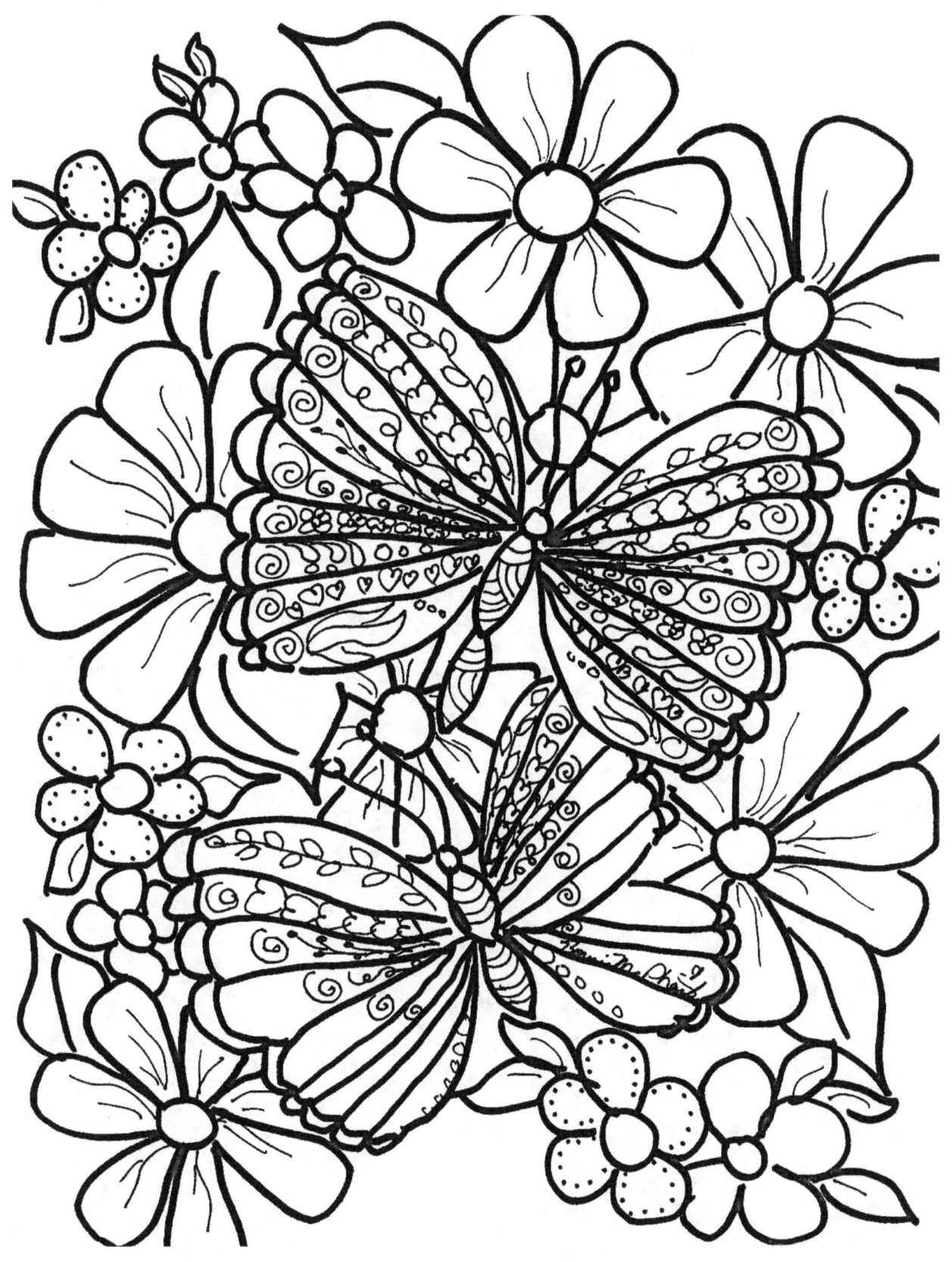

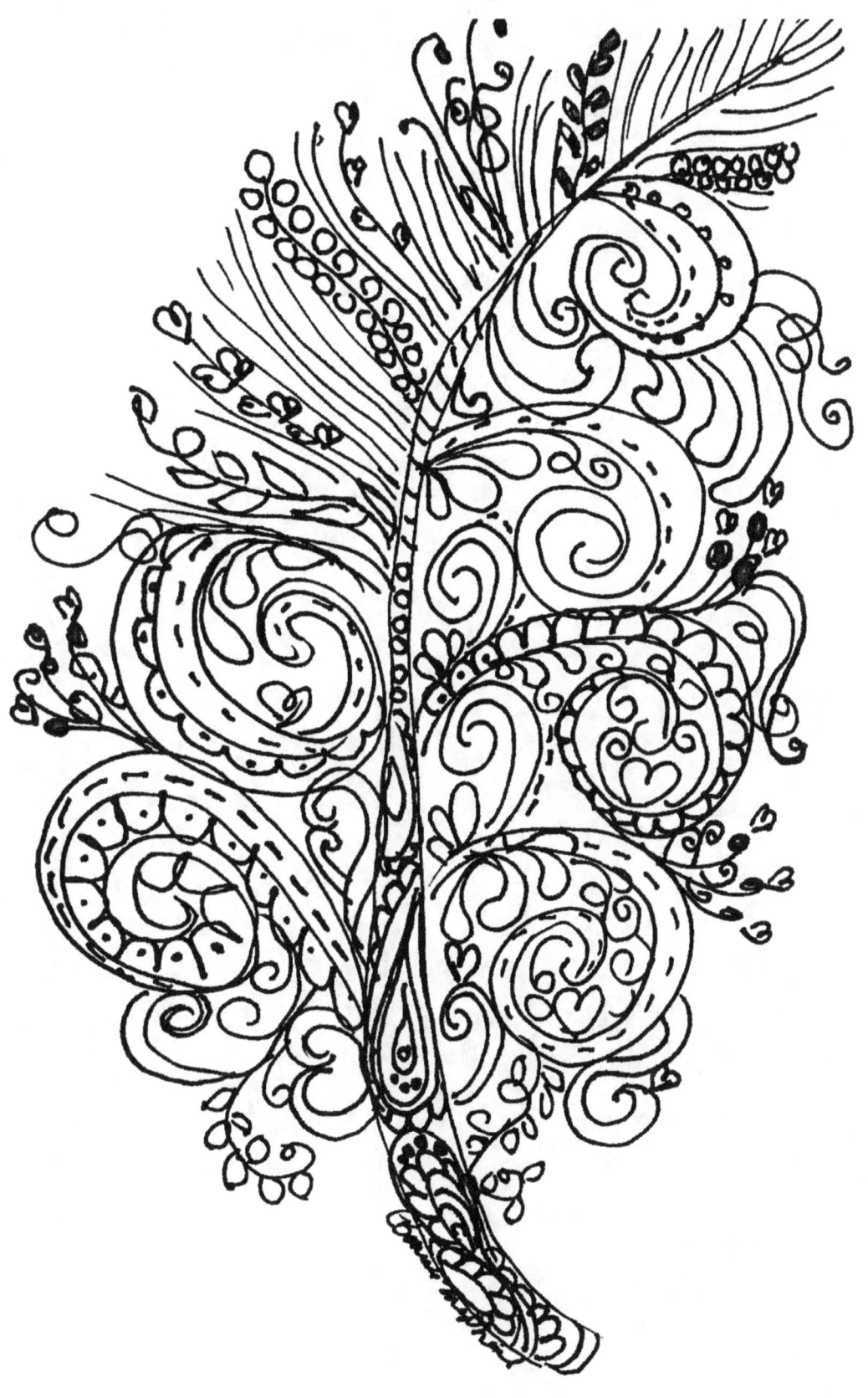

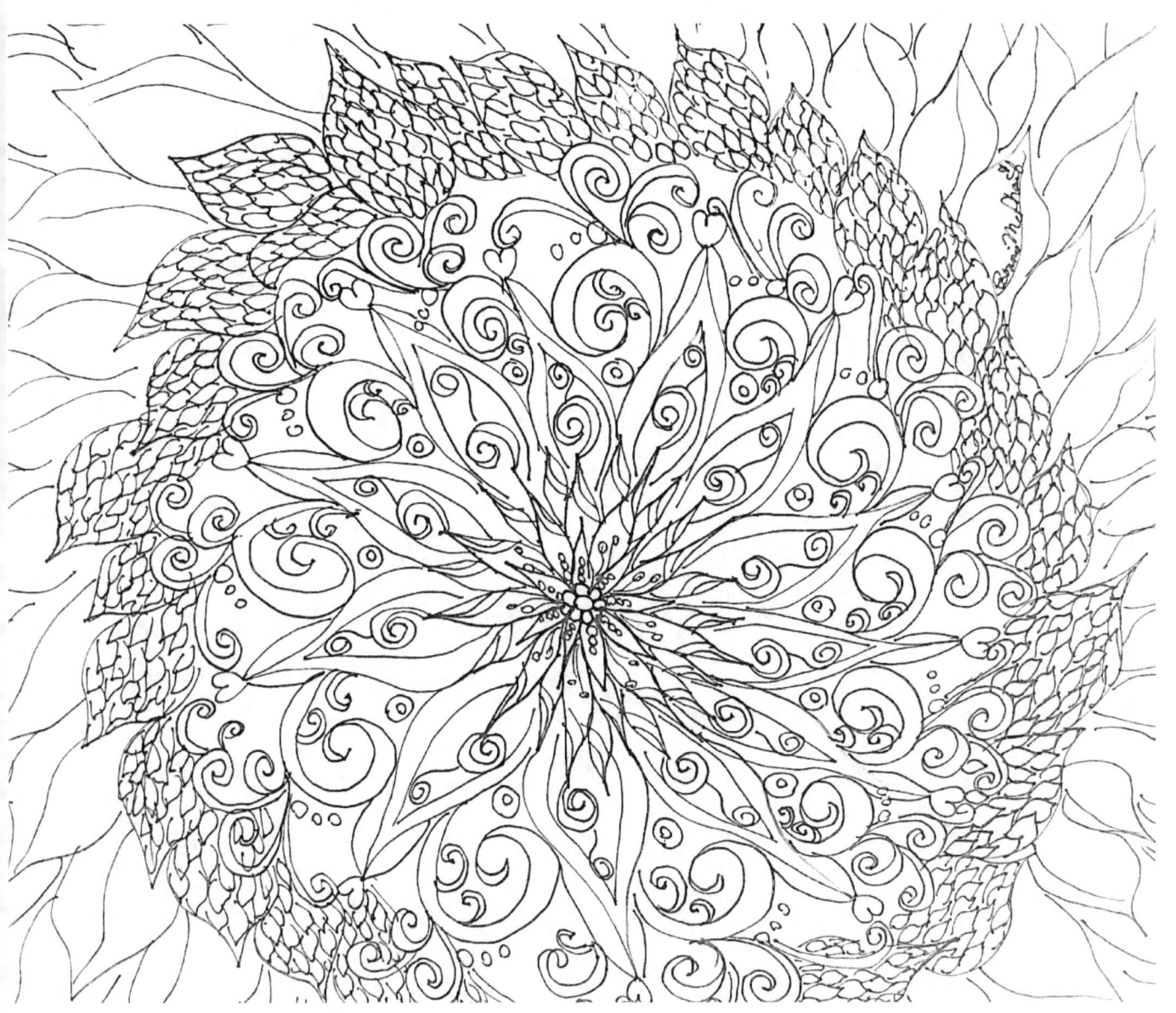

"Finally brothers and sisters, whatever is true, whatever is noble, whatever is right, whatever is pure, whatever is lovely, whatever is admirable-if anything is excellent or praiseworthy-think about such things." Philippians 4:8

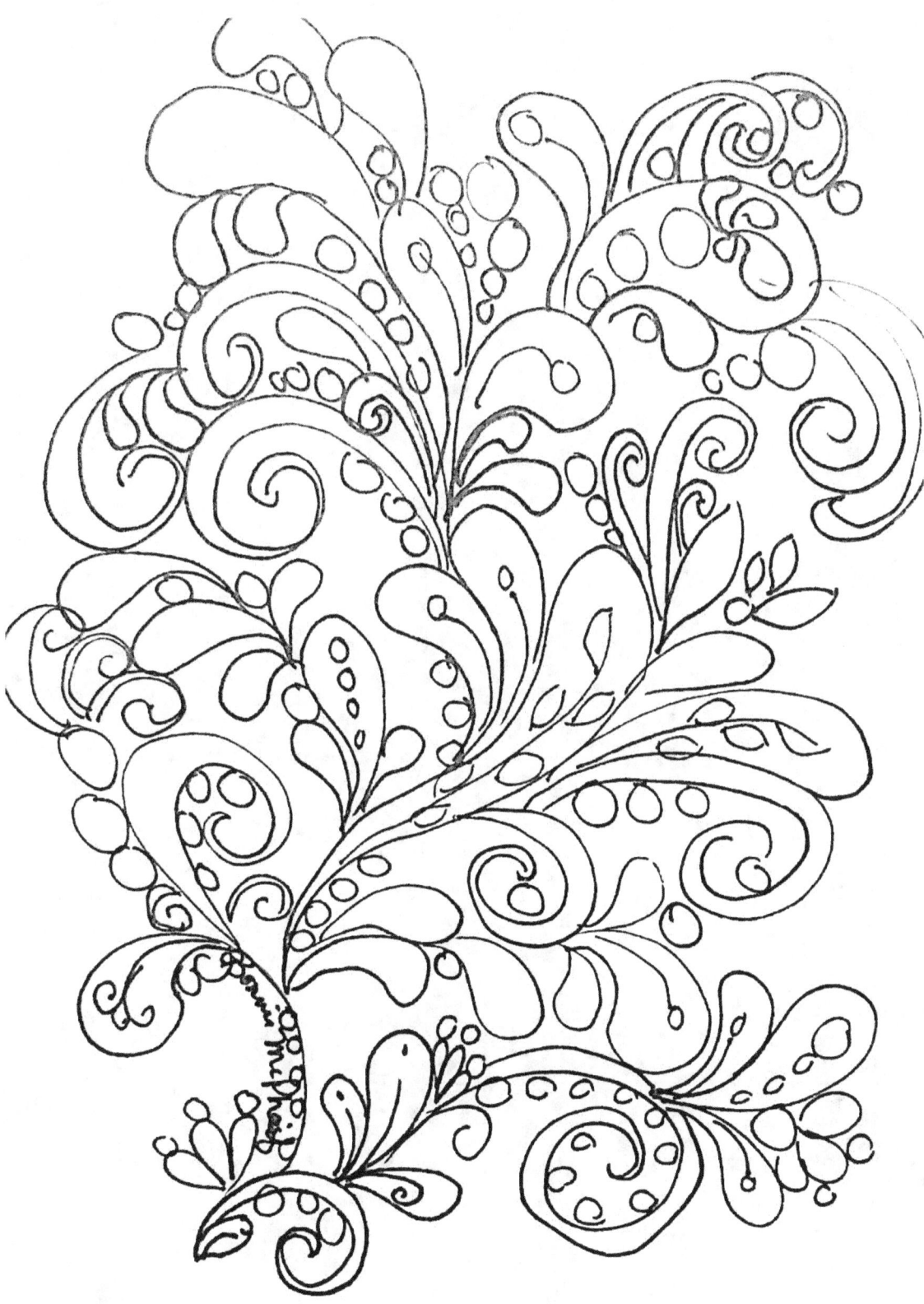

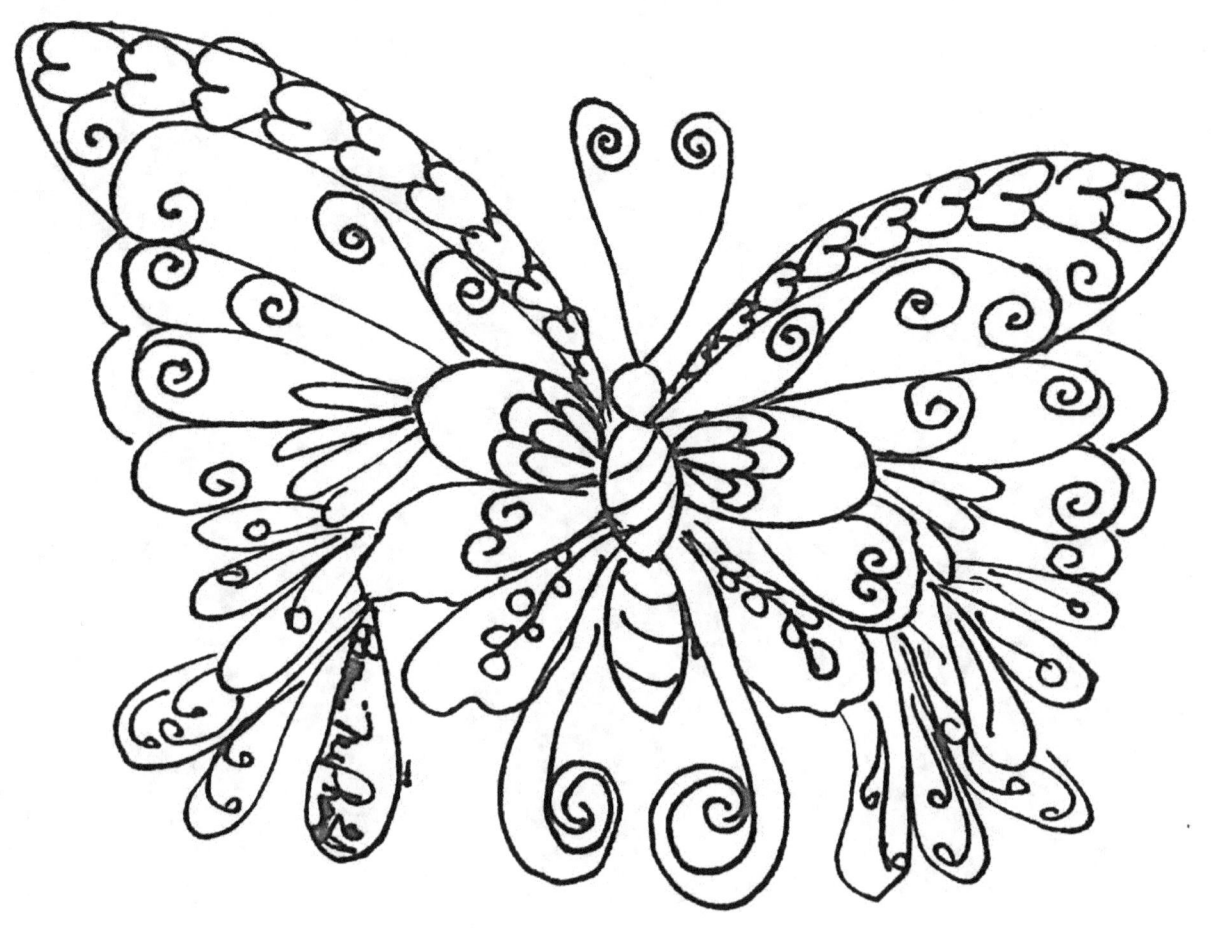

"Come to me, all you who are weary and burdened,

and I will give you rest." Matthew 11:28

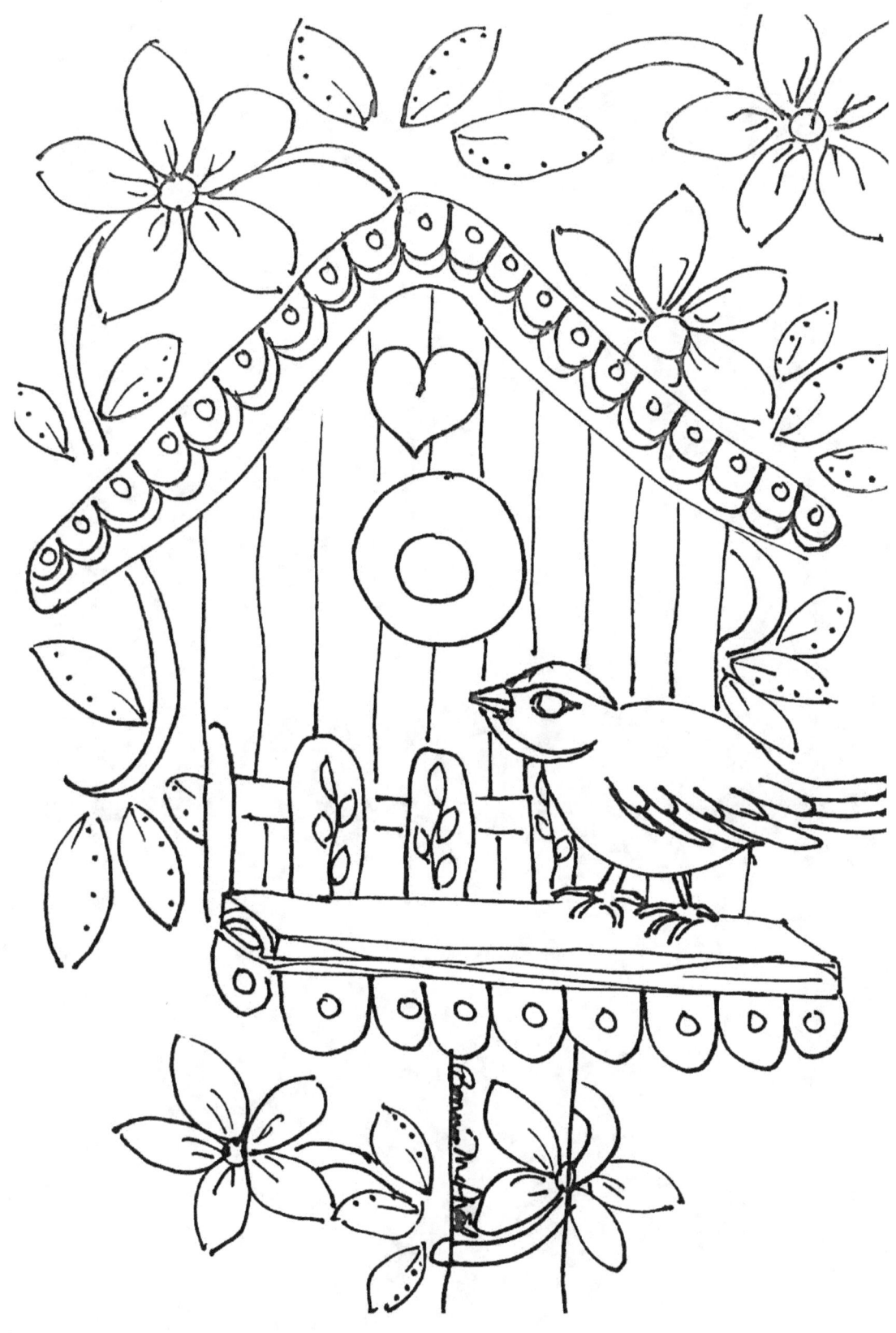

20 20

20

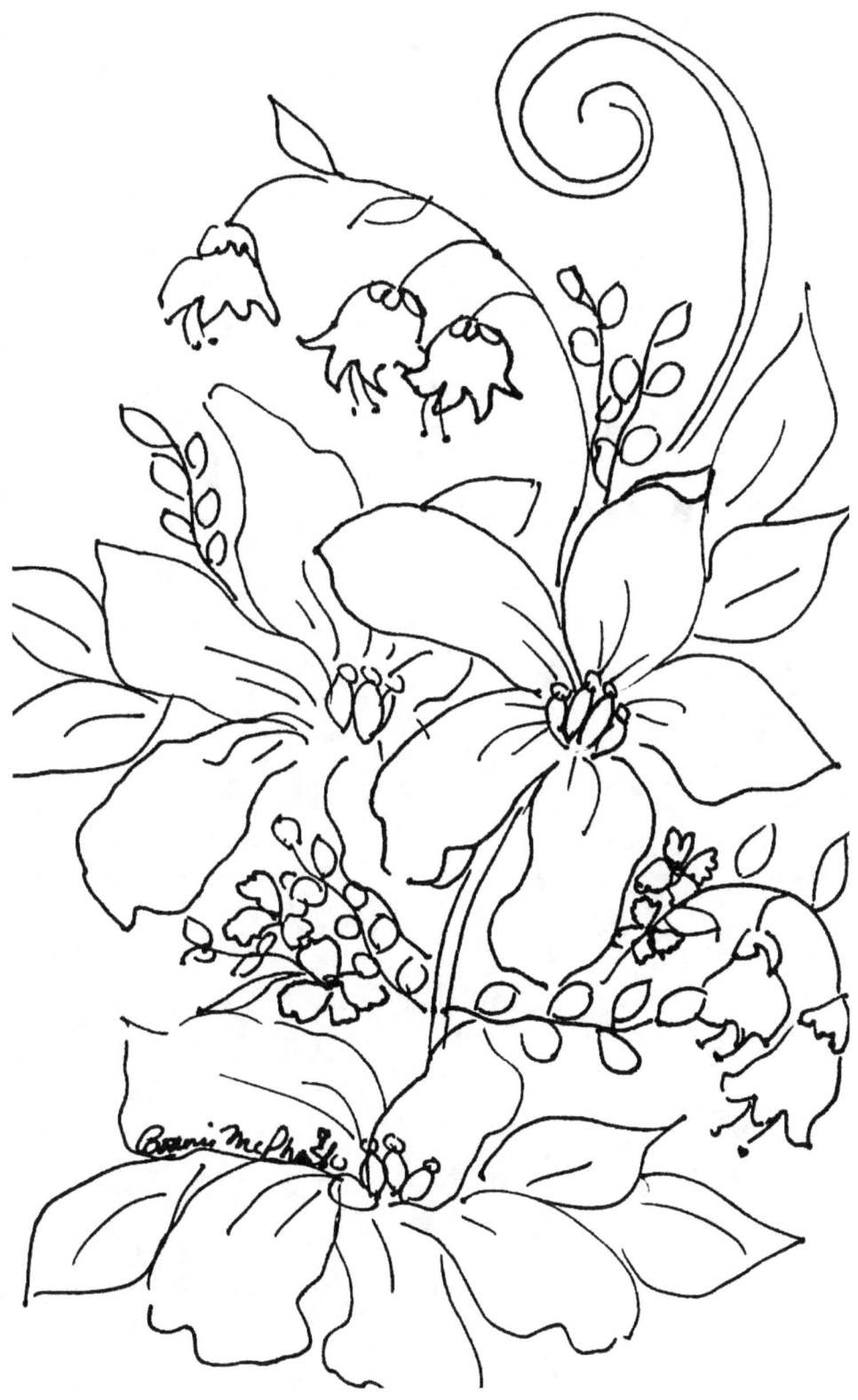

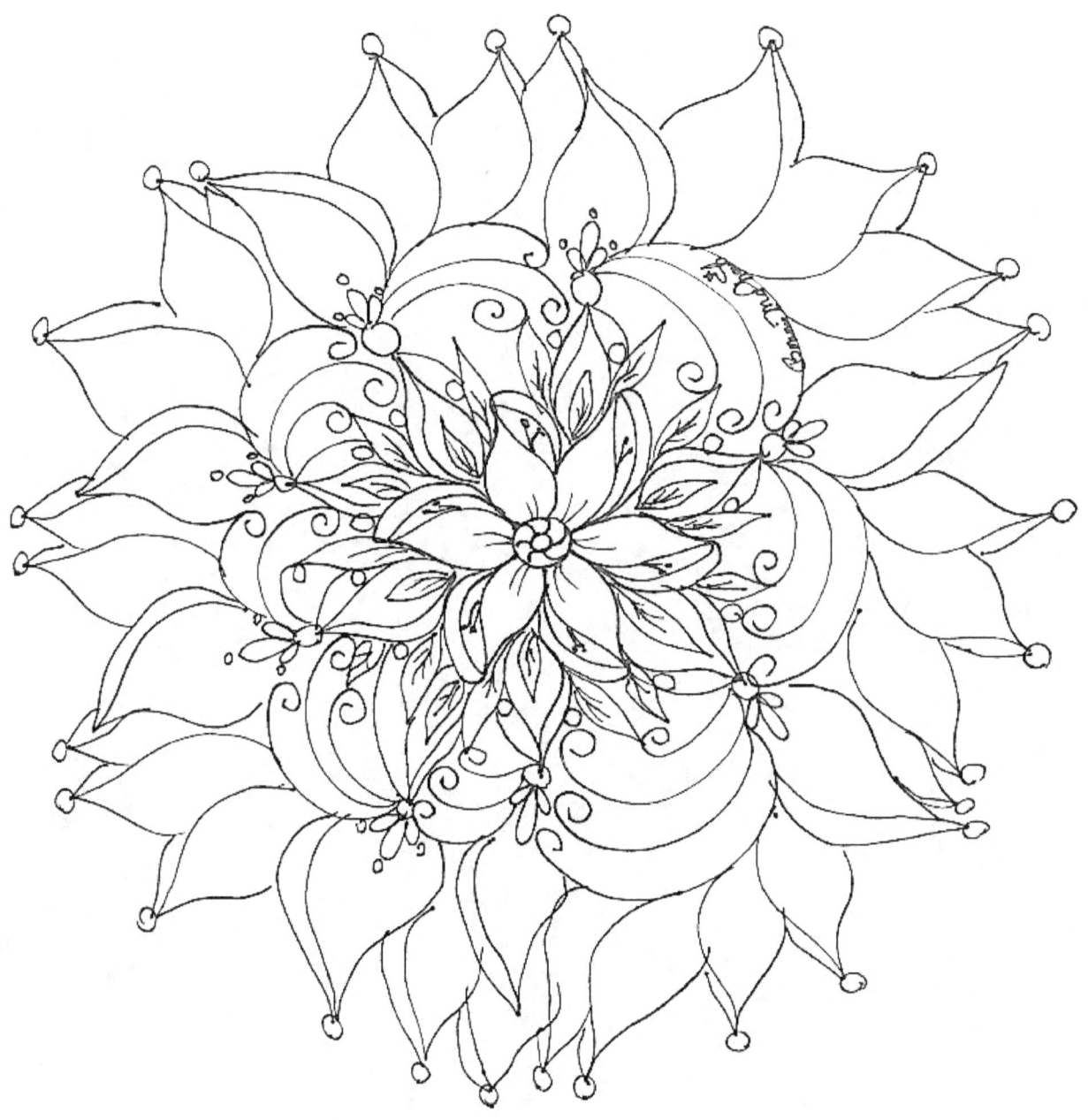

"Therefore, if anyone is in Christ, the new creation has come: The old has gone, the new is here!" 2 Corinthians 5:17

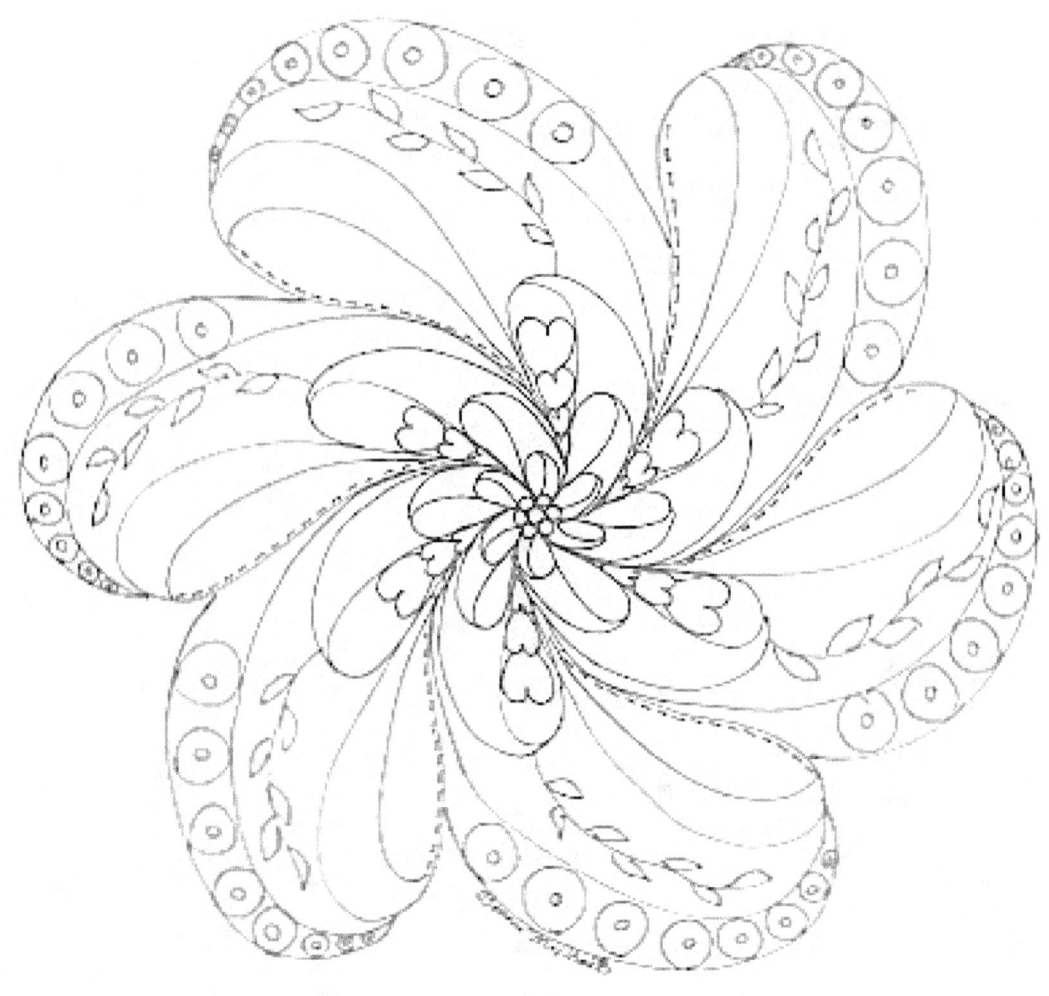

"The thief comes only to steal and kill and destroy; I have come that they may have life, and have it to the full." John 10:10

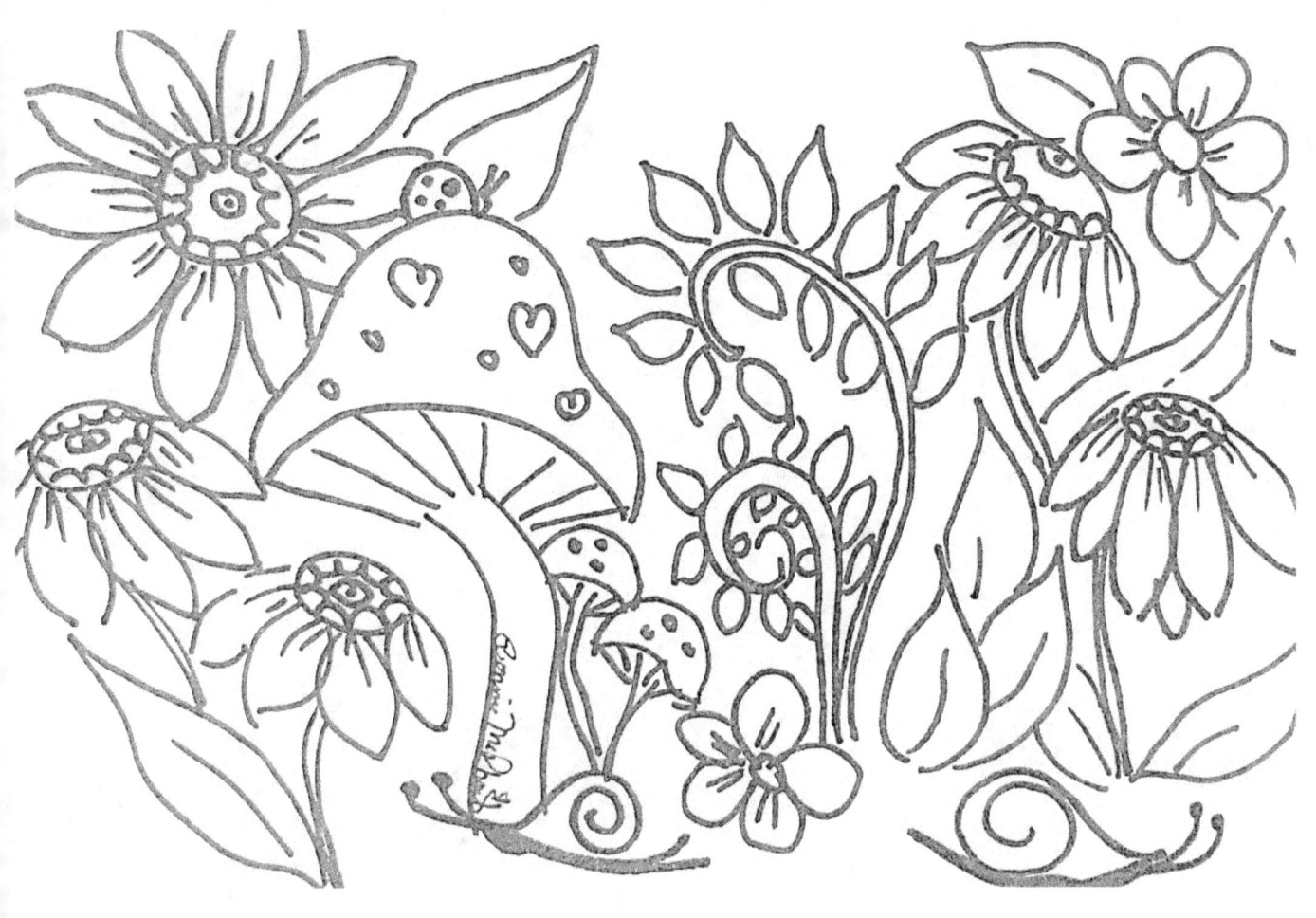

"No tempation has overtaken you except what is common to mankind. And God is faithful; he will not let you be tempted beyond what you can bear. But when you are tempted, he will also provide a way out so that you can endure it." 1 Corinthians 10:13

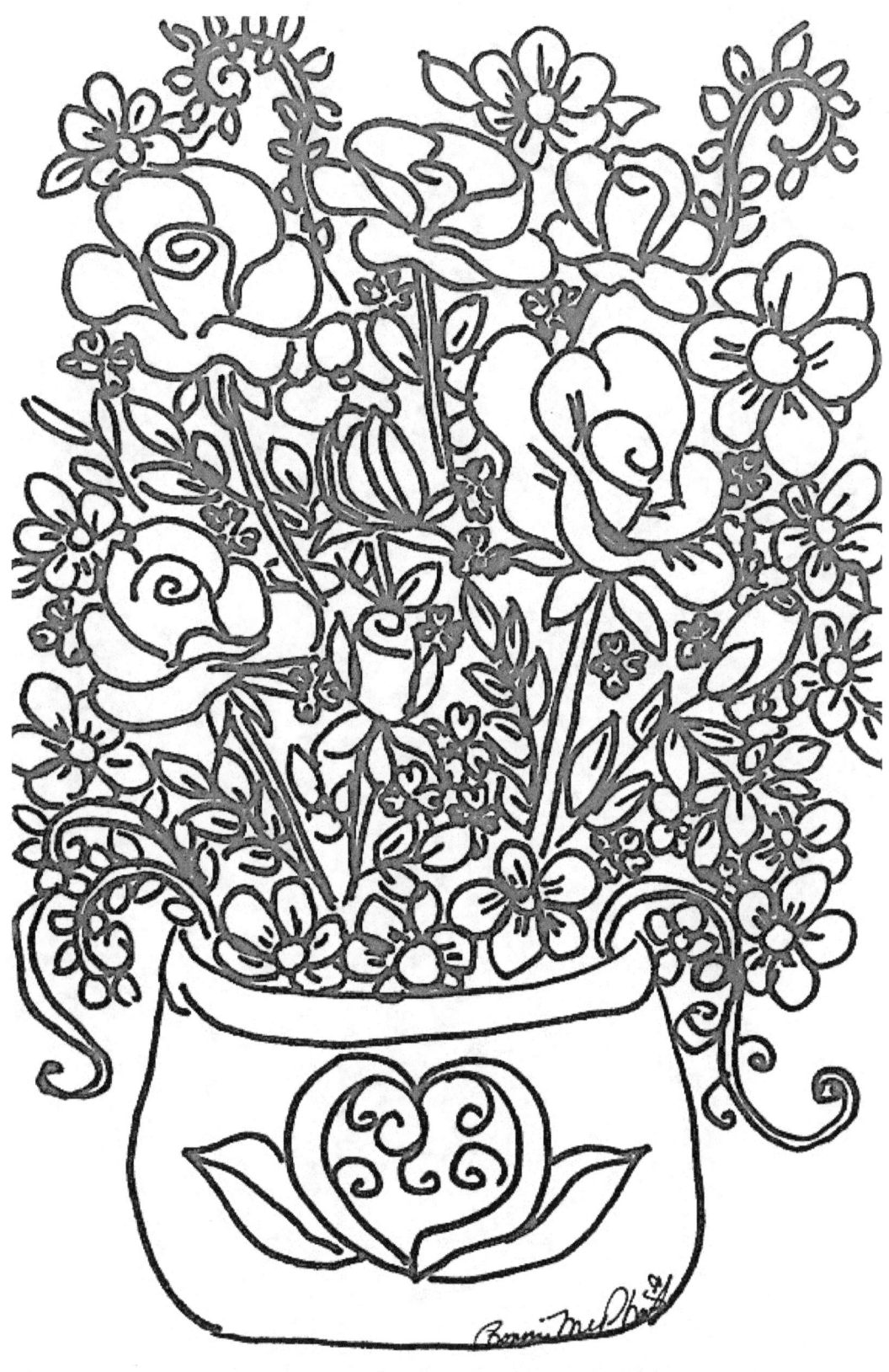

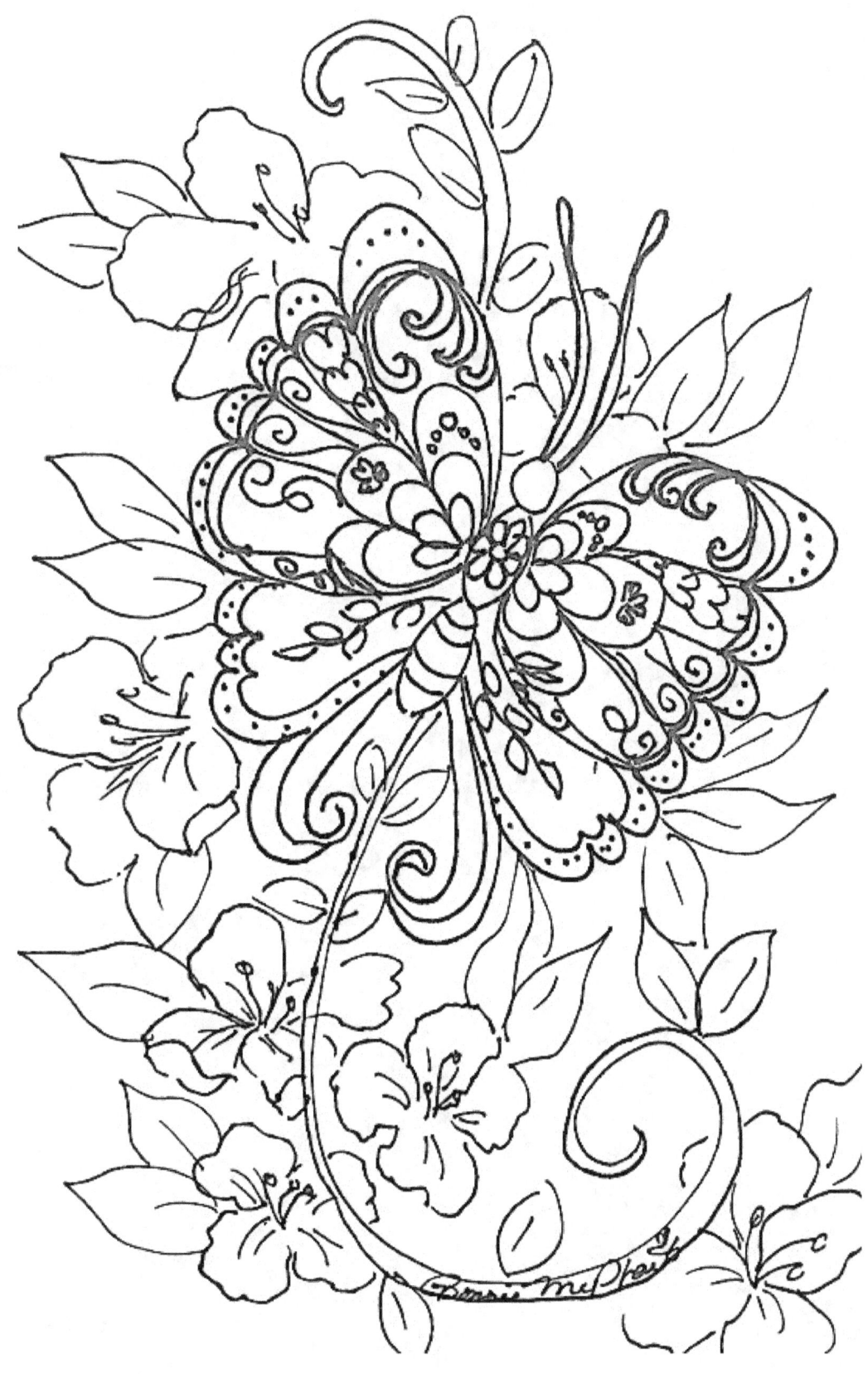

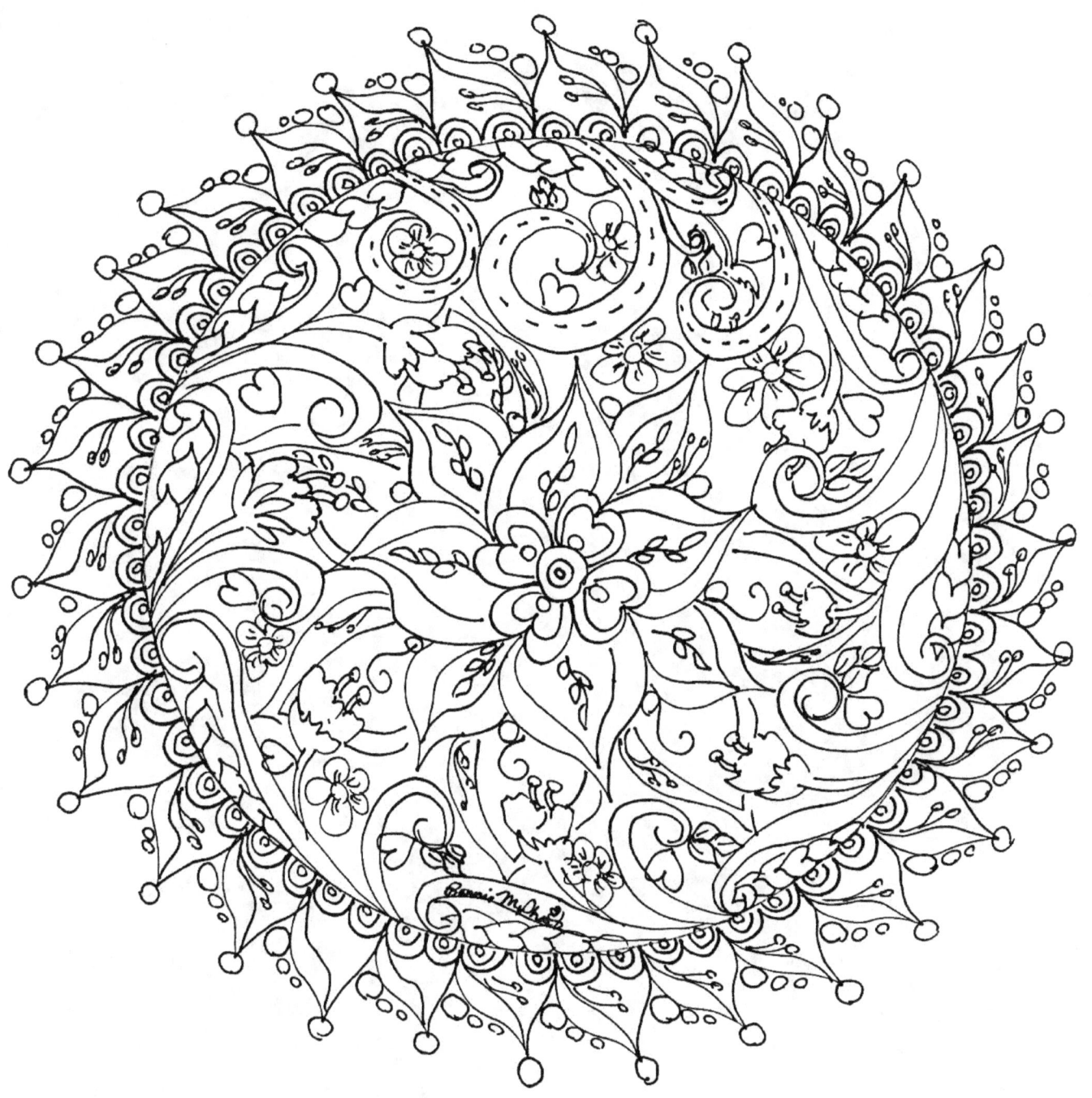

"For the Spirit of God gave does not make us timid, but gives us power, love and self-discipline."

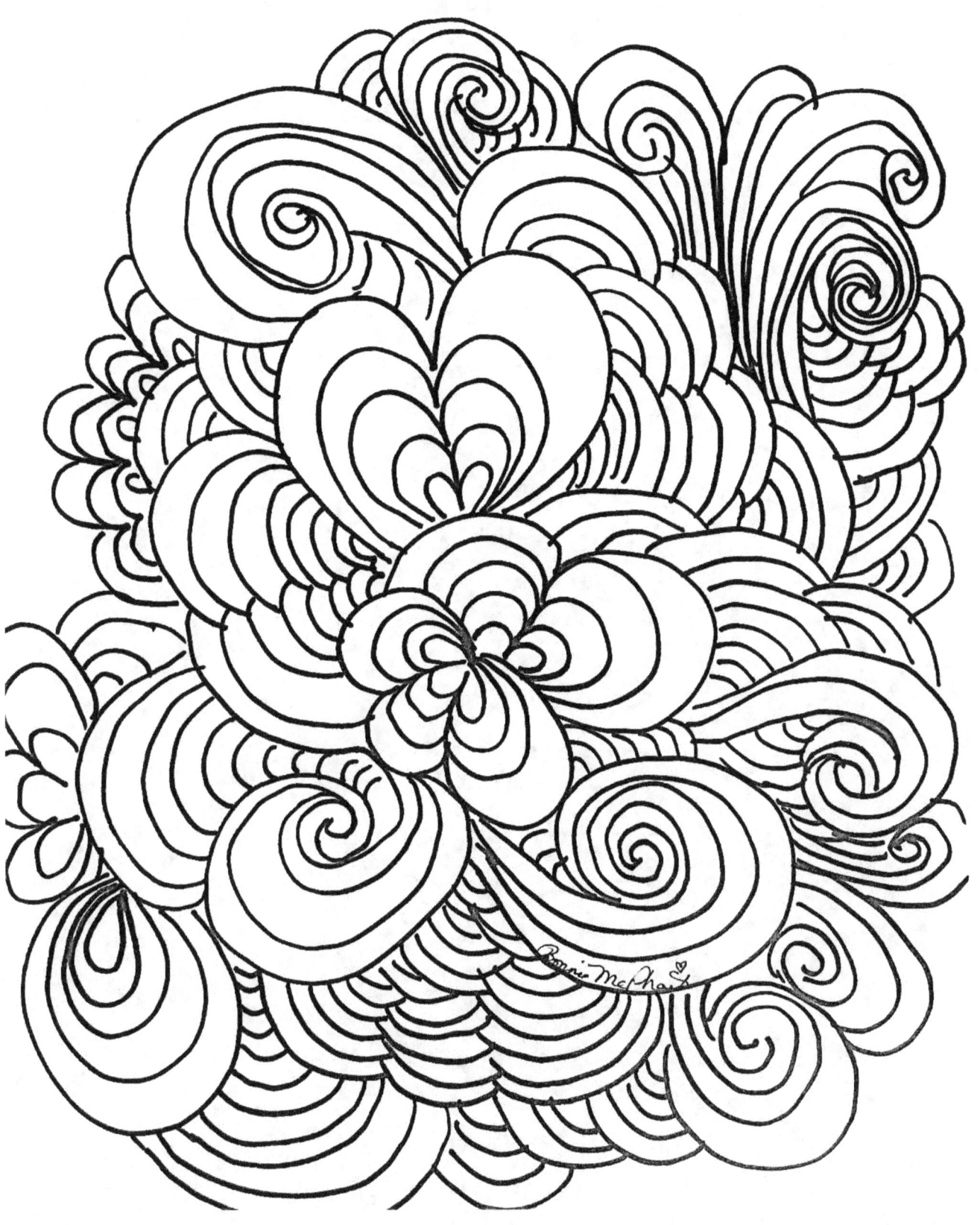

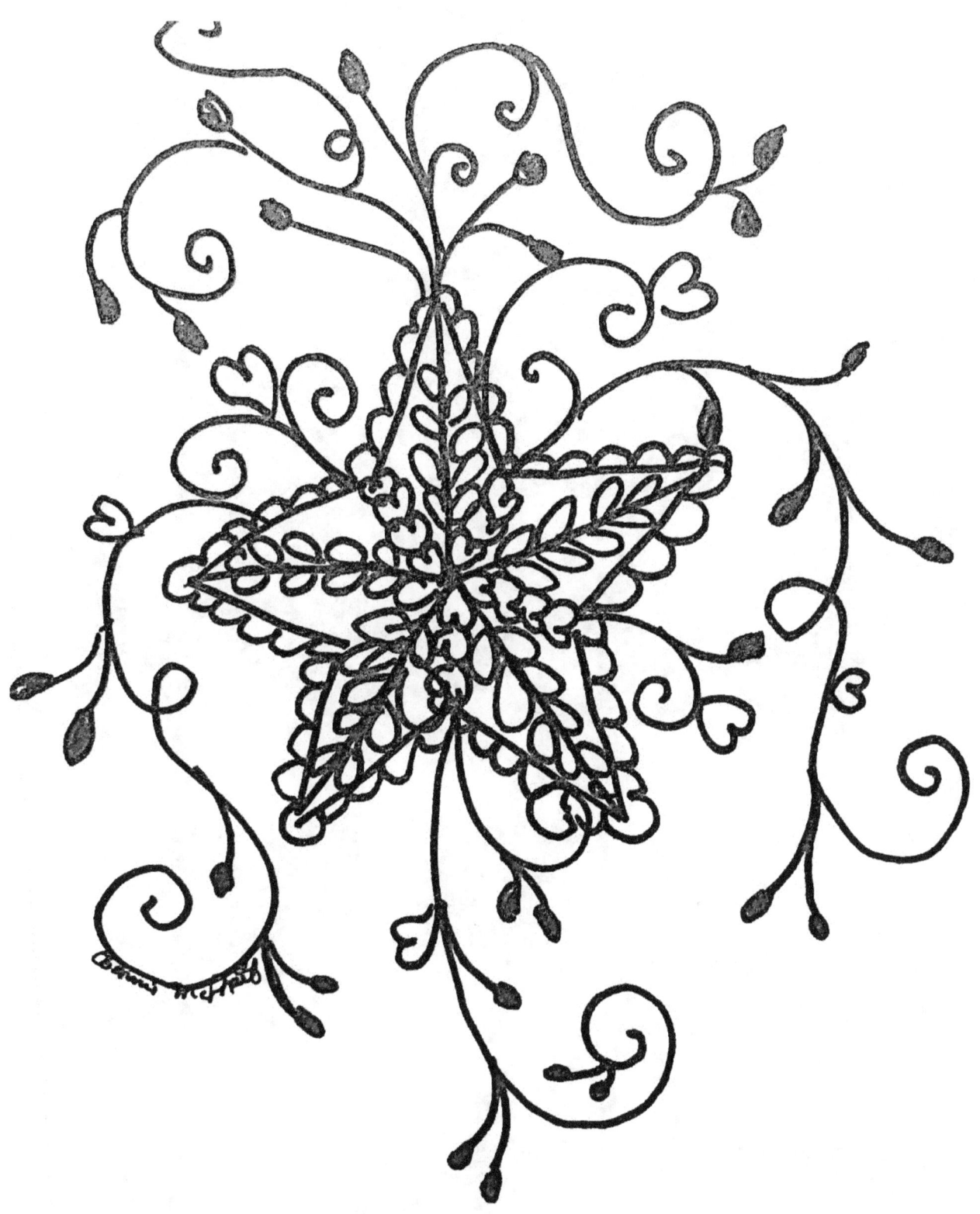

39

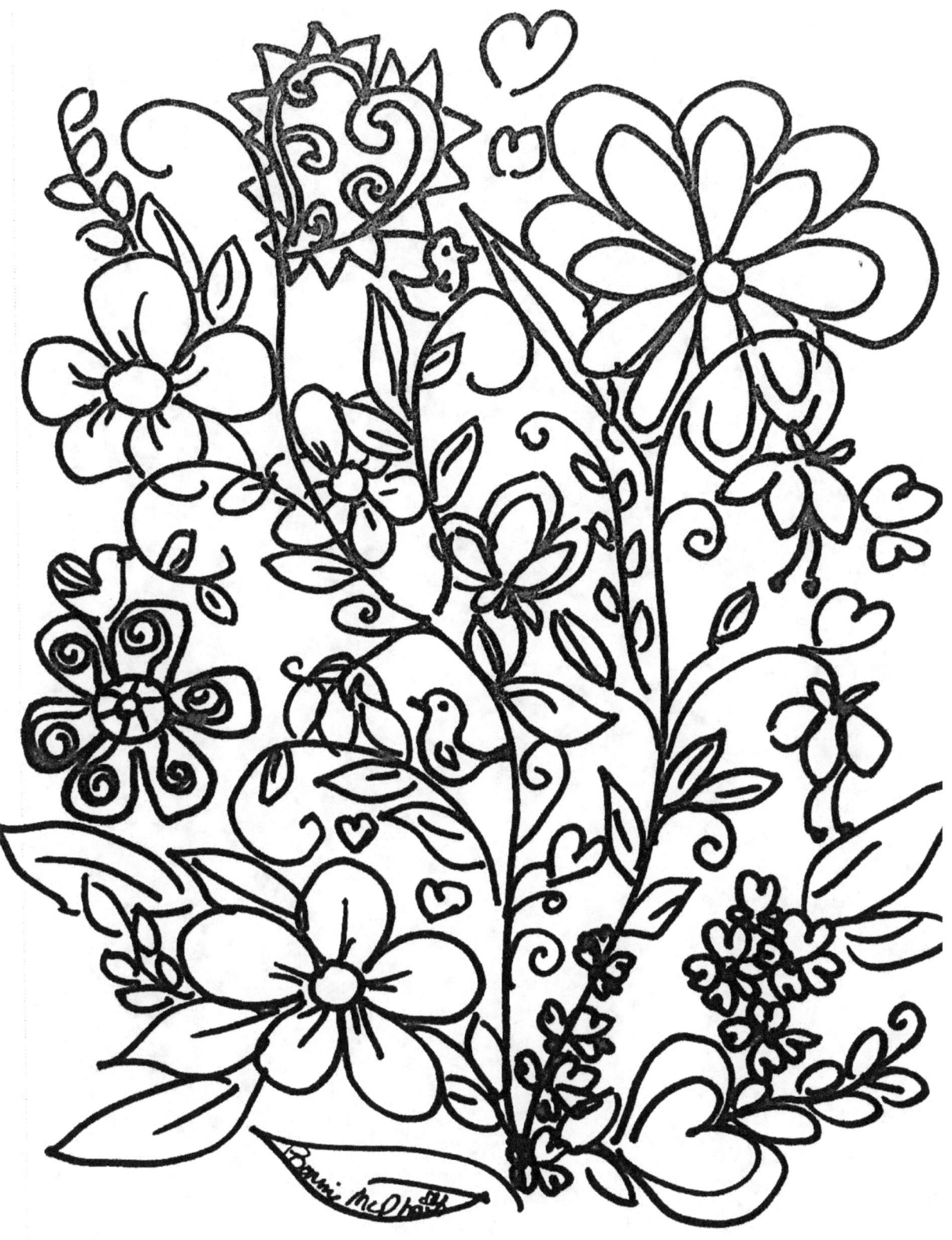

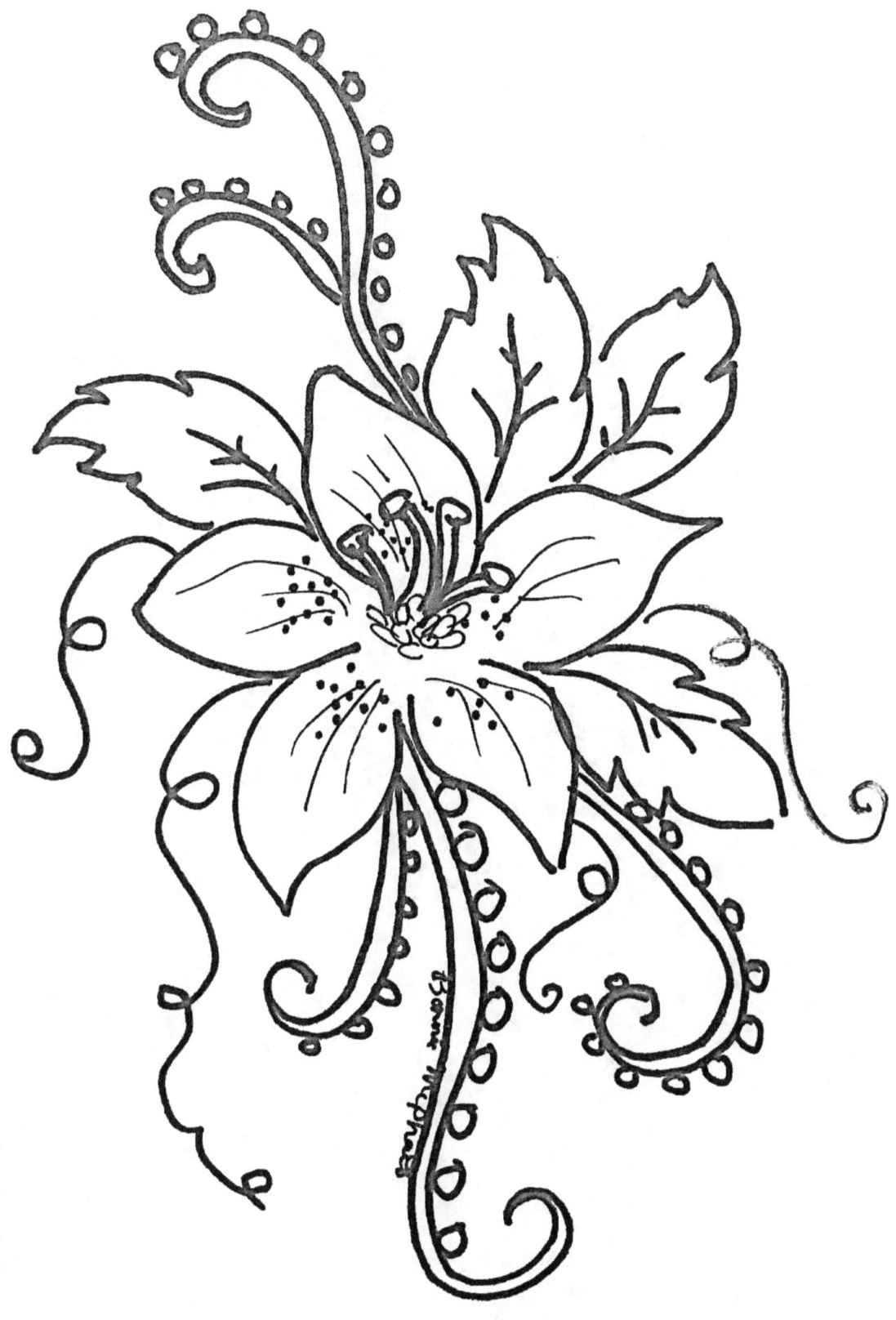

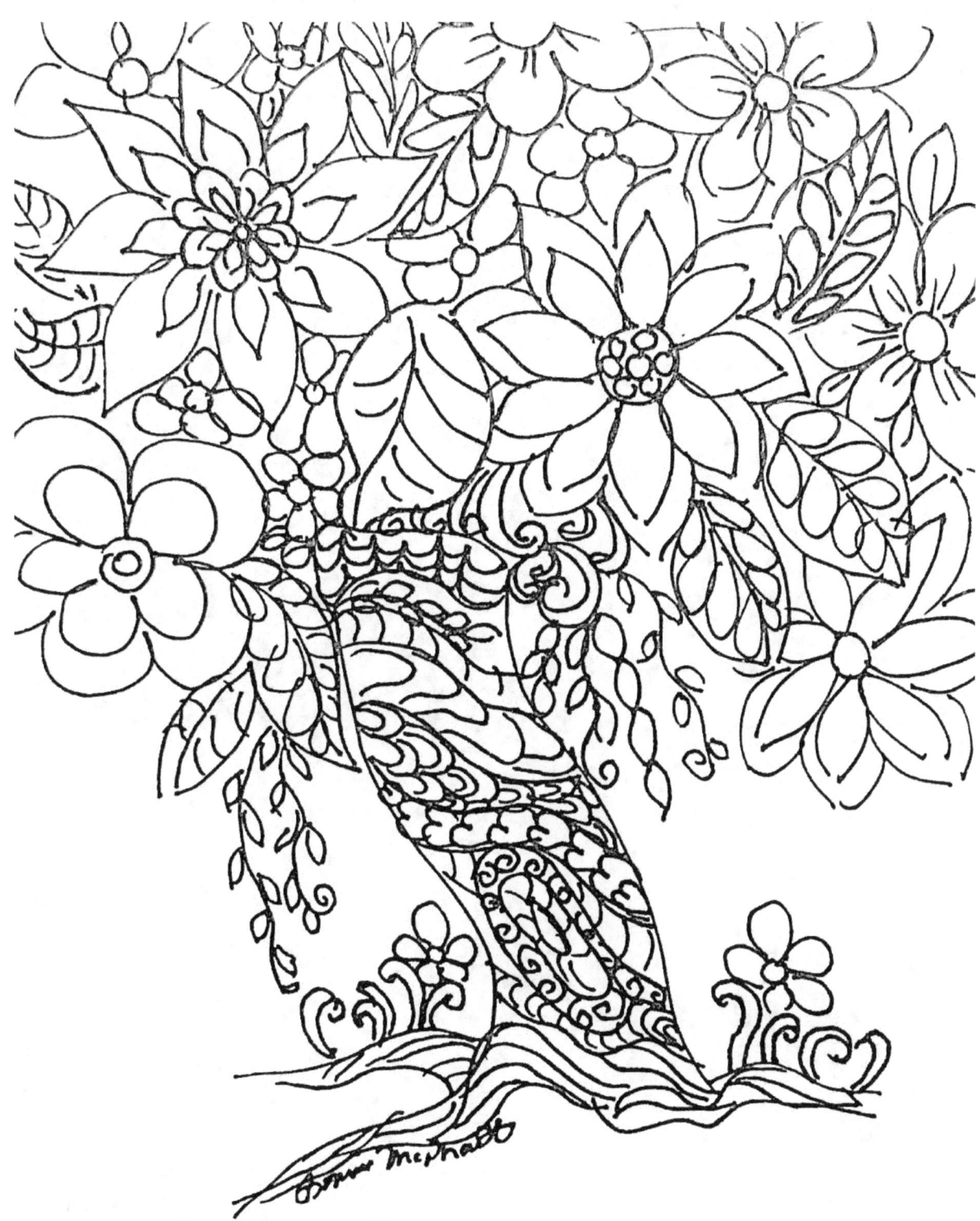

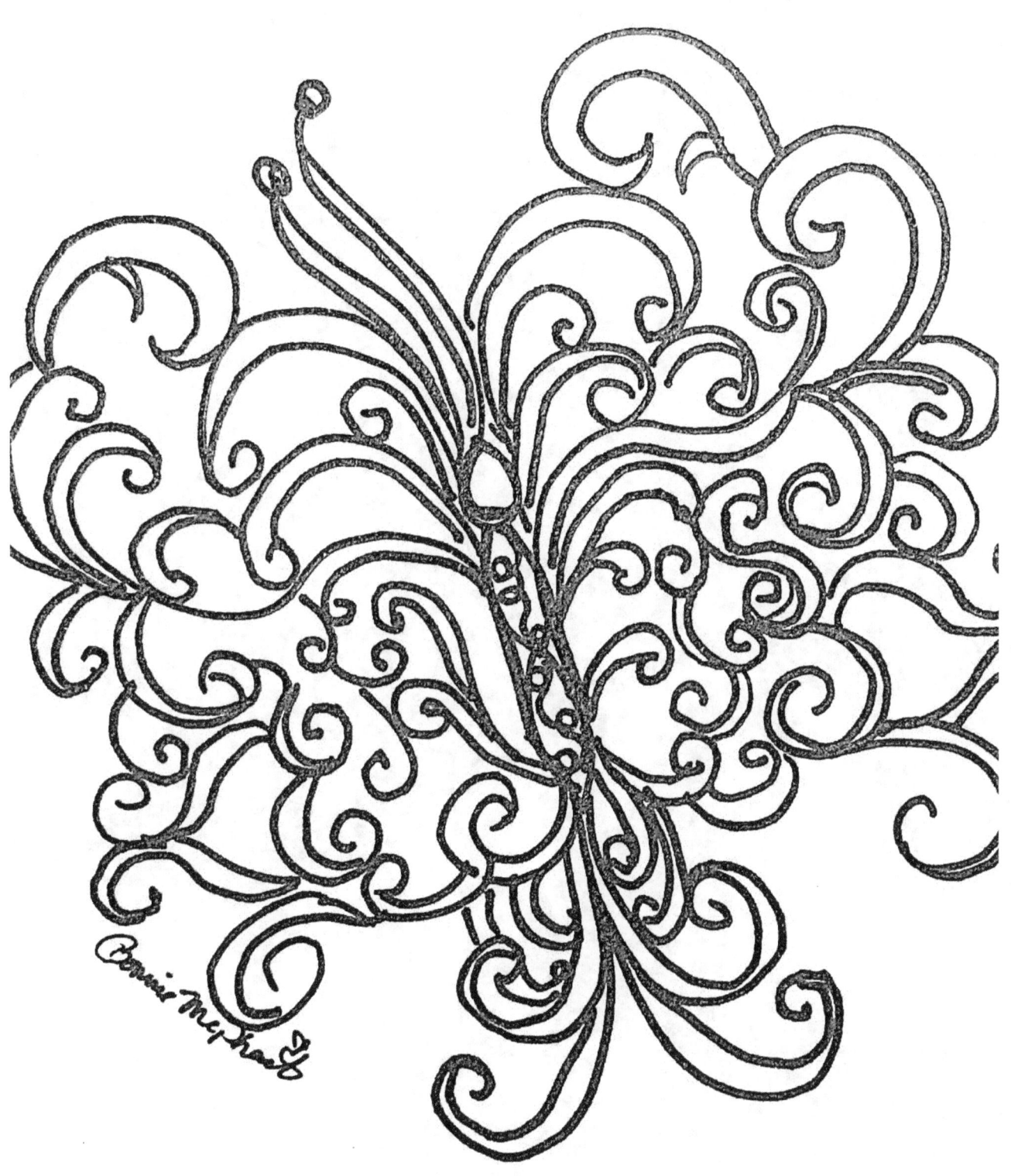

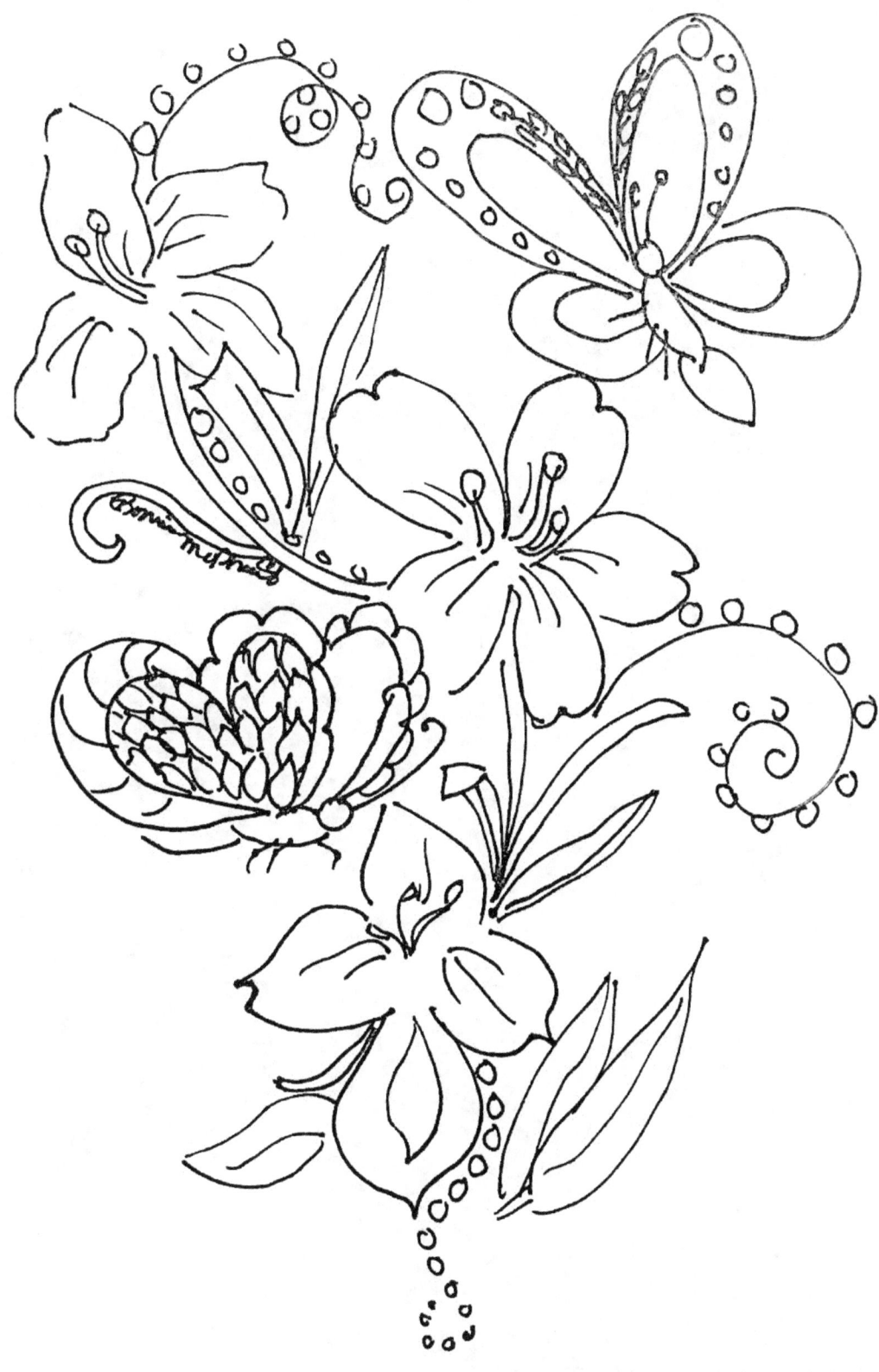

49

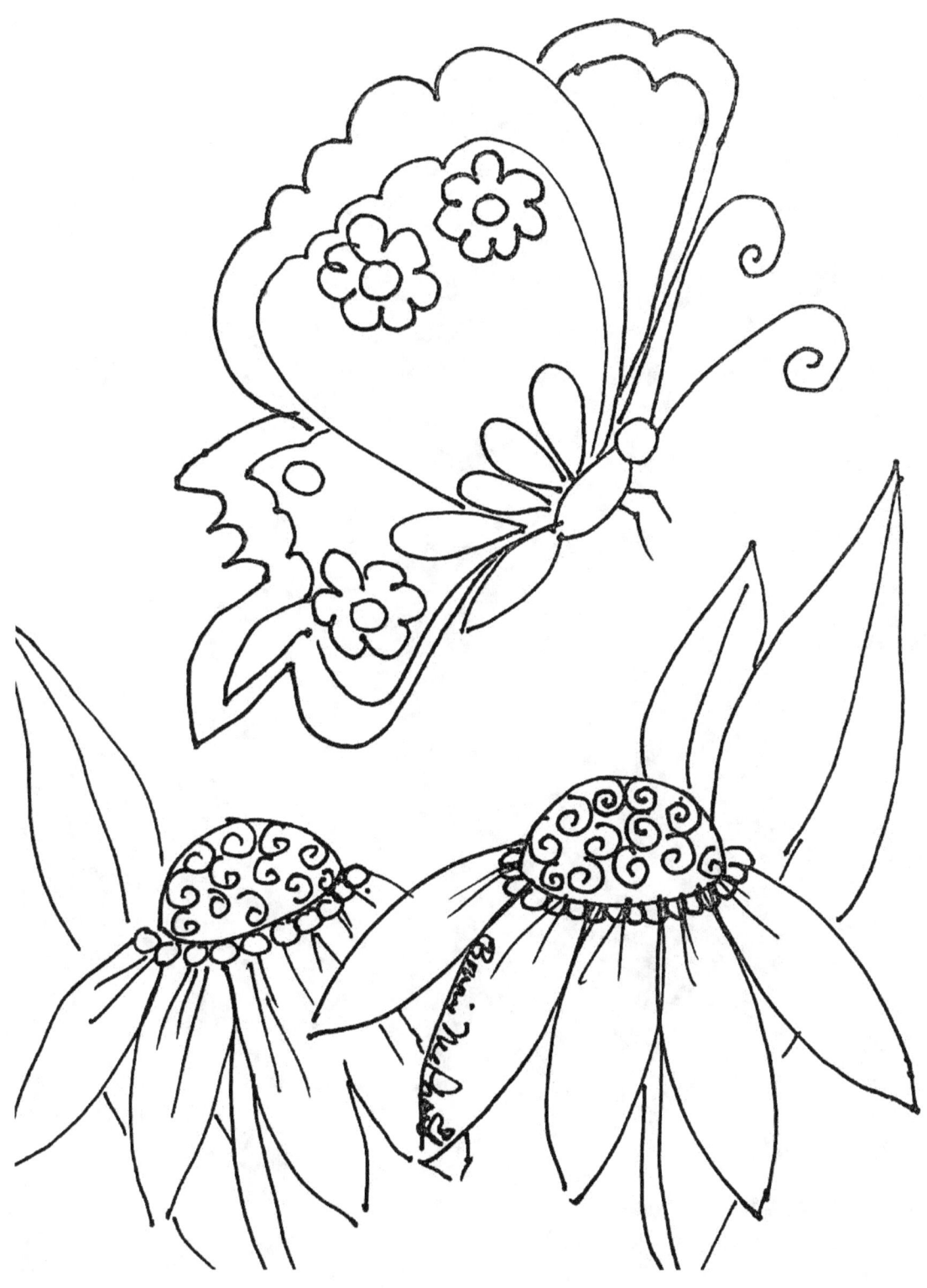

"God is our refuge and strength, an ever-present help in trouble."

Psalm 46:1

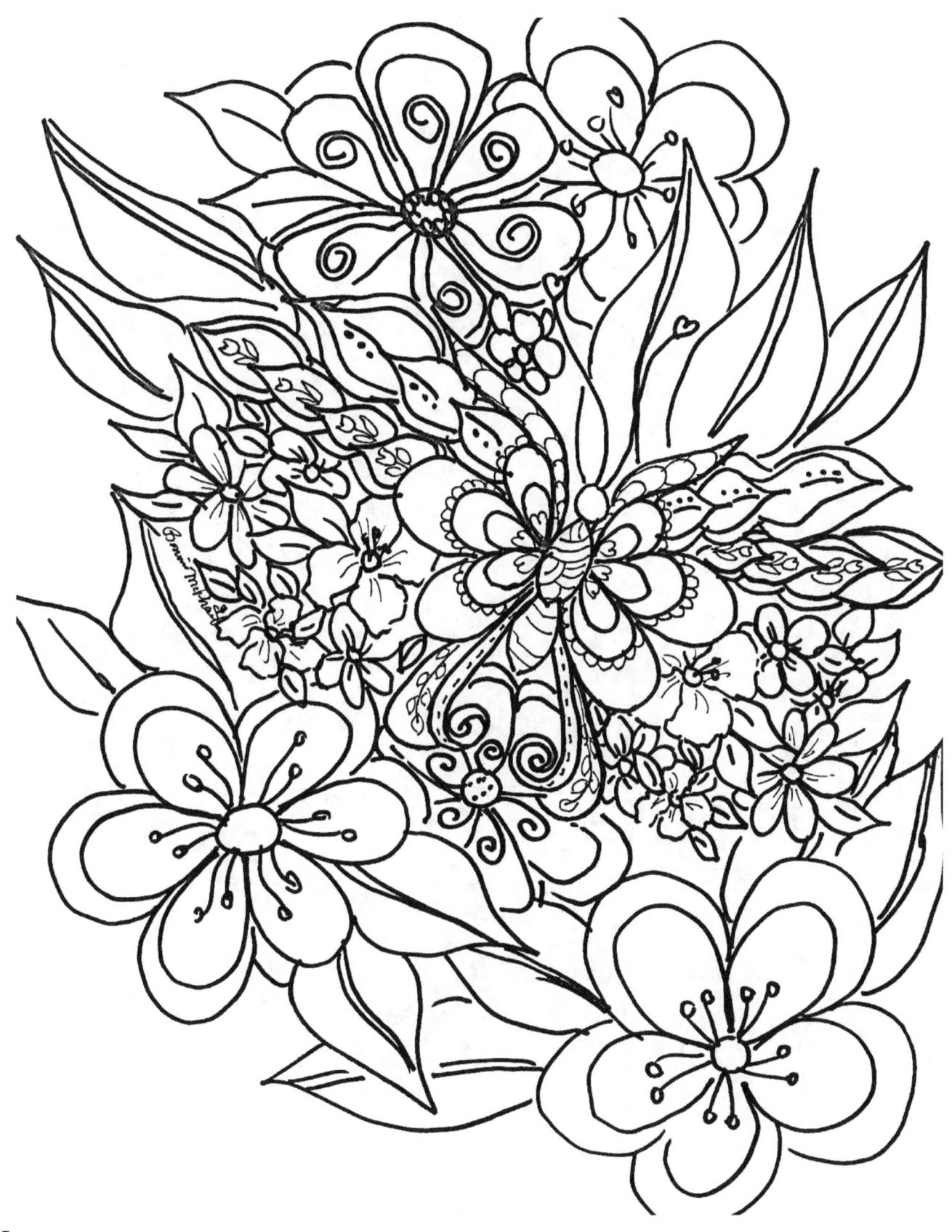

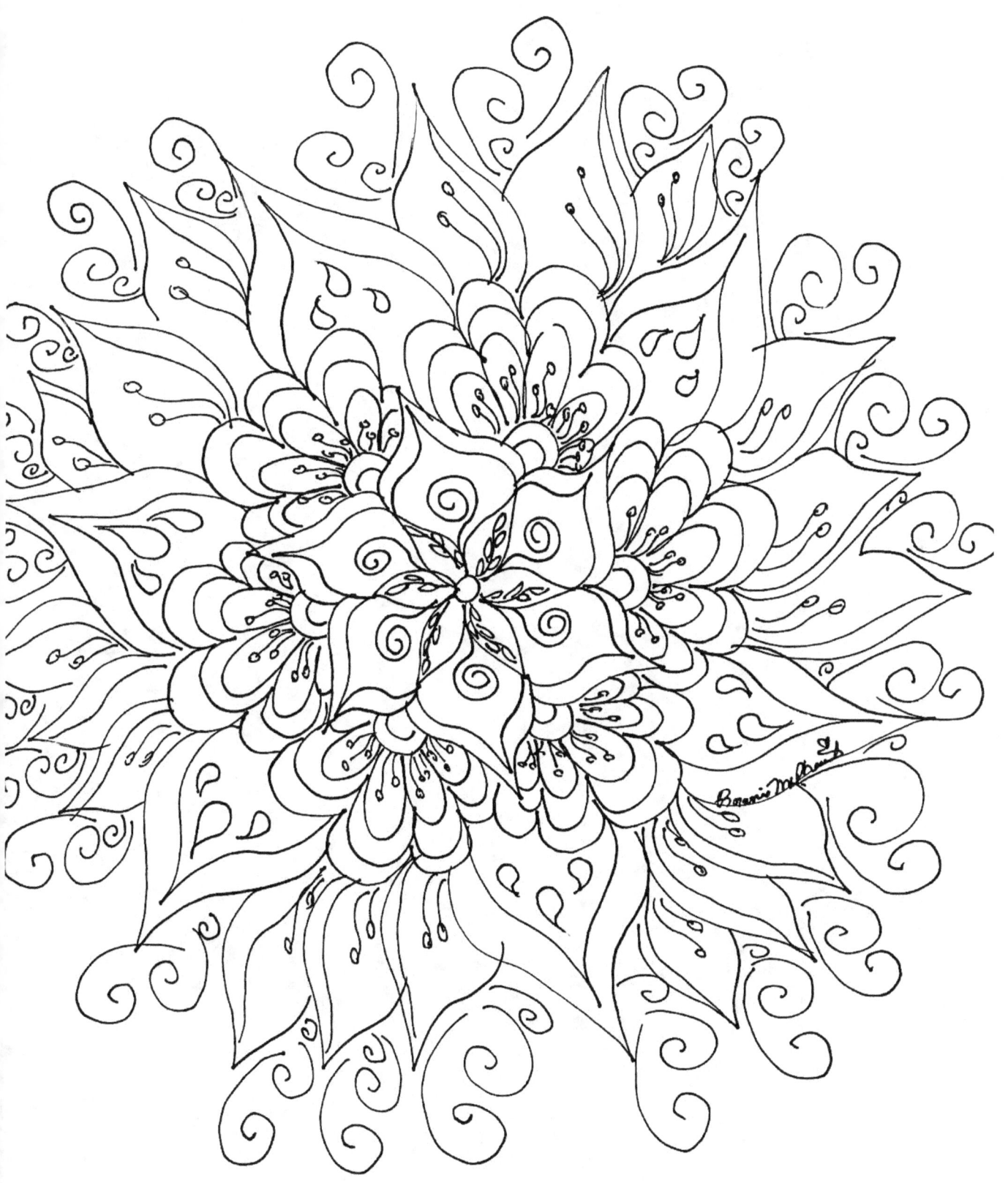

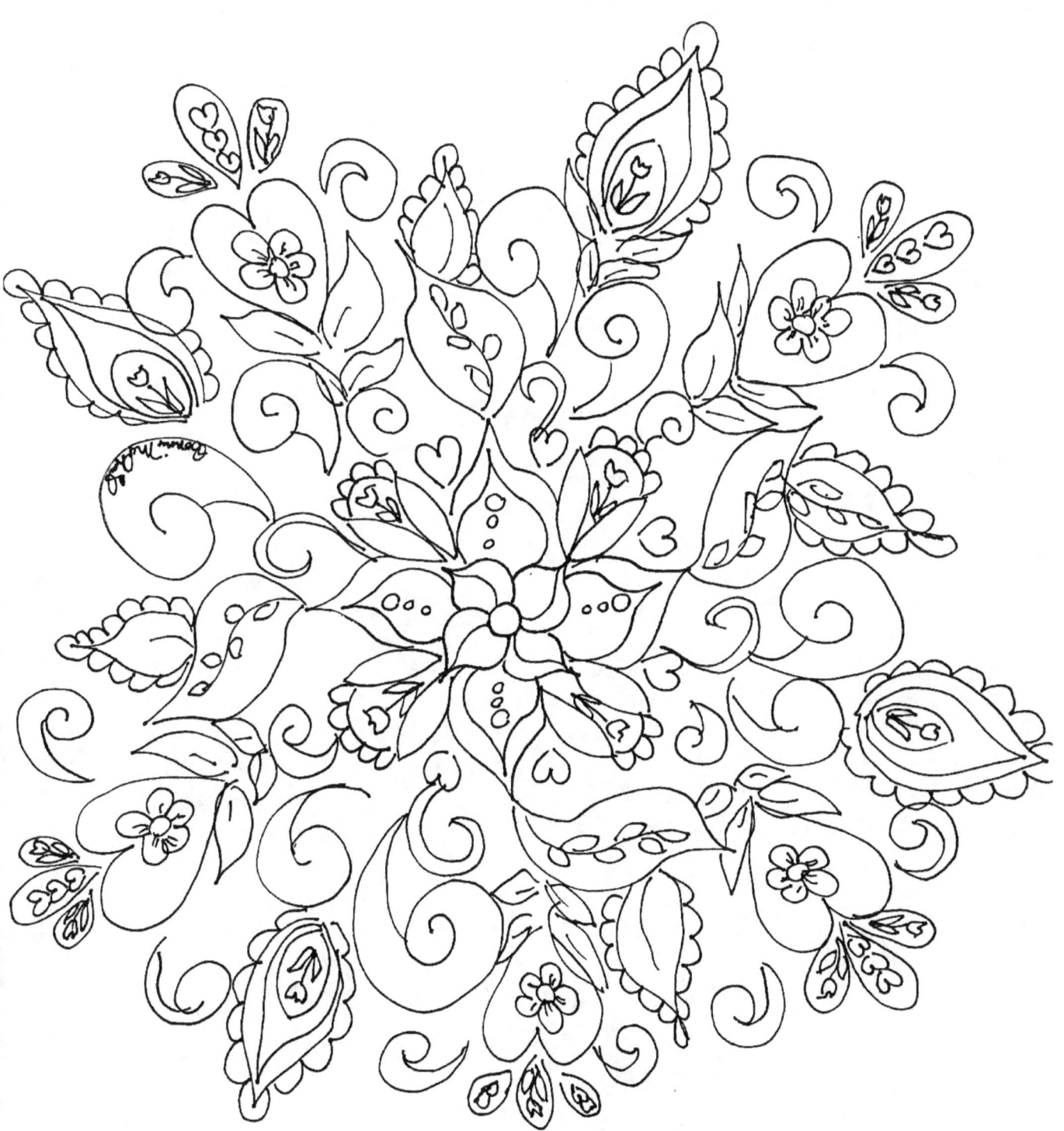

59

"Now to him who is able to do immeasurably more than all we ask or imagine, according to his power that is at work within us."

Ephesians 3:20

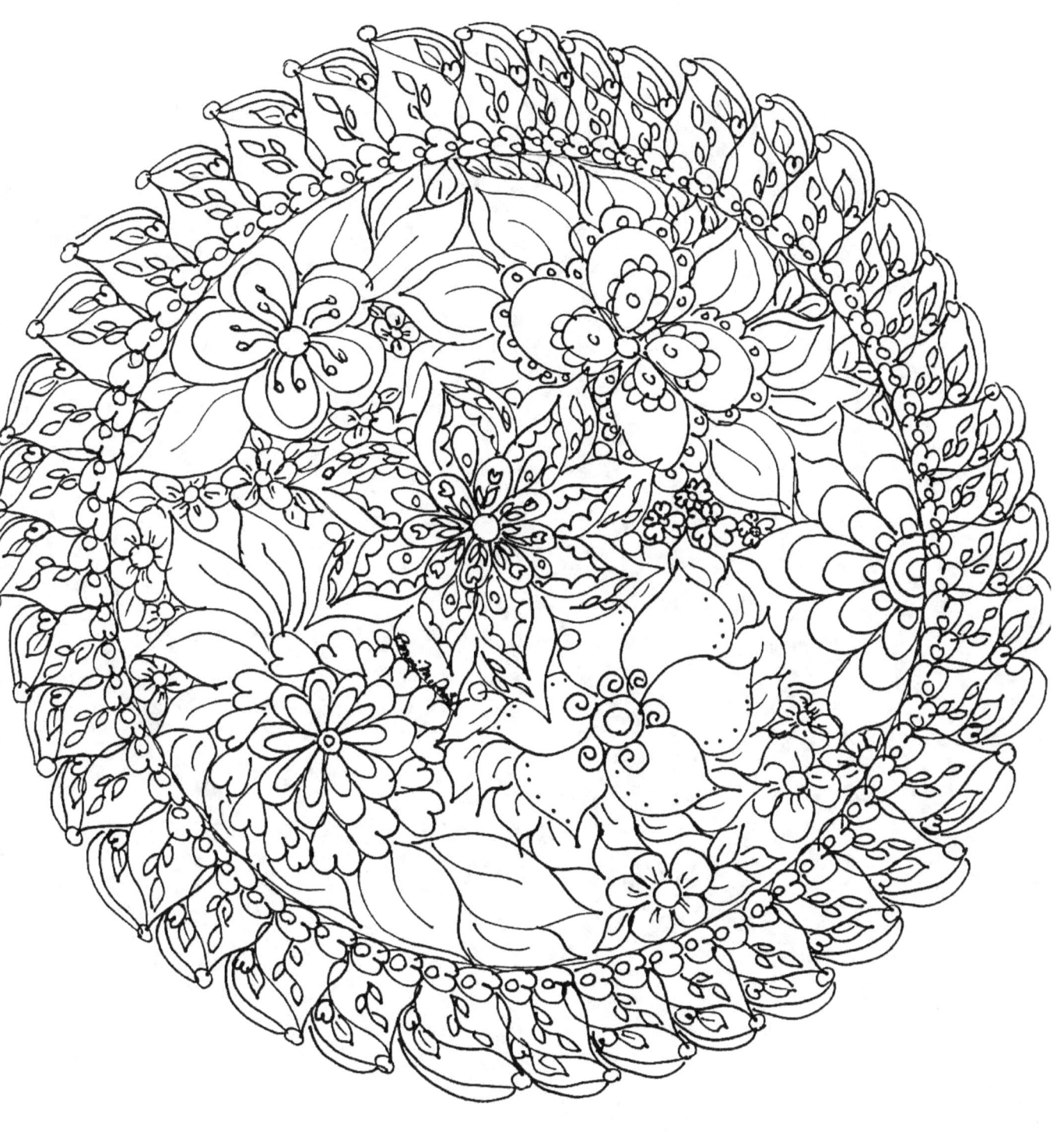

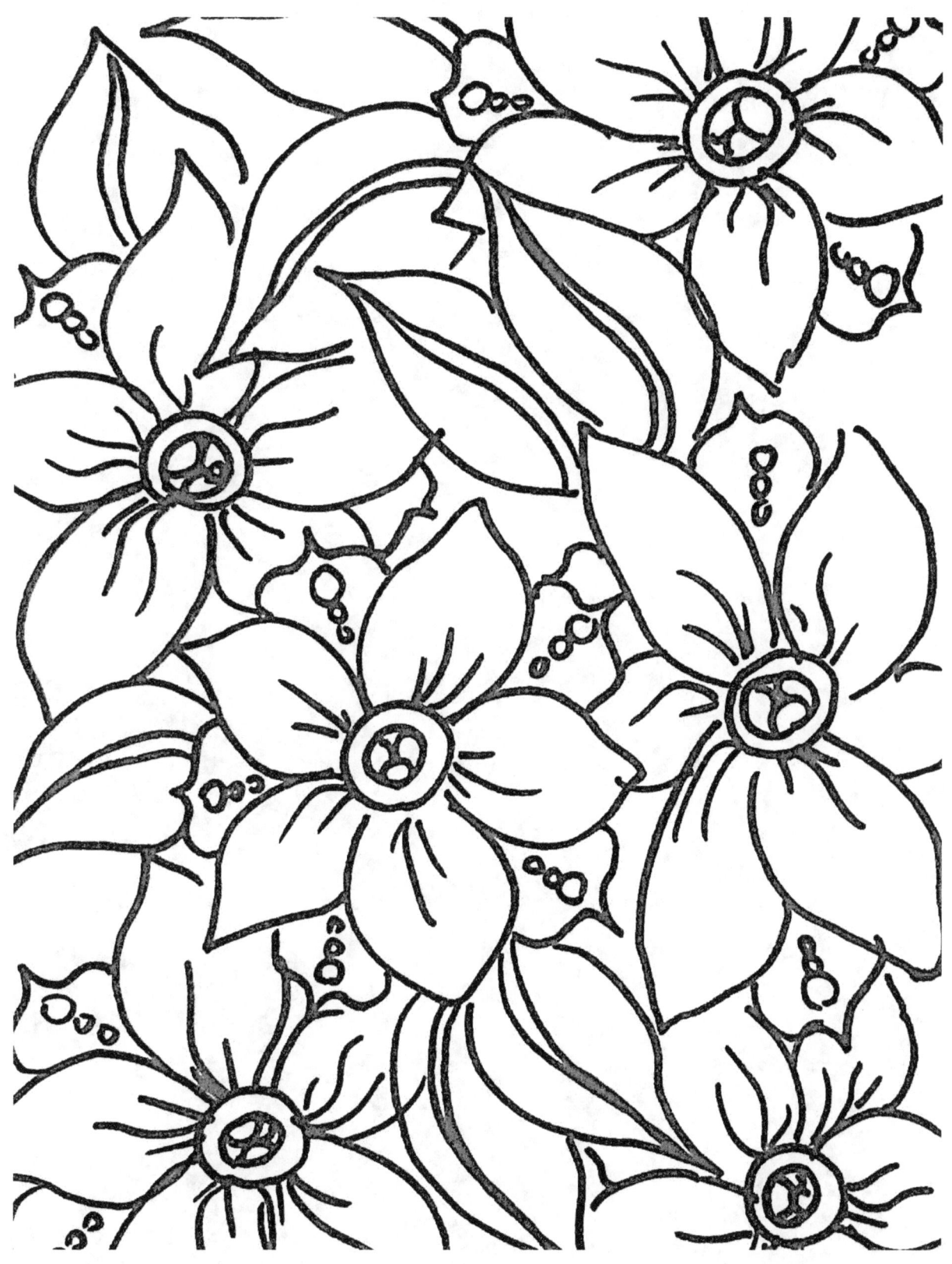

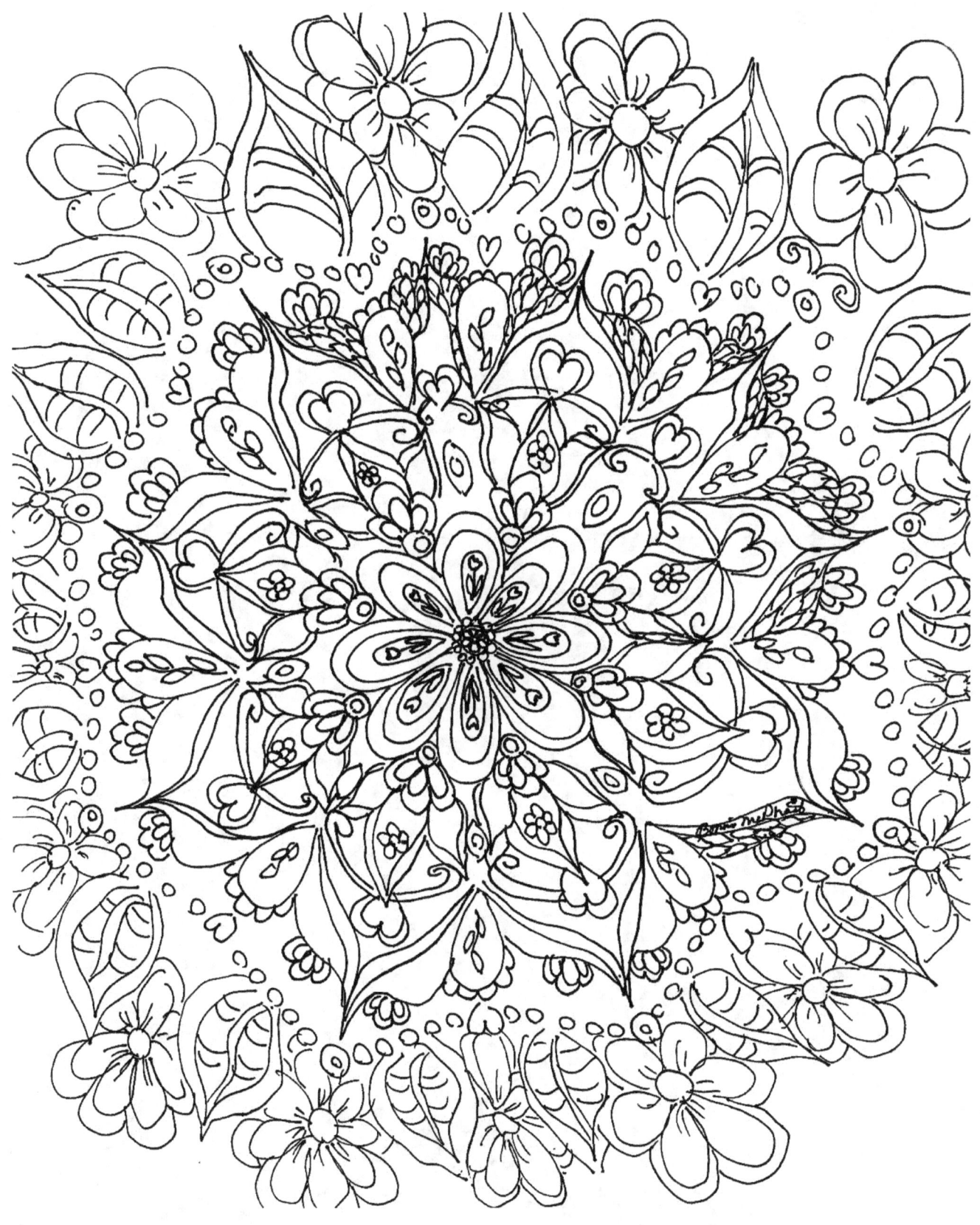

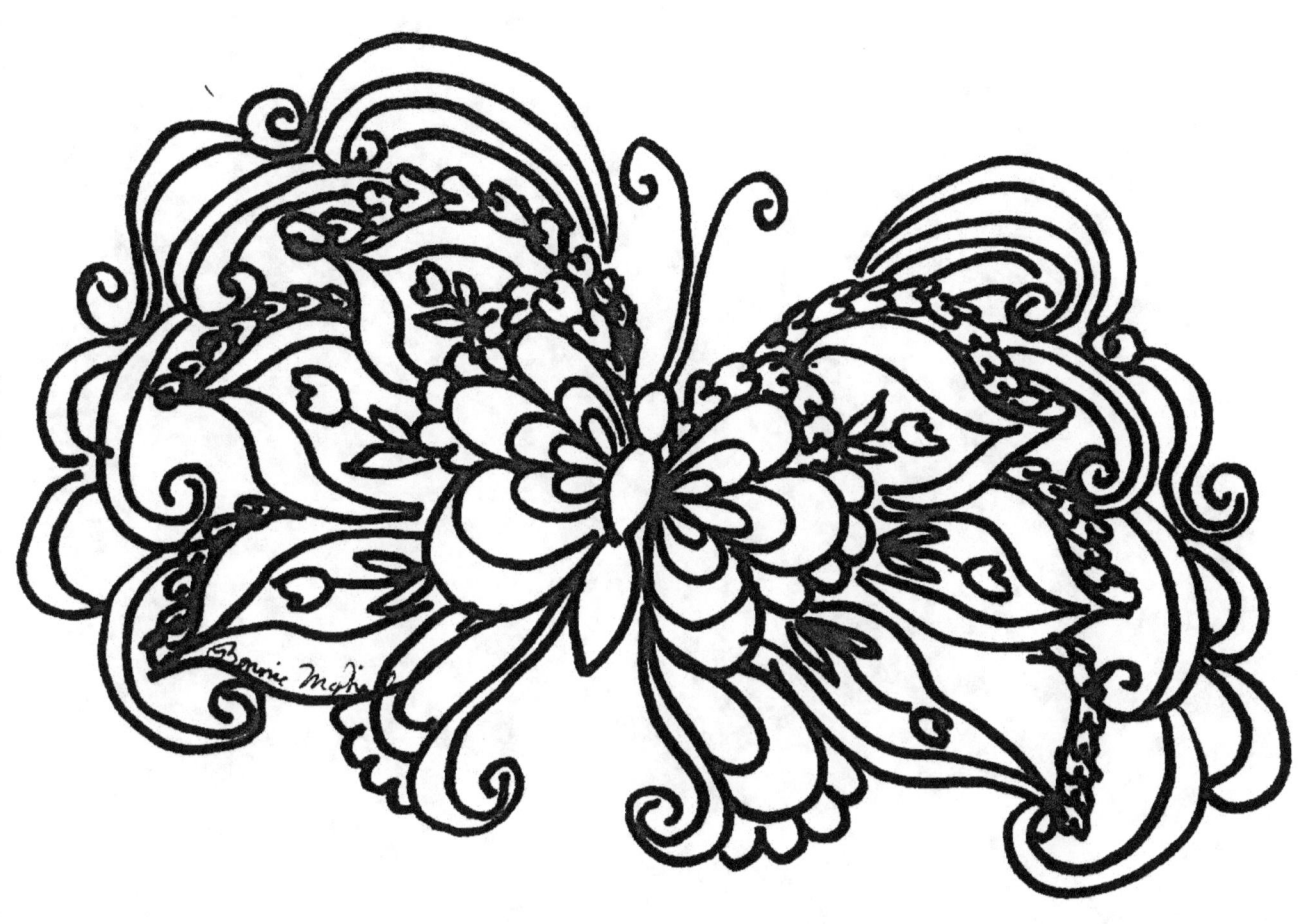

"Therefore we do not lose heart. Though outwardly we are wasting away, yet inwardly we are being renewed day by day. For our light and momentary troubles are achieving for us an eternal glory that far outweighs them all. So we fix our eyes not on what is seen, but on what is unseen, since what is seen is temporary, but what is unseen is eternal." 2 Corinthians 4:16-18

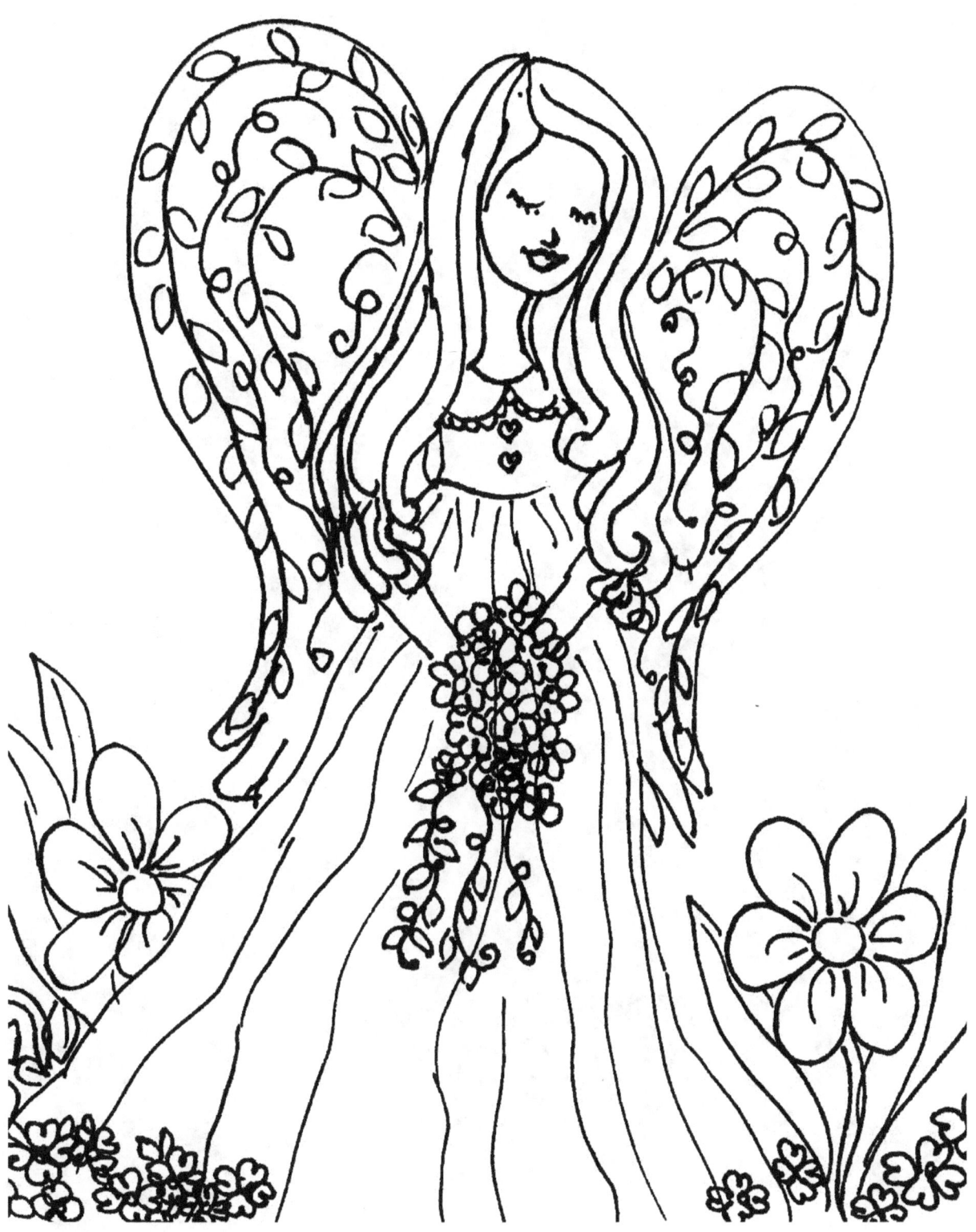

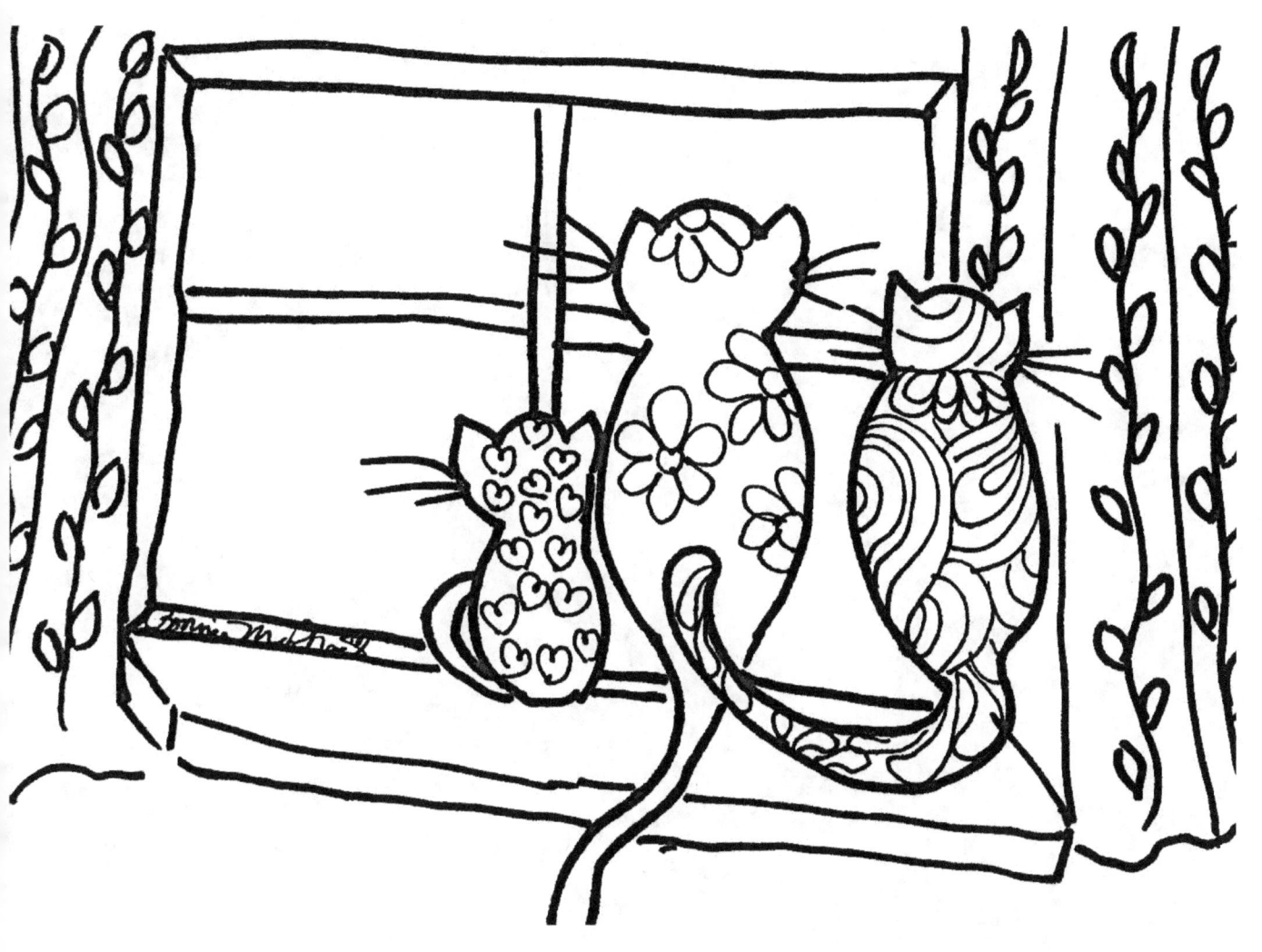

"Because of the LORD'S great love we are not consumed, for his compassions never fail. They are new every morning; great is your faithfulness." Lamentations 3:22-23

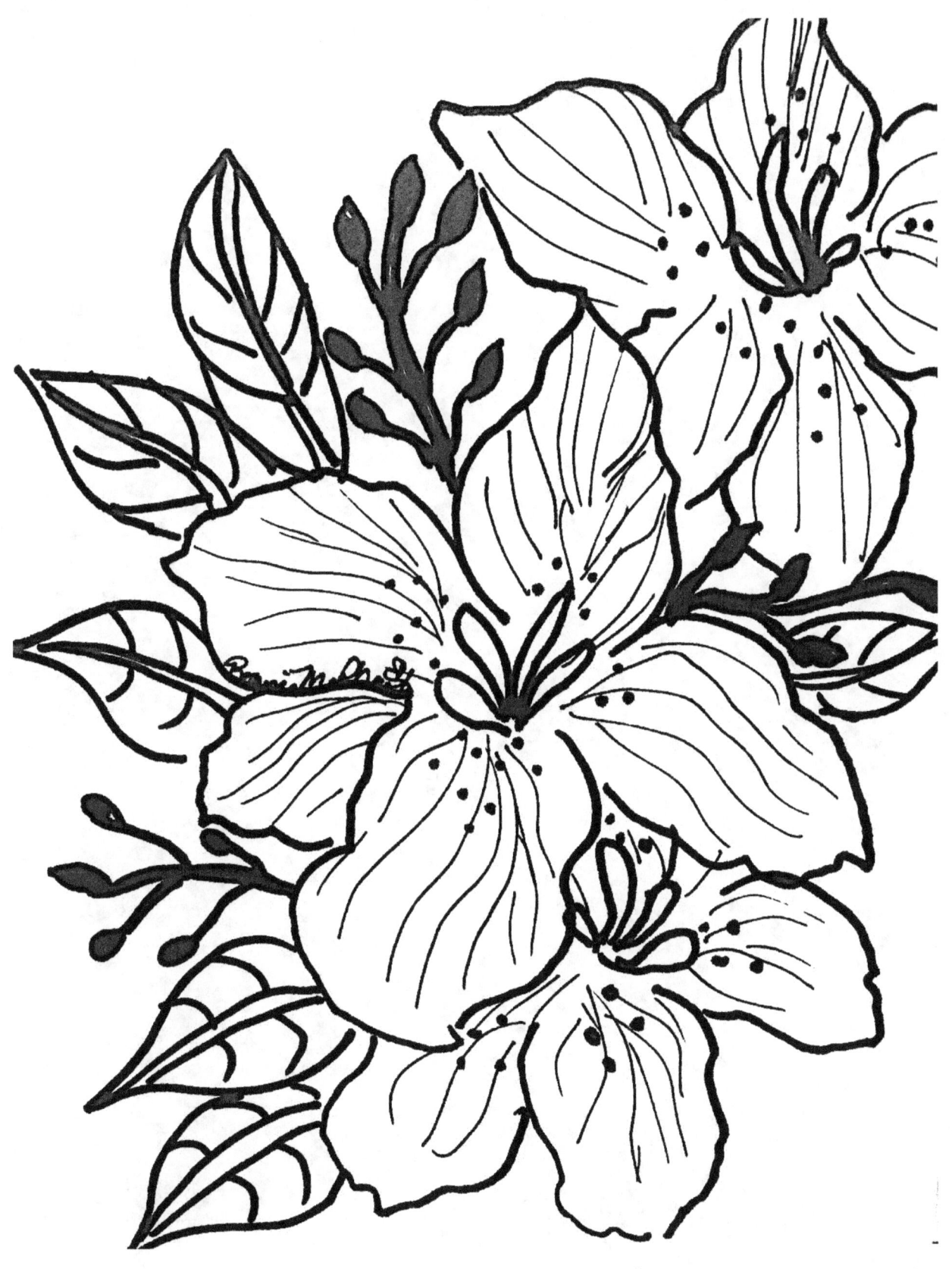

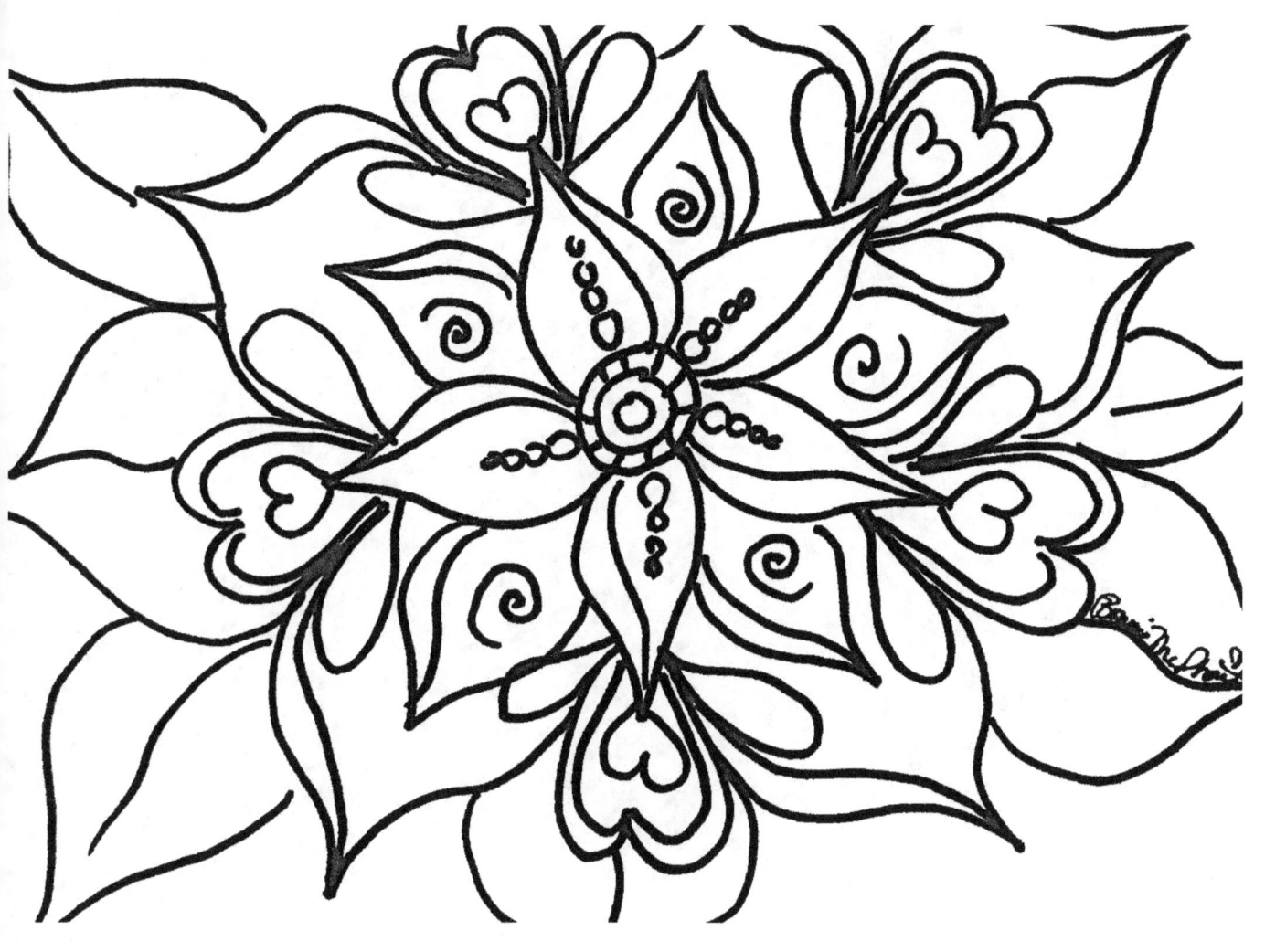

"For now we see only a reflection as in a mirror; then we shall see face to face. Now I know in part; then I shall know fully even as I am fully known." 1 Corinthians 13:12

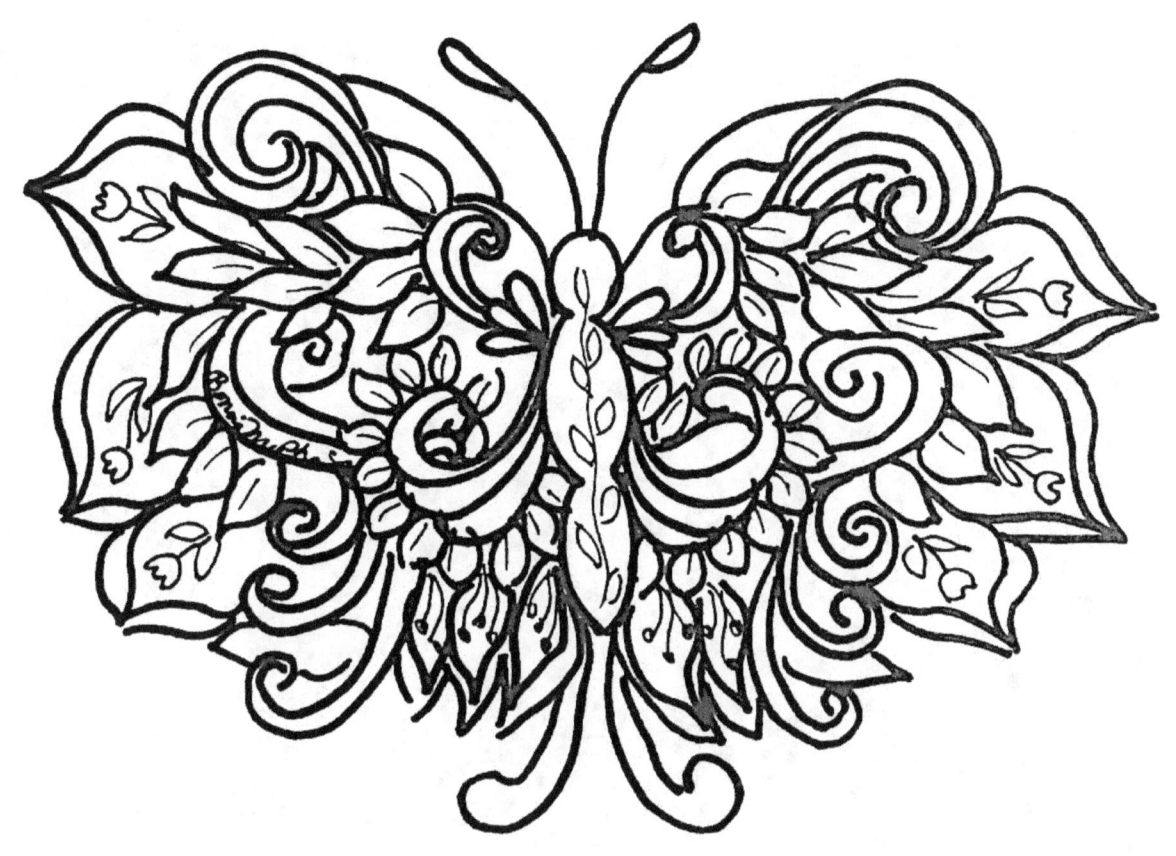

"For I am convinced that neither death nor life, neither angels nor demons, neither the present nor the future, nor any powers, neither height nor depth, nor anything else in all creation, will be able to separate us from the love of God that is in Christ Jesus our Lord."
Romans 8:38-39

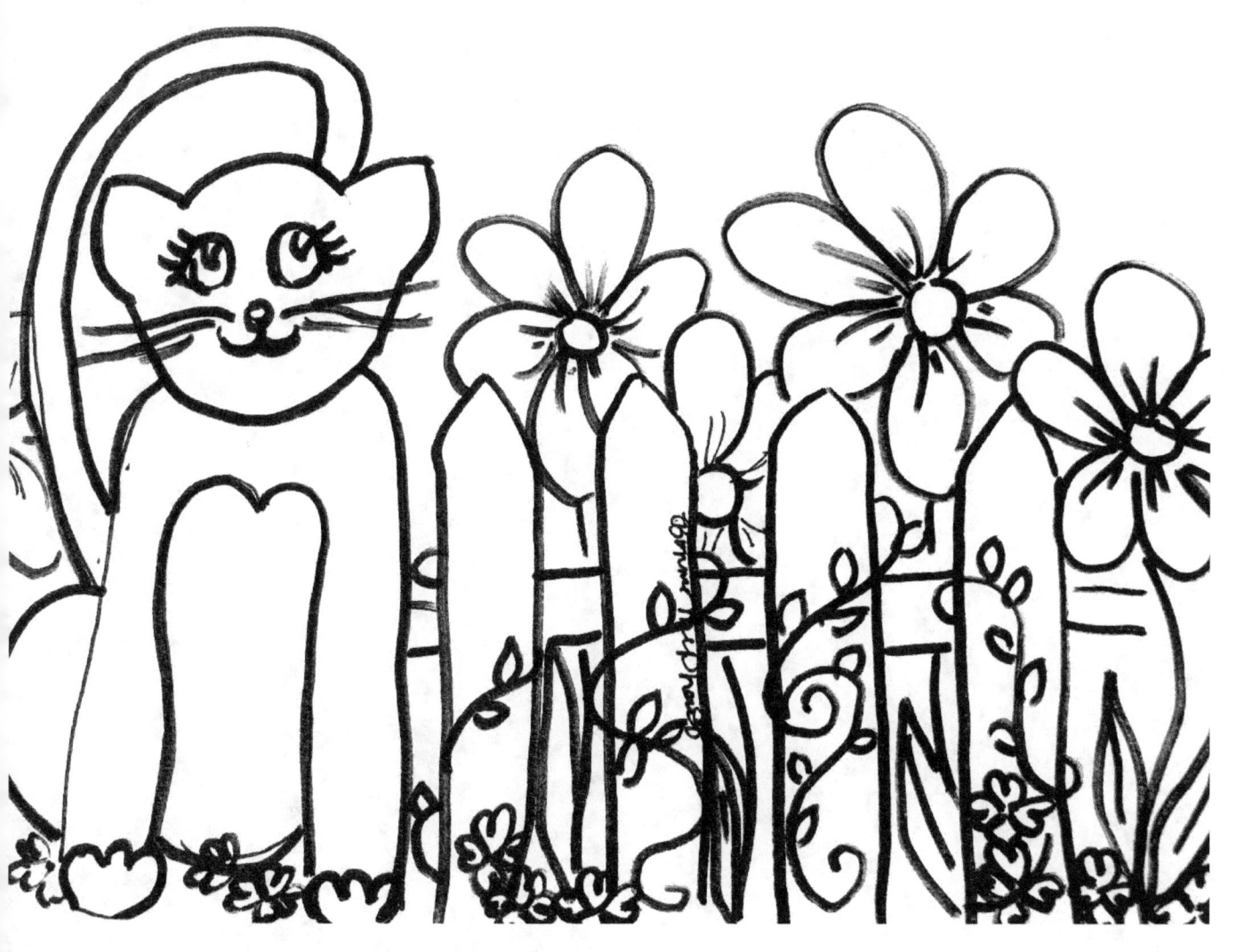

"May the God of hope fill you with all joy and peace as you trust in him, so that you may overflow with hope by the power of the Holy Spirit."
Romans 15:13

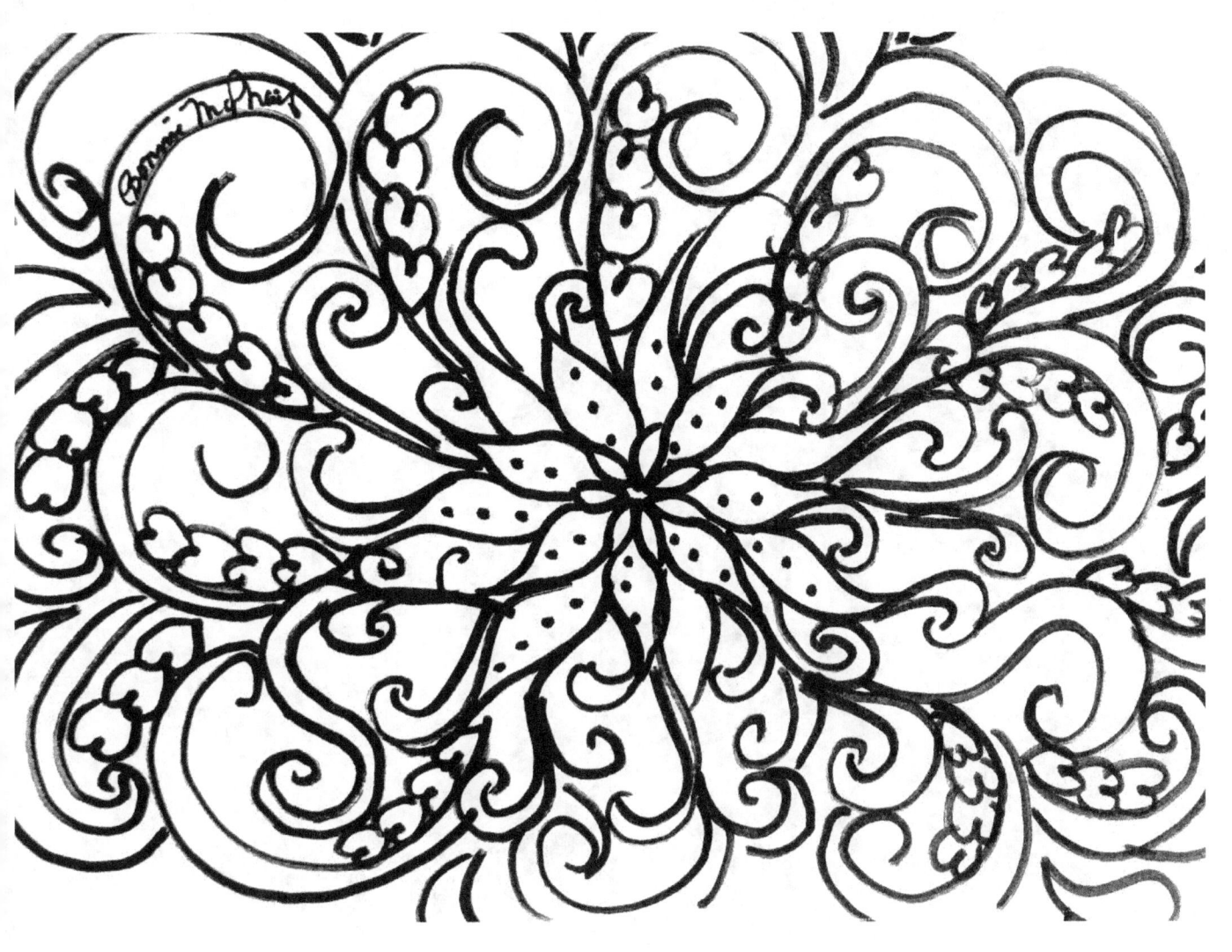

"What, then, shall we say in response to these things? If God is for us, who can be against us?" Romans 8:31

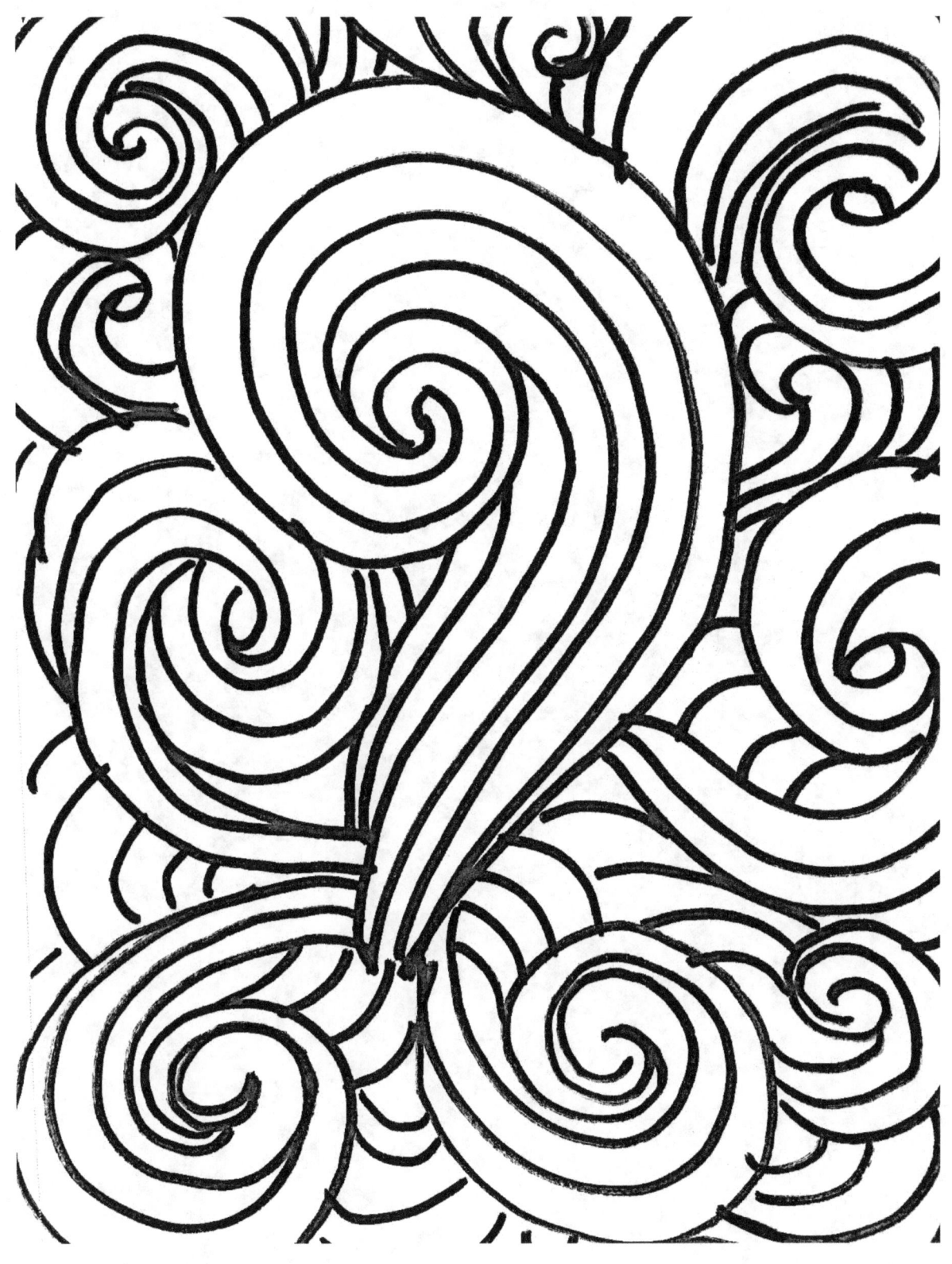

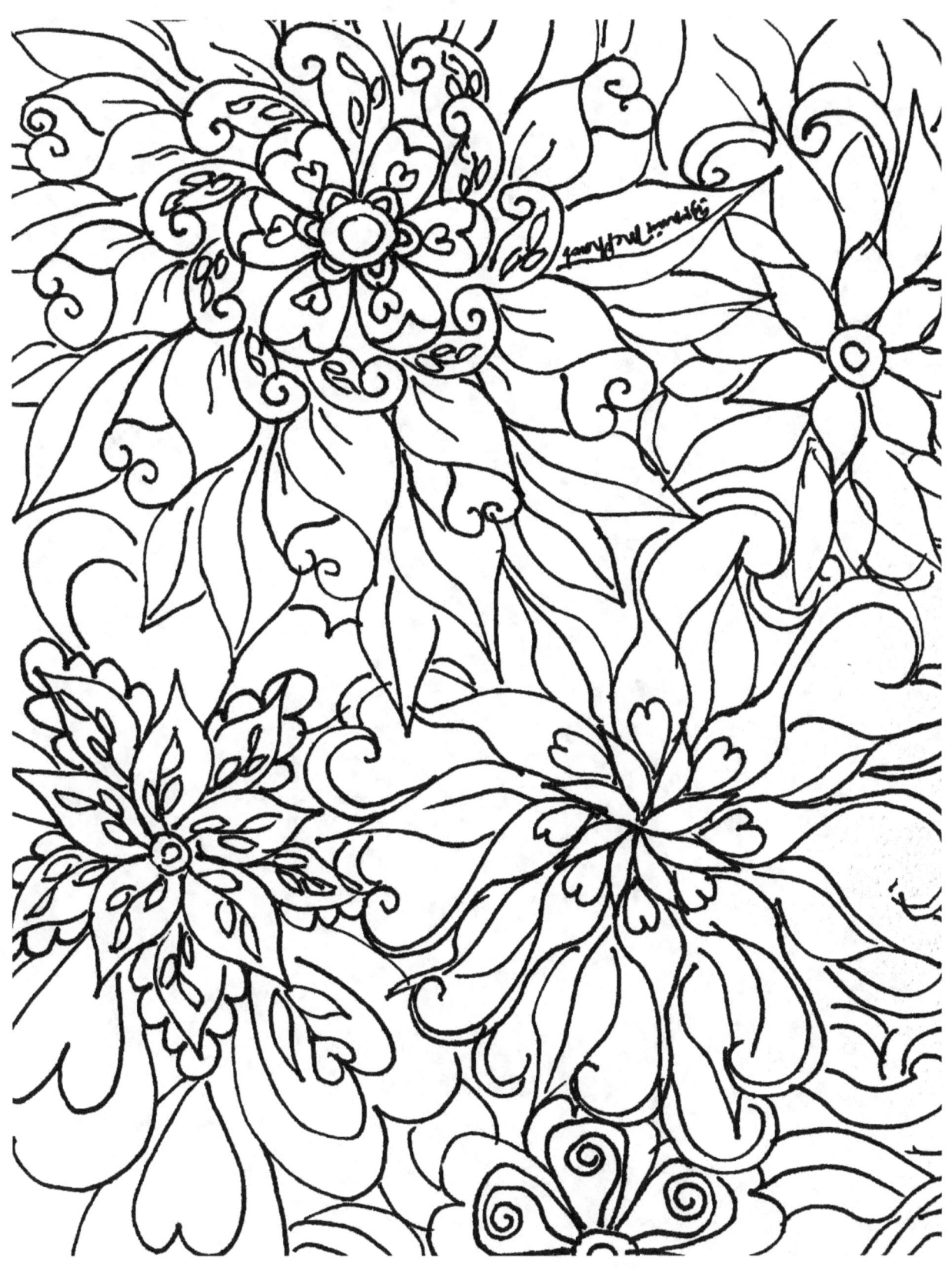

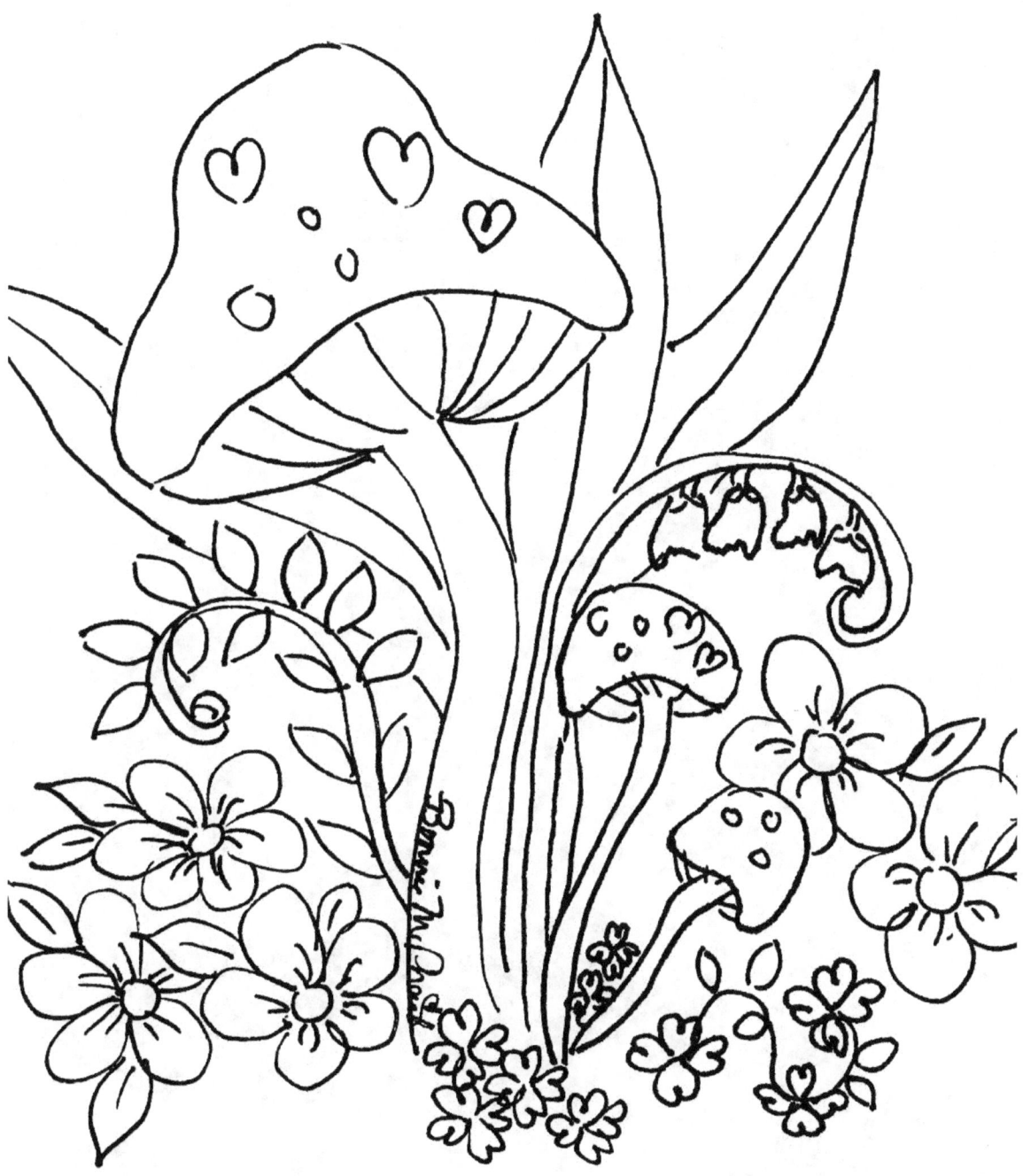

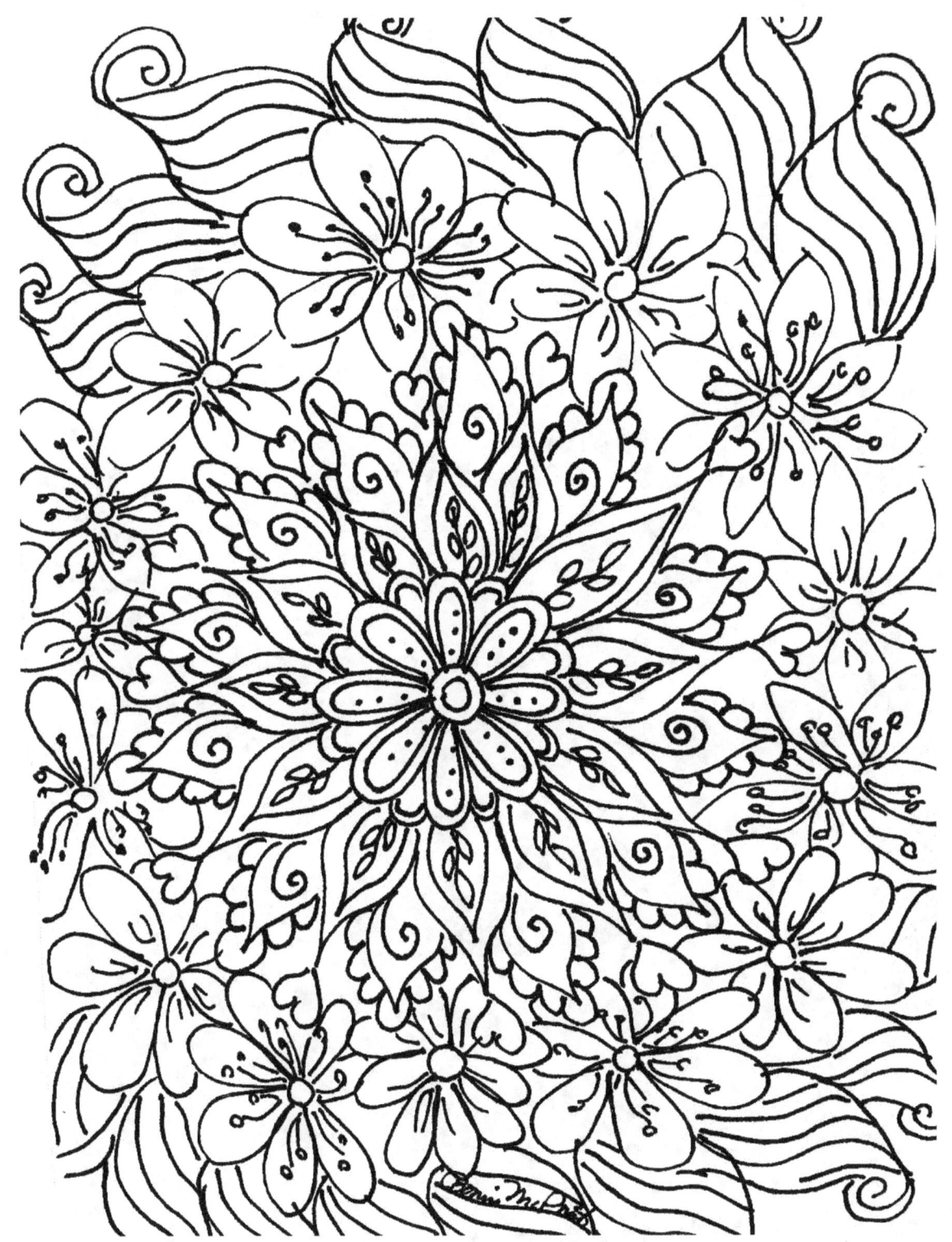

"He gives strength to the weary and increases the power of the weak." Isaiah 40:29

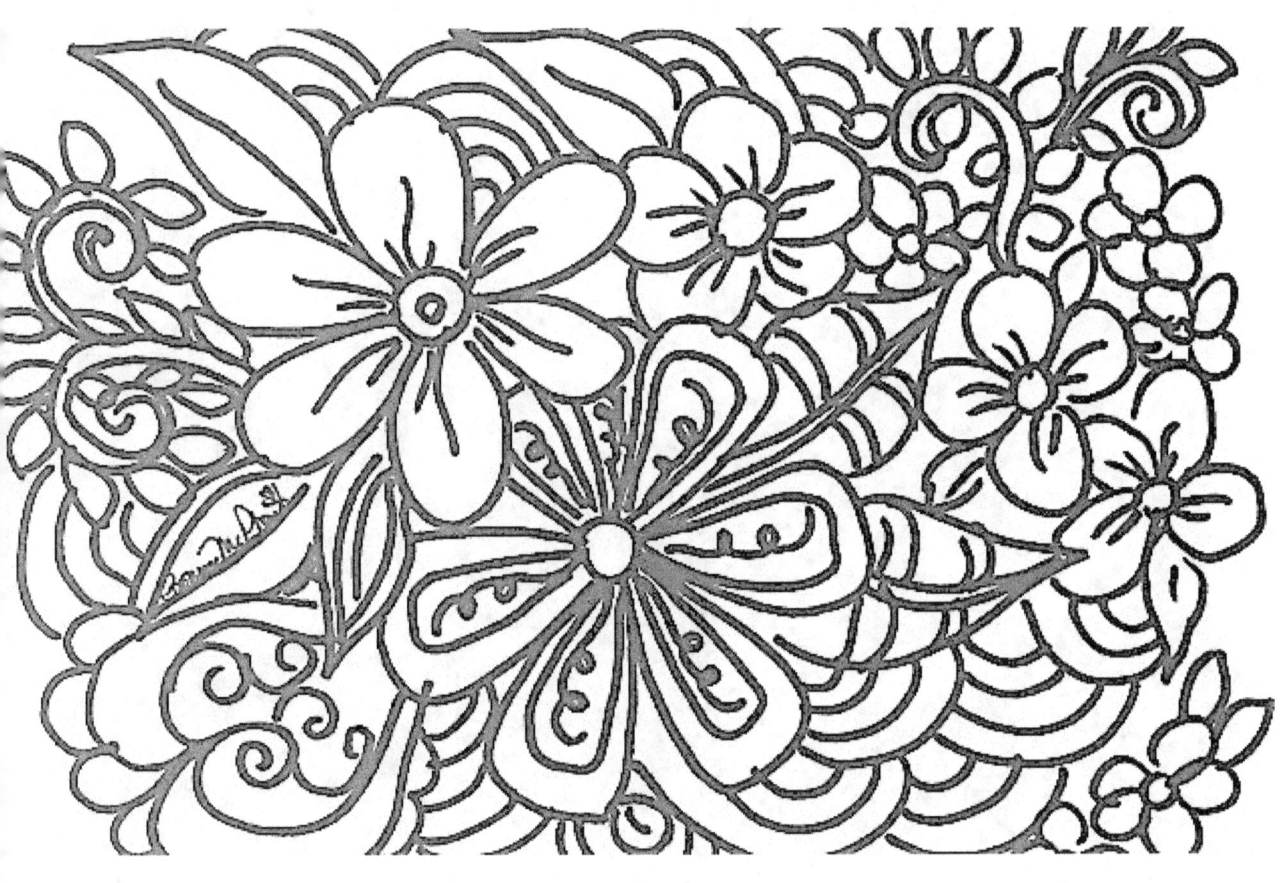

"One thing I ask from the LORD, this only do I seek: that I may dwell in the house of the LORD all the days of my life, to gaze on the beauty of the LORD and to seek him in his temple." Psalm 27:4

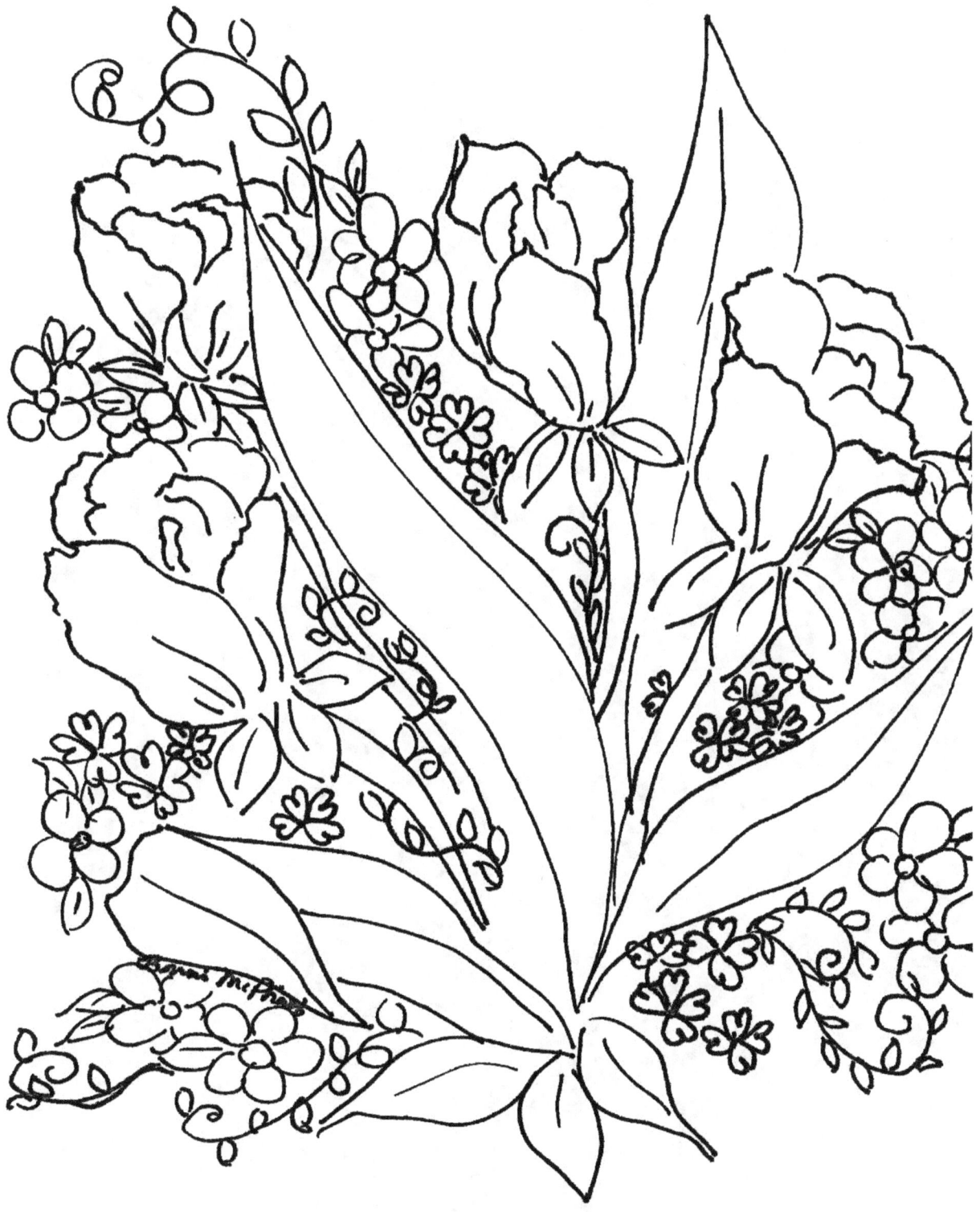

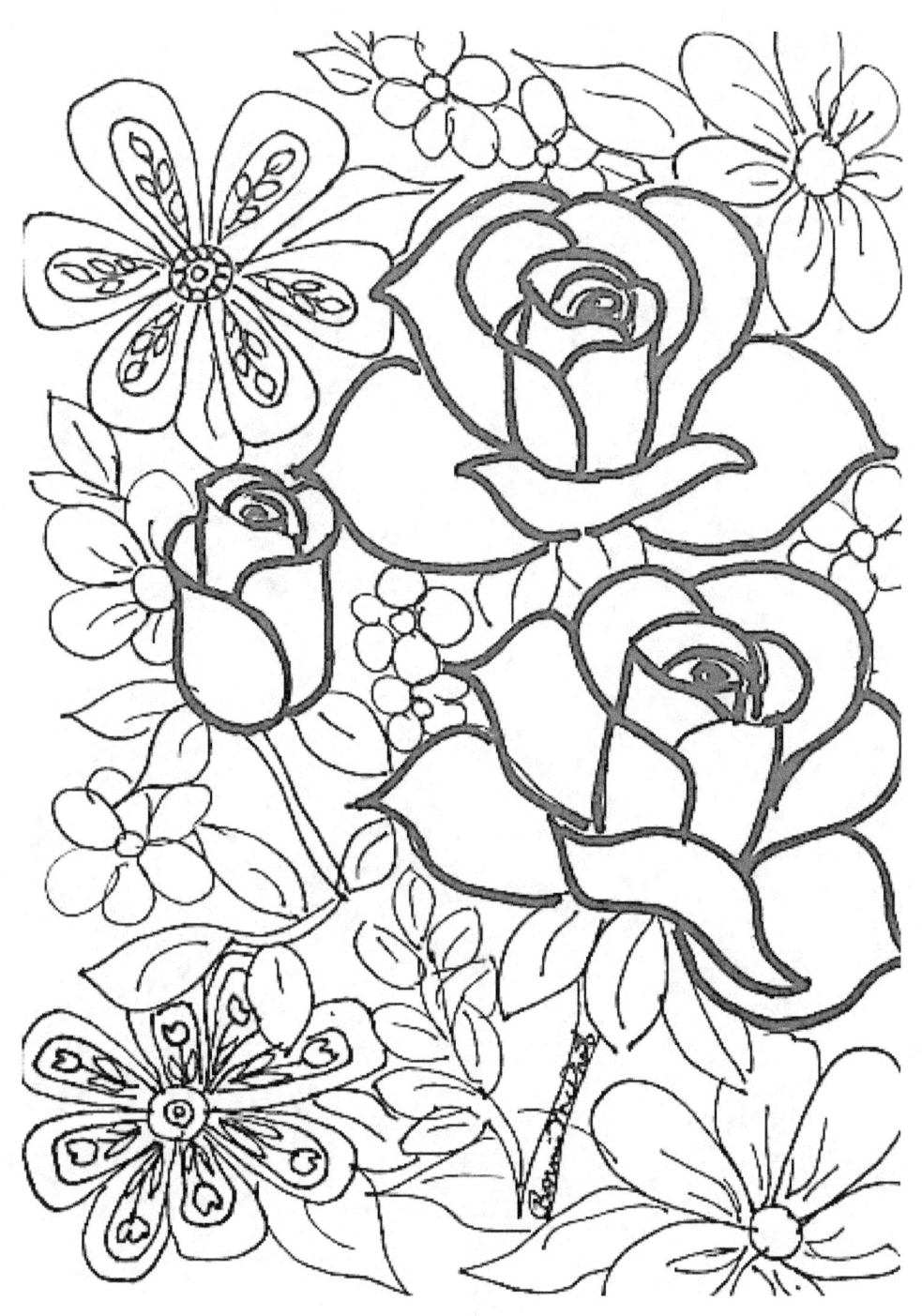

"All scripture is inspired by God and useful for teaching, rebuking, correcting, and training in righteousness." 2 Timothy 3:16

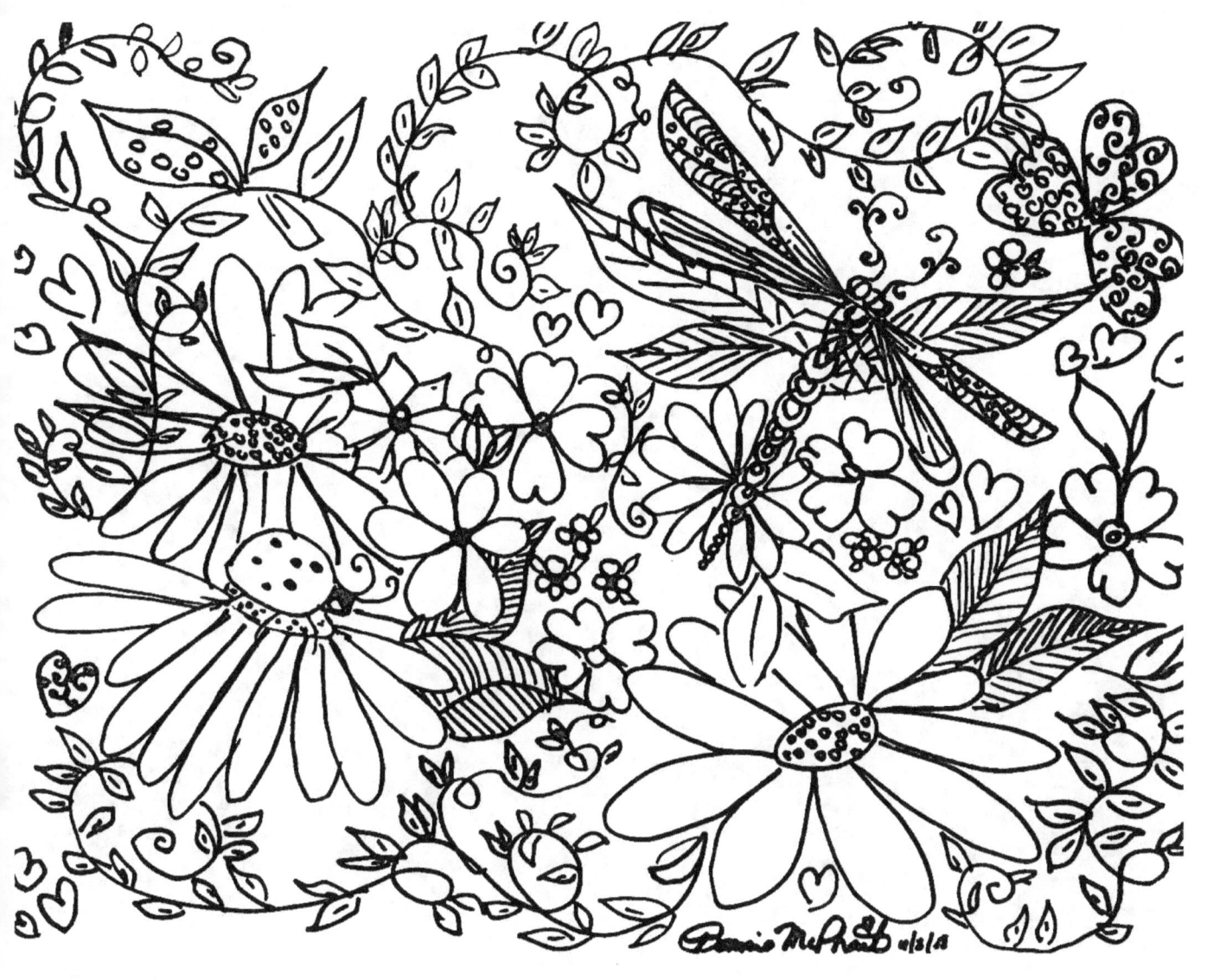

"For I know the plans I have for you," declares the LORD,"

Plans to prosper you and not to harm you, plans to give you hope and a future."

Jeremiah 29:11

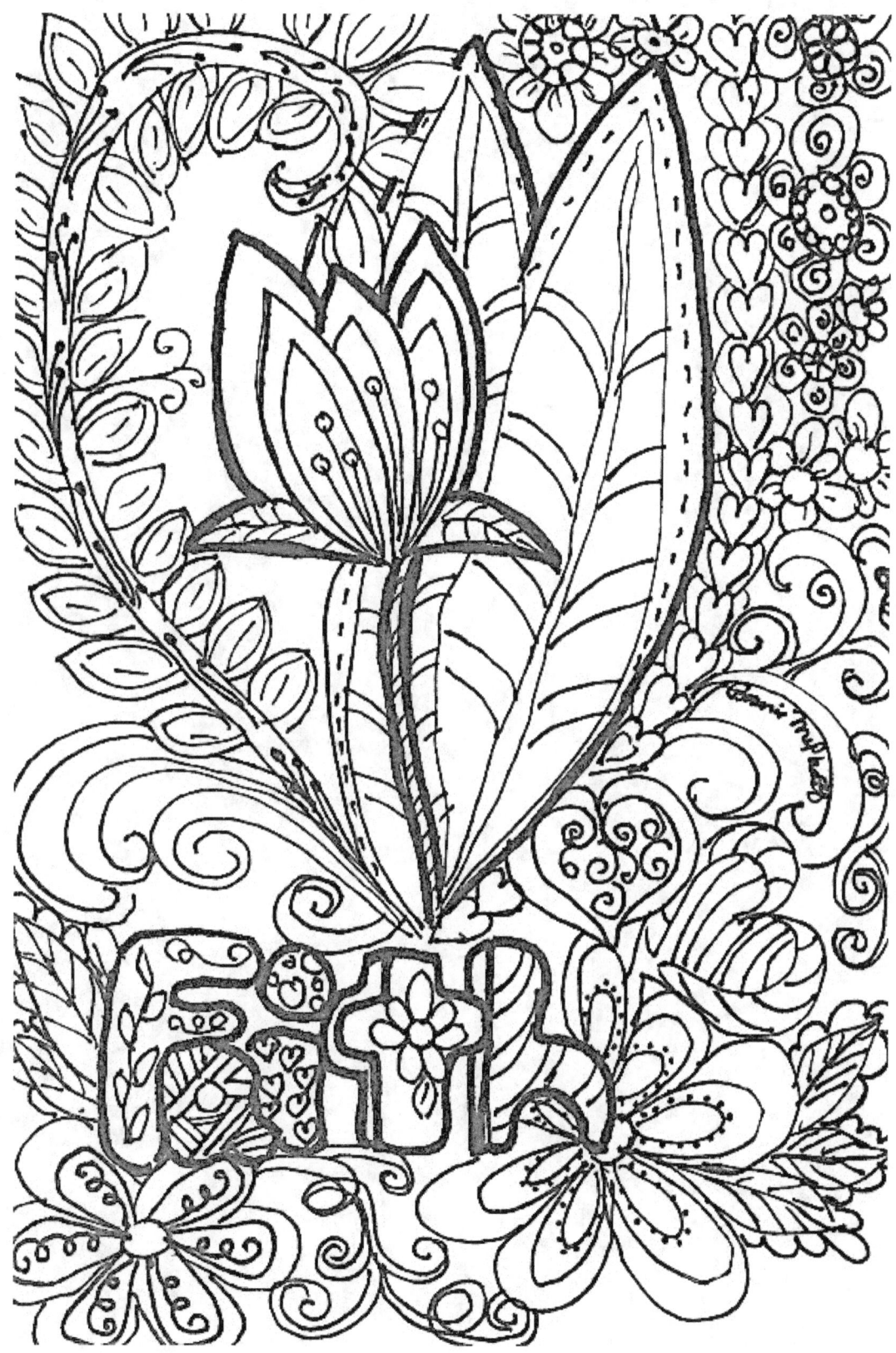

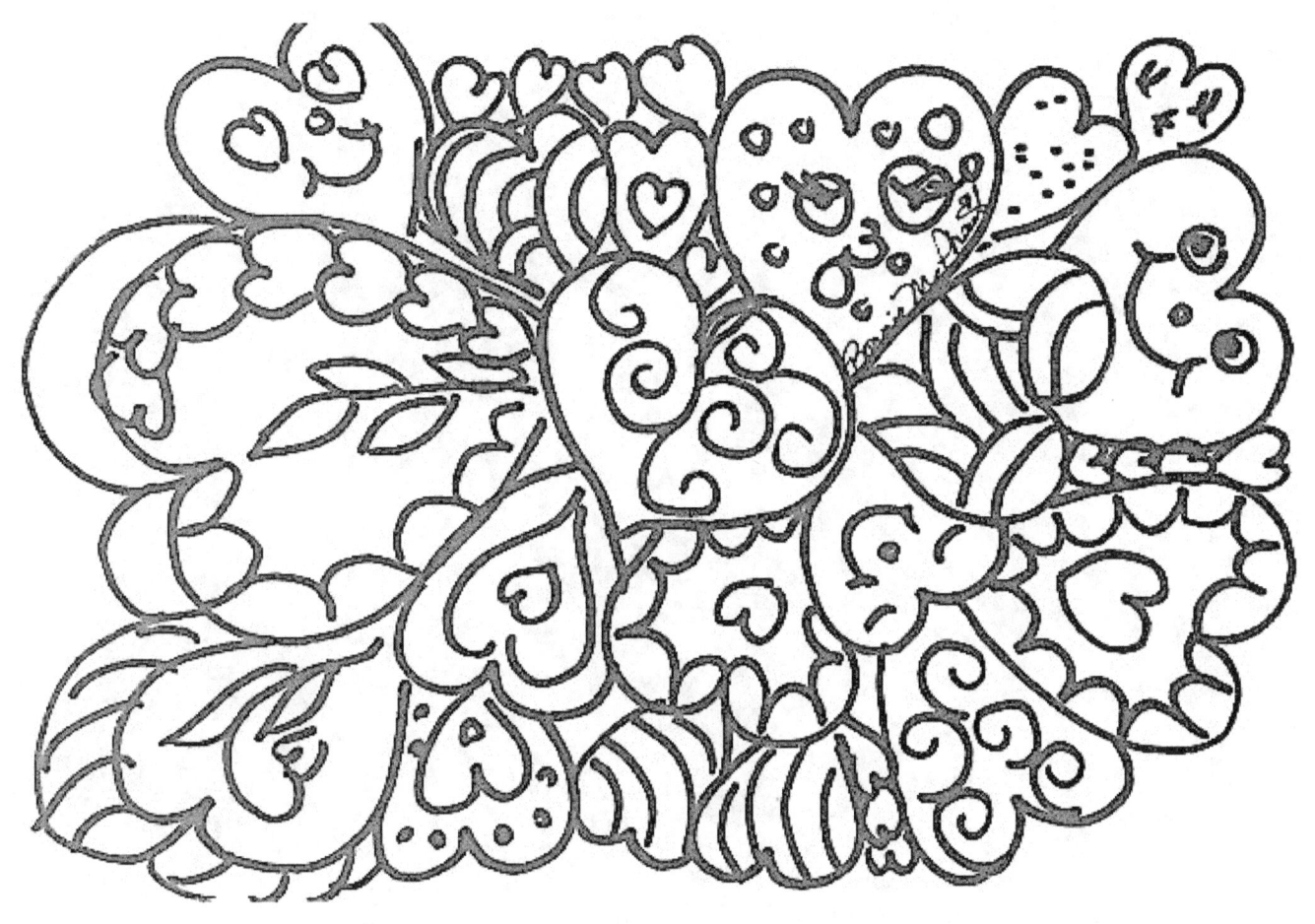

"Taste and see that the LORD is good; blessed is the one who takes refuge in him."
Psalm 34:8

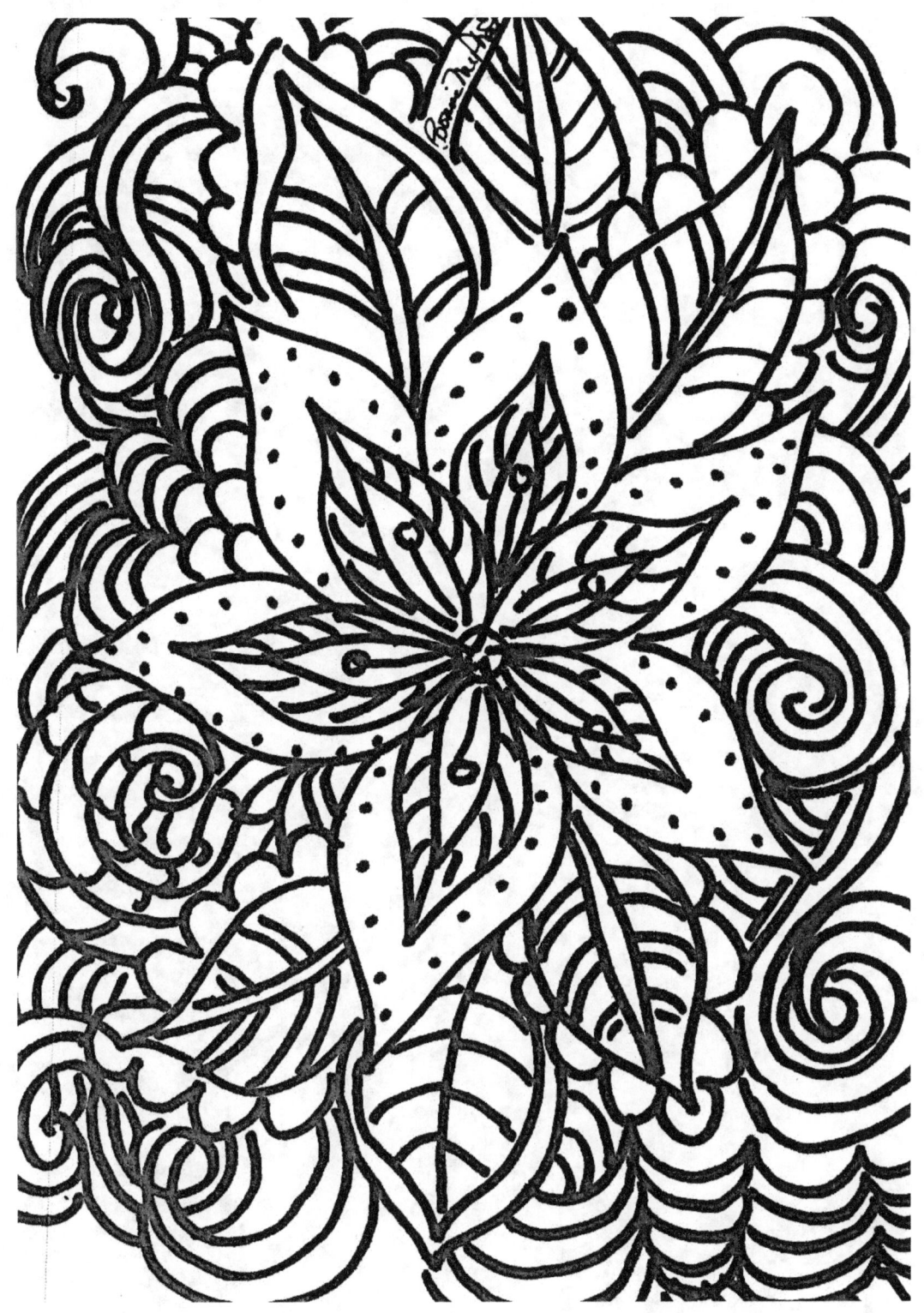

"I can do all this through him who gives me strength." Phil 4:13

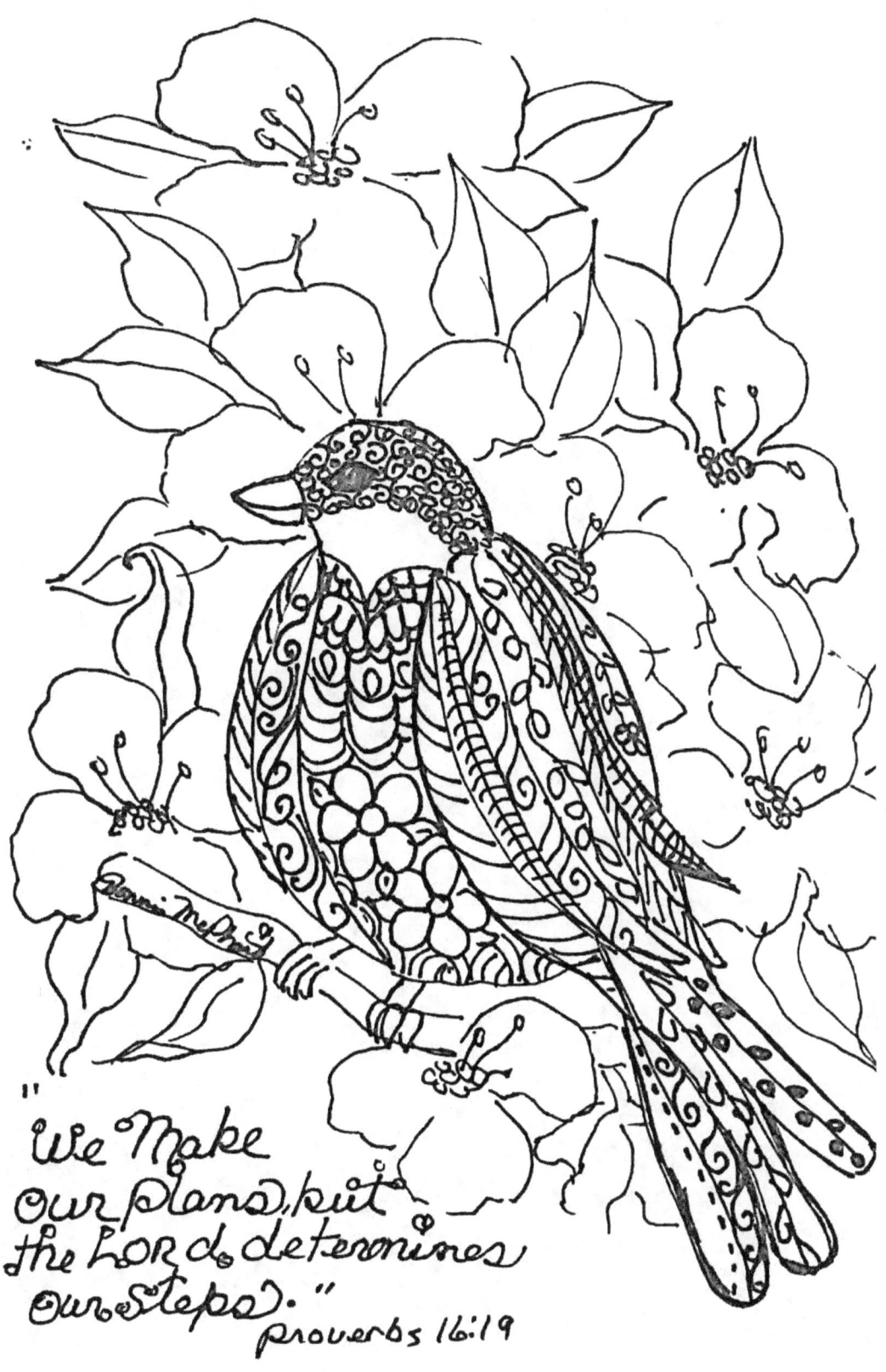

"We make
our plans, but
the Lord determines
our steps."
                proverbs 16:19

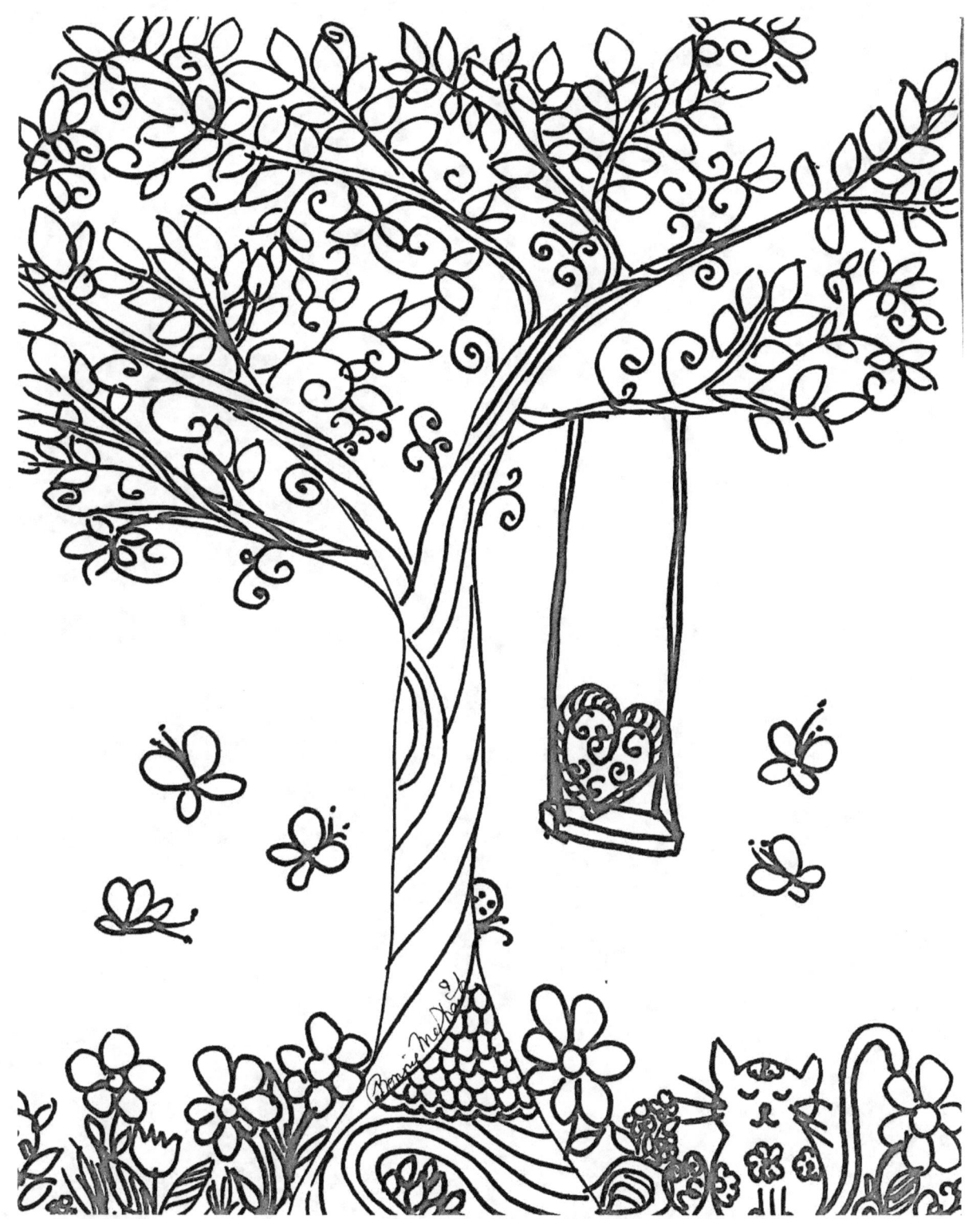

"Take delight in the LORD, and he will give you the desires of your heart."

Psalm 37:4

"Taste and see the LORD is good;

Blessed is the one who takes refuge in him."

Psalm 34:8

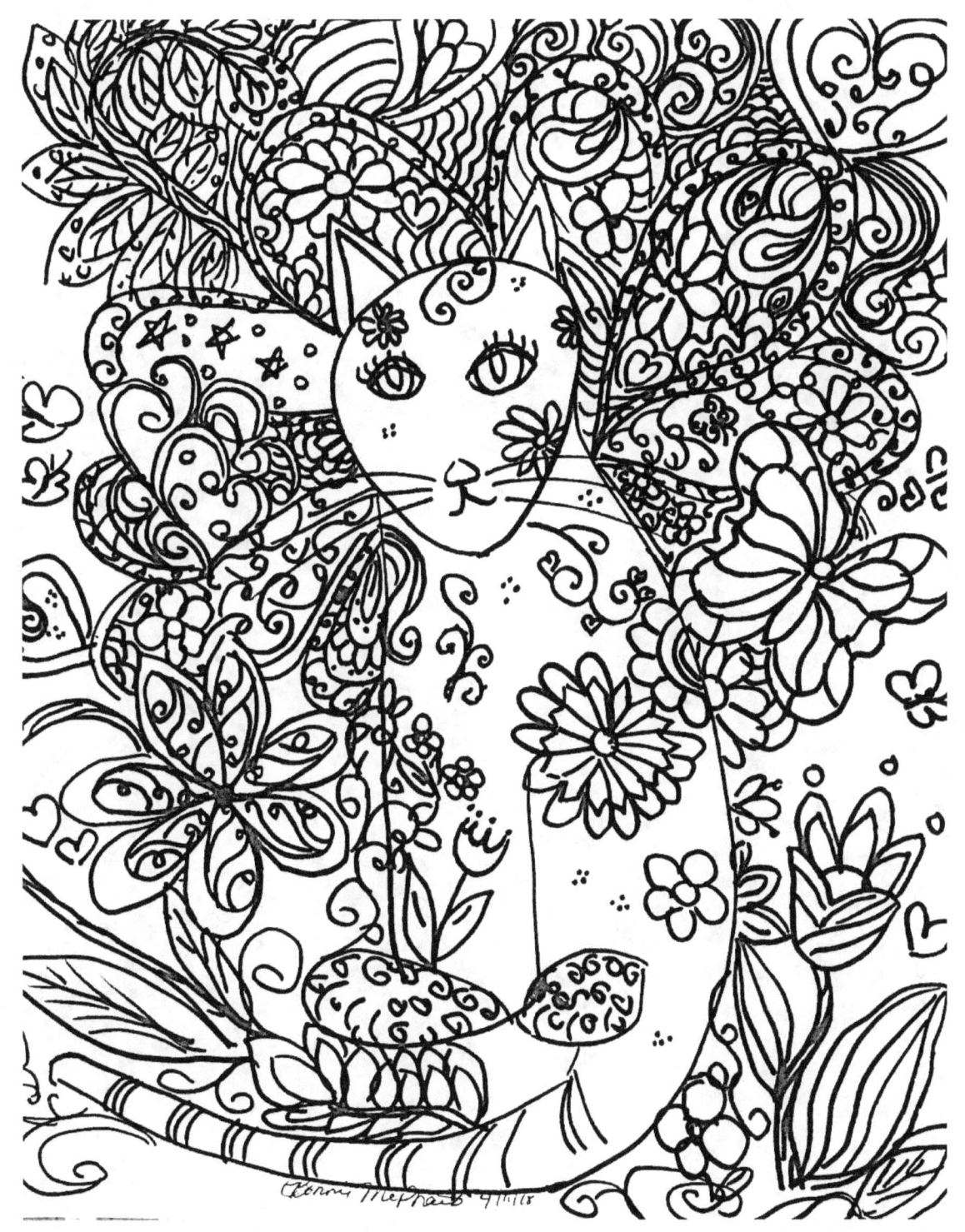

"Commit to the LORD whatever you do, and he will establish your plans."

Proverbs 16:3

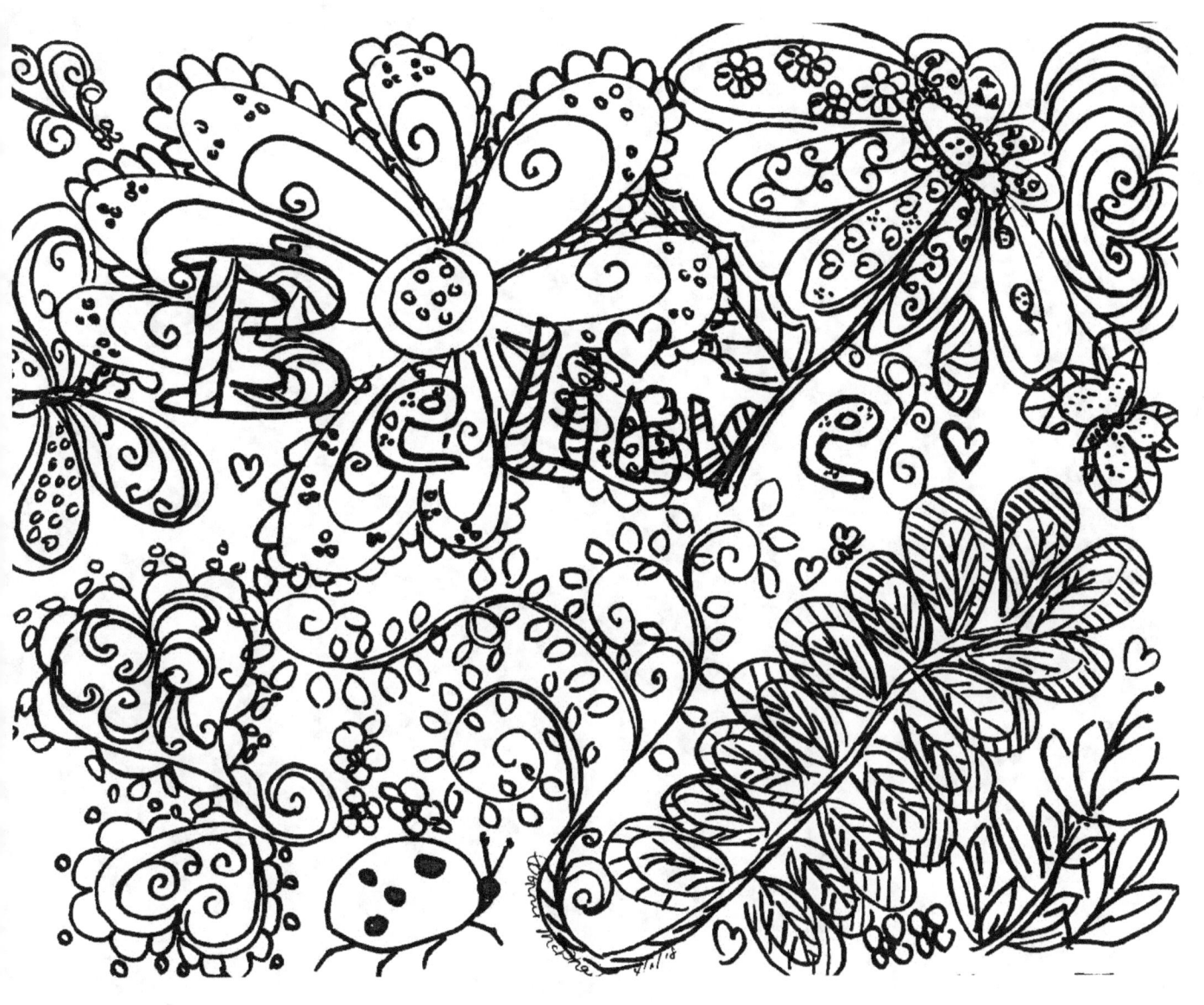

"God is our refuge and strength, an ever-present help in trouble."

Psalm 46:1

119

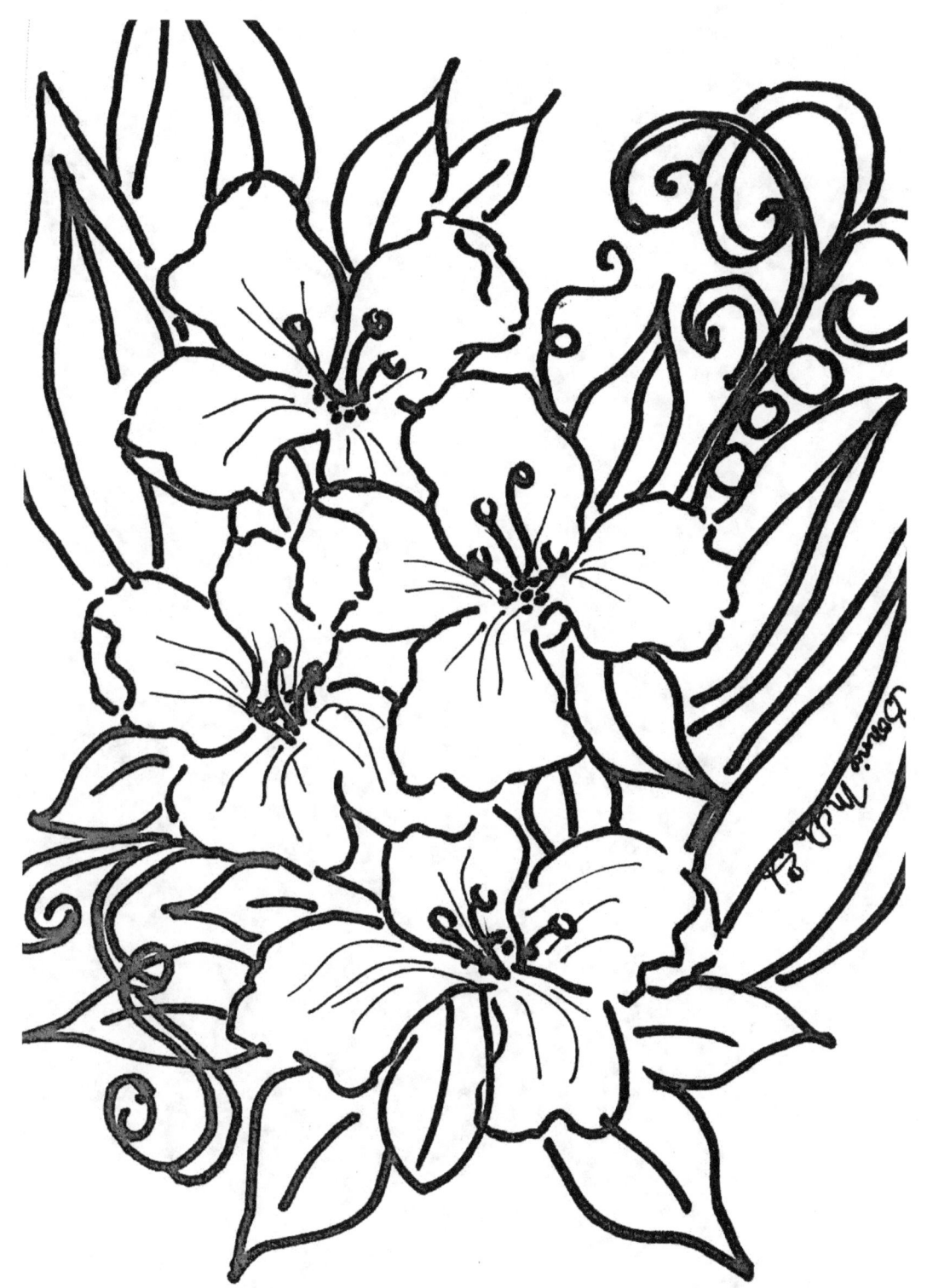

"So do not fear, for I am with you; do no be dismayed for I am your God. I will strengthen you and help you I will uphold you with my righteous right hand."

Isaiah 41:10

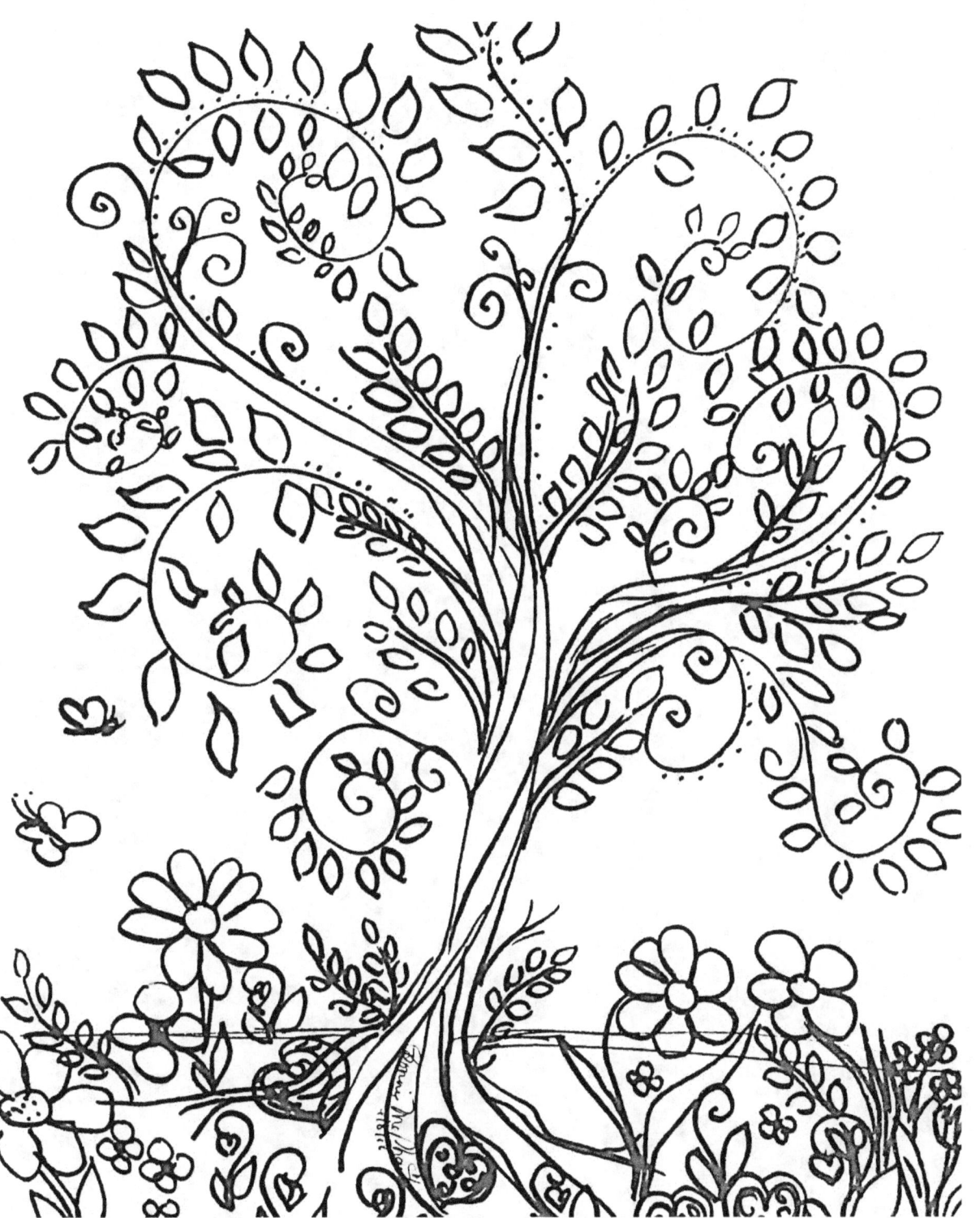

"Do not be anxious about anything, but in every situation, by prayer and petition, with thanksgiving, present your requests to God."

Philippians 4:6

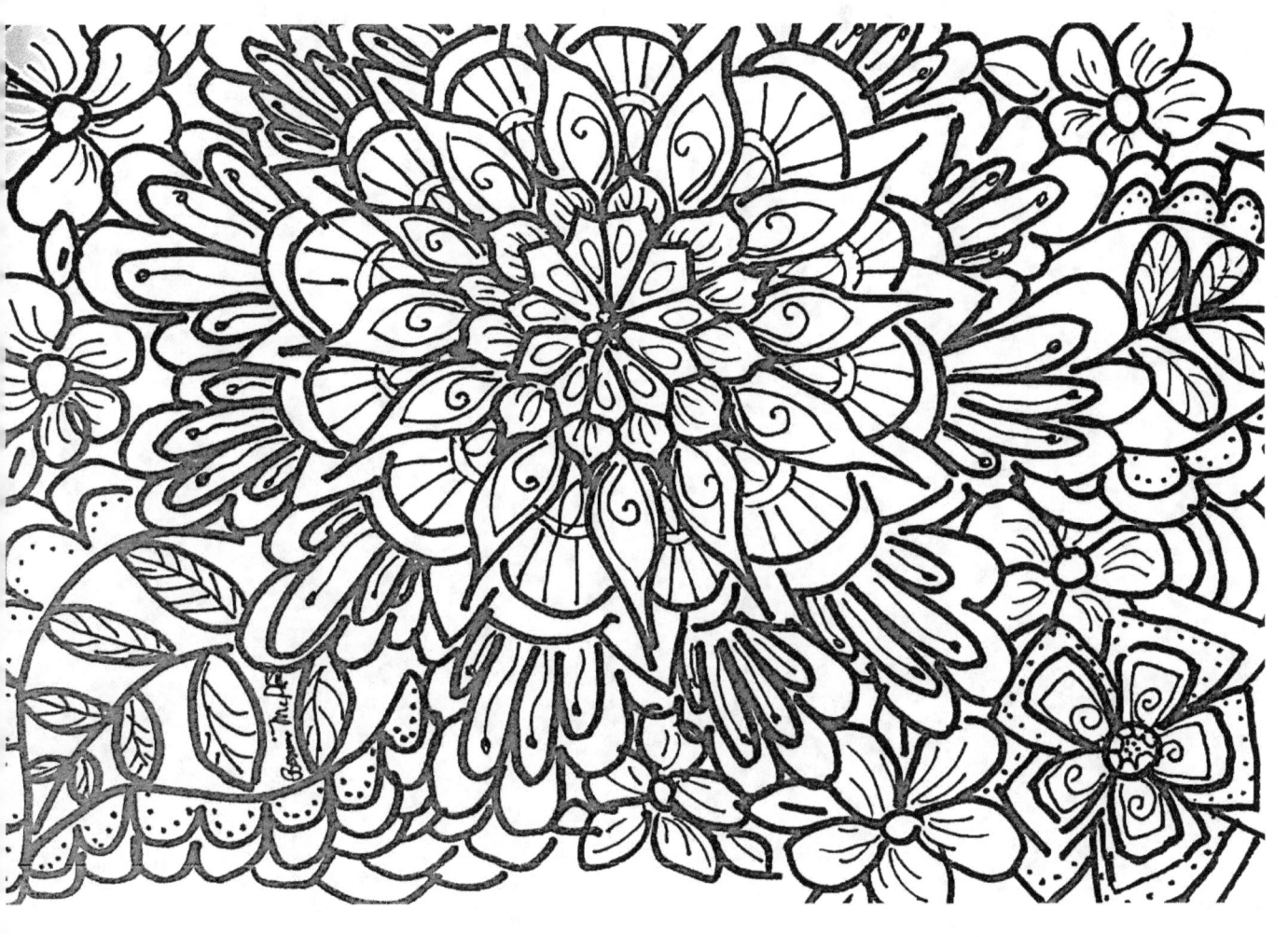

"And we know that in all things God works for the good of those who love him, who have been called according to his purpose."
Romans 8:28

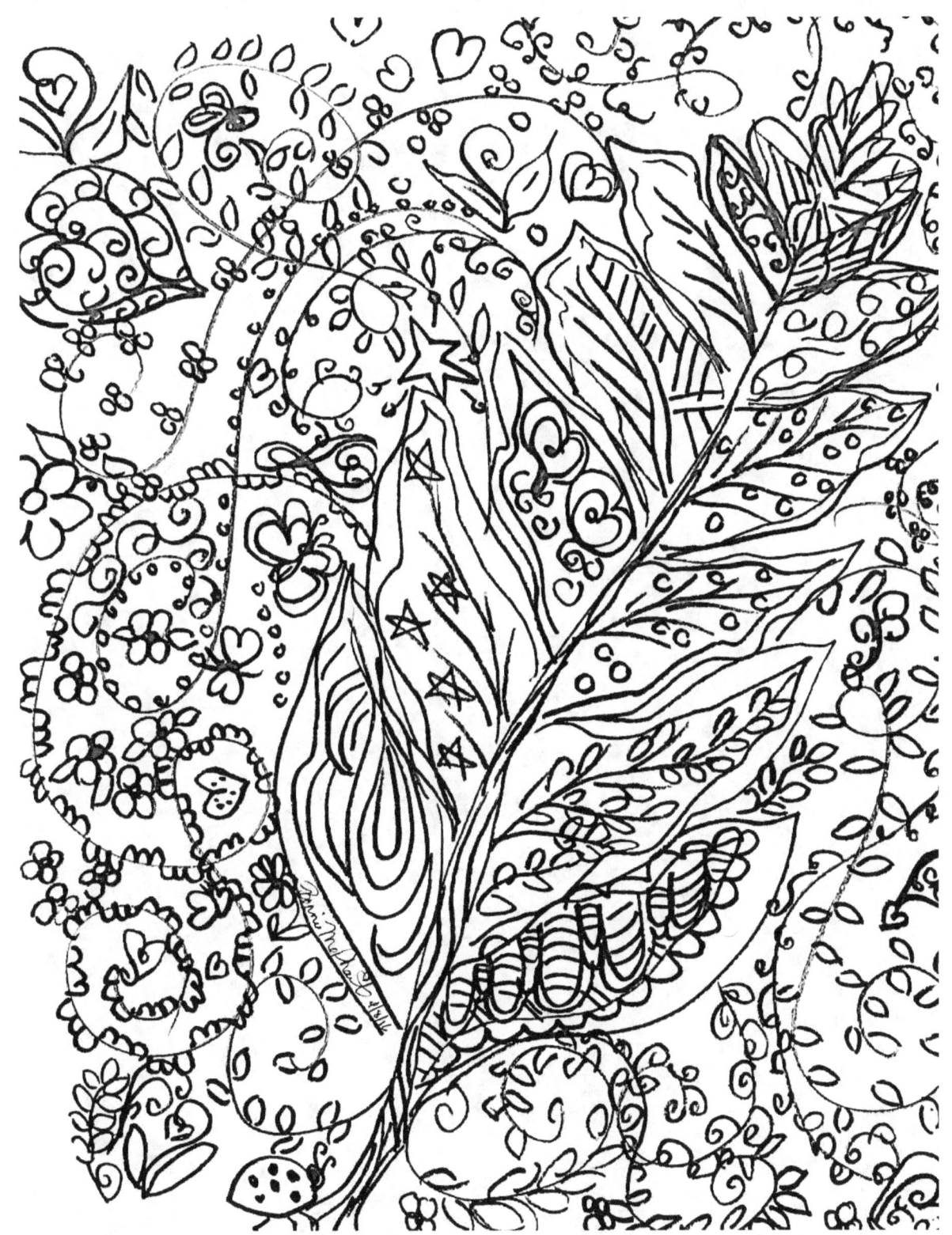

"But remember the LORD your God, for it is he who gives you the ability to produce wealth, and so confirms his covenant, which he swore to your ancestors, as it is today." Deuteronomy 8:18

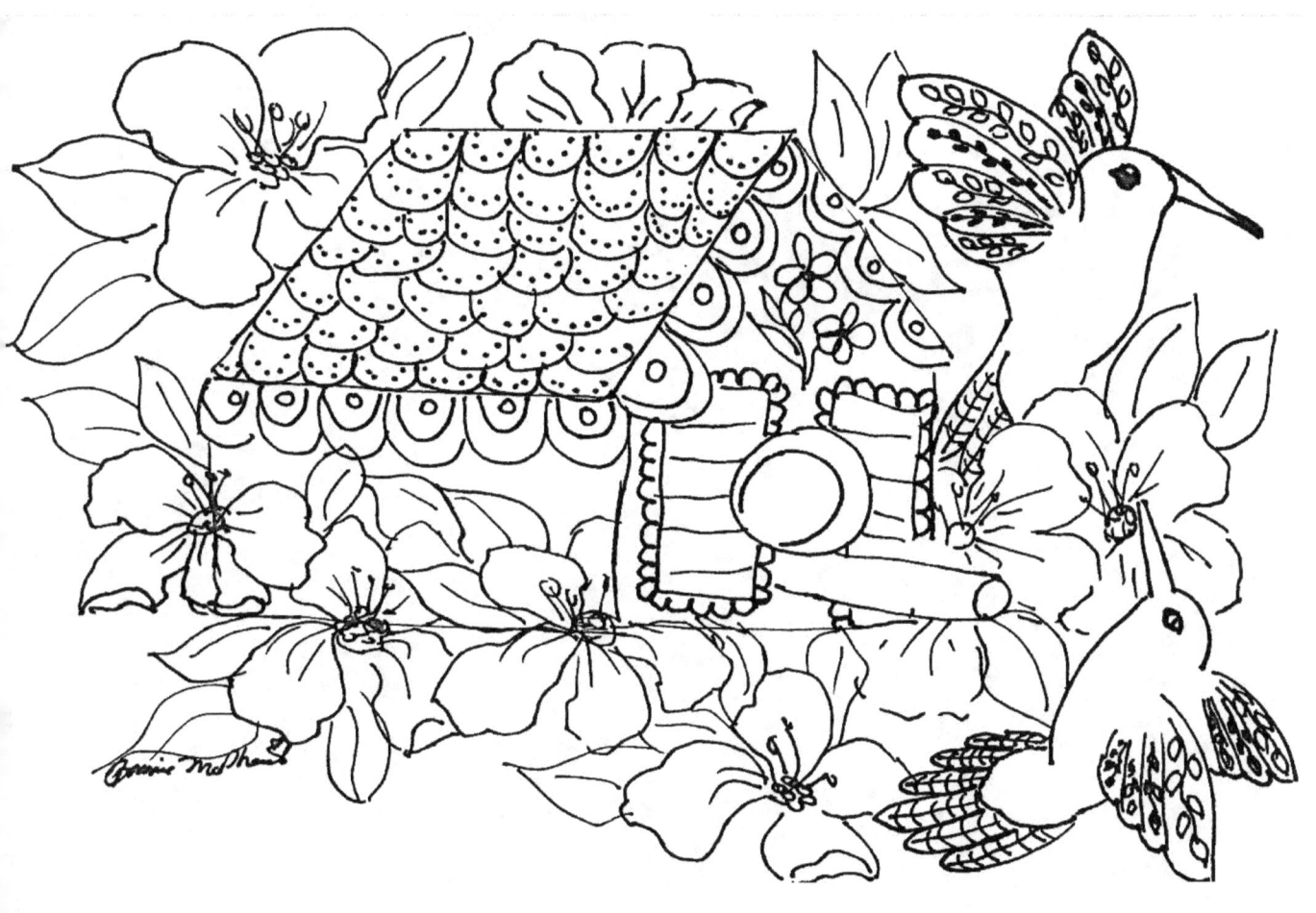

"Love is patient, love is kind. It does not envy, it does not boast, it is not proud. It does not dishonor others, it is not self-seeking, it is not easily angered, it keeps no record of wrongs. Love does not delight in evil but rejoices with the truth. It always protects, always trusts, always hopes, always perseveres. Love never fails..."

1 Corinthians 13:1-7

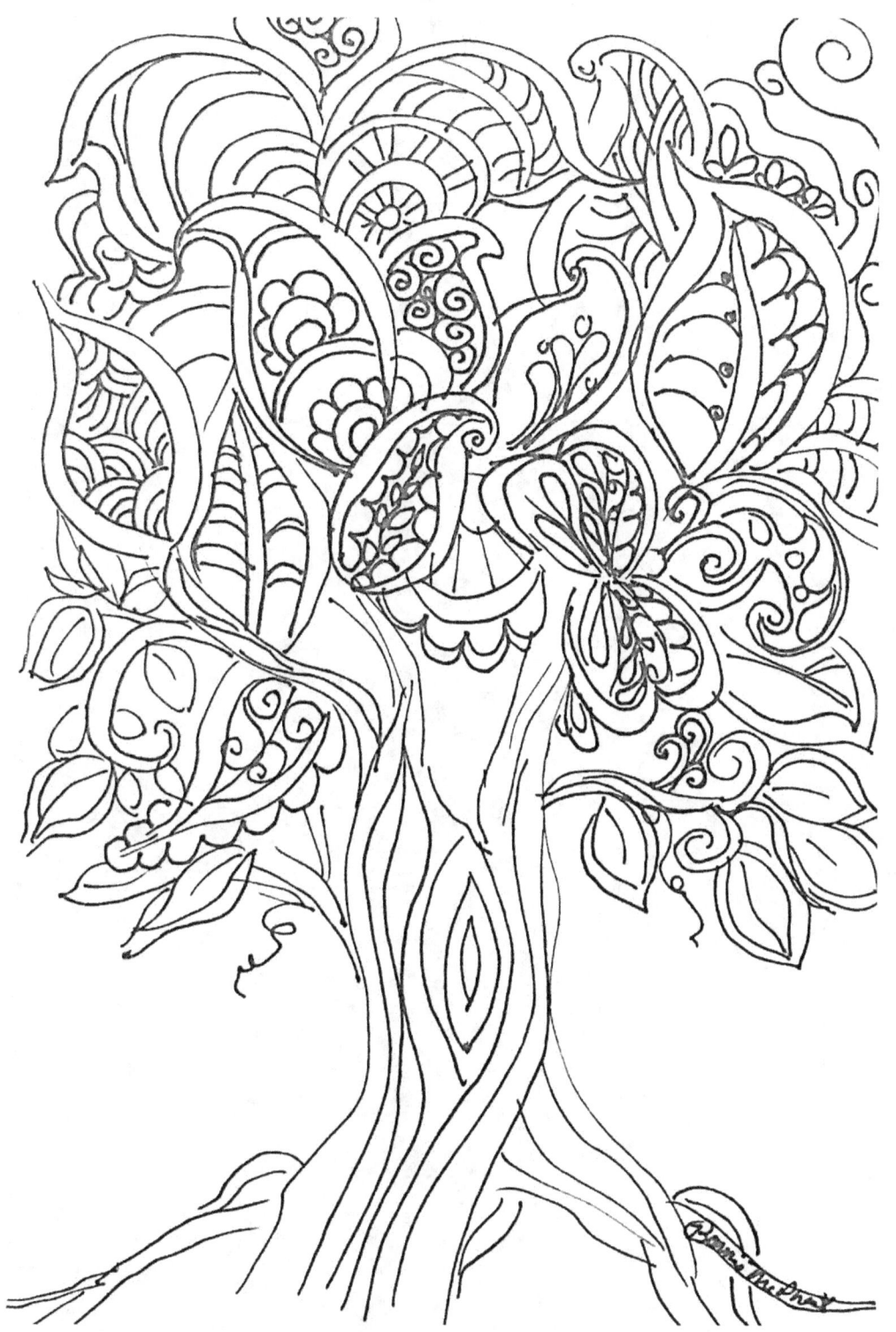

"But blessed is the one who trusts in the LORD, whose confidence is in him."

Jeremiah 17:7

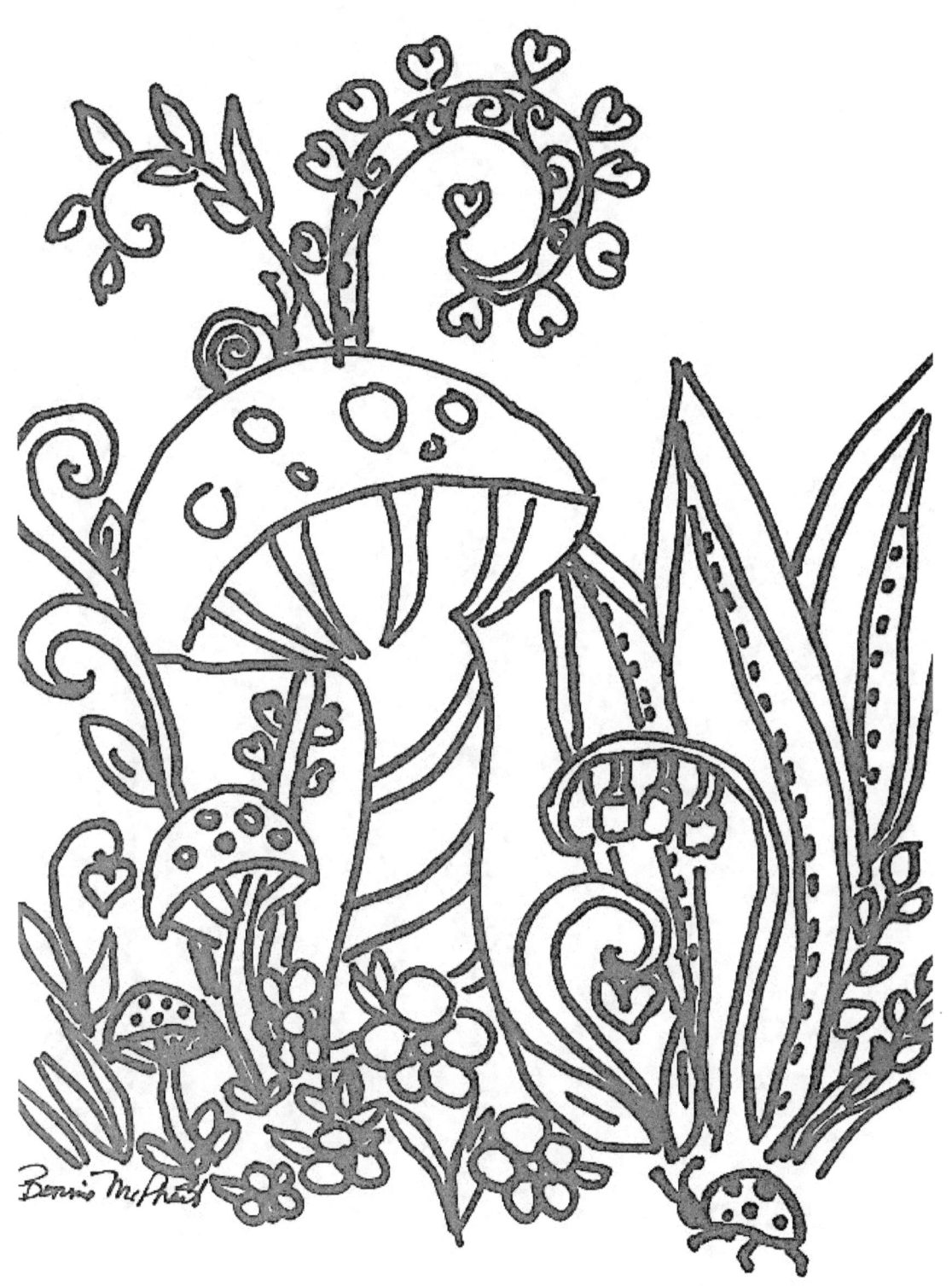

"God blessed them and said to them, "Be fruitful and increase in number..."

Genesis 1:28

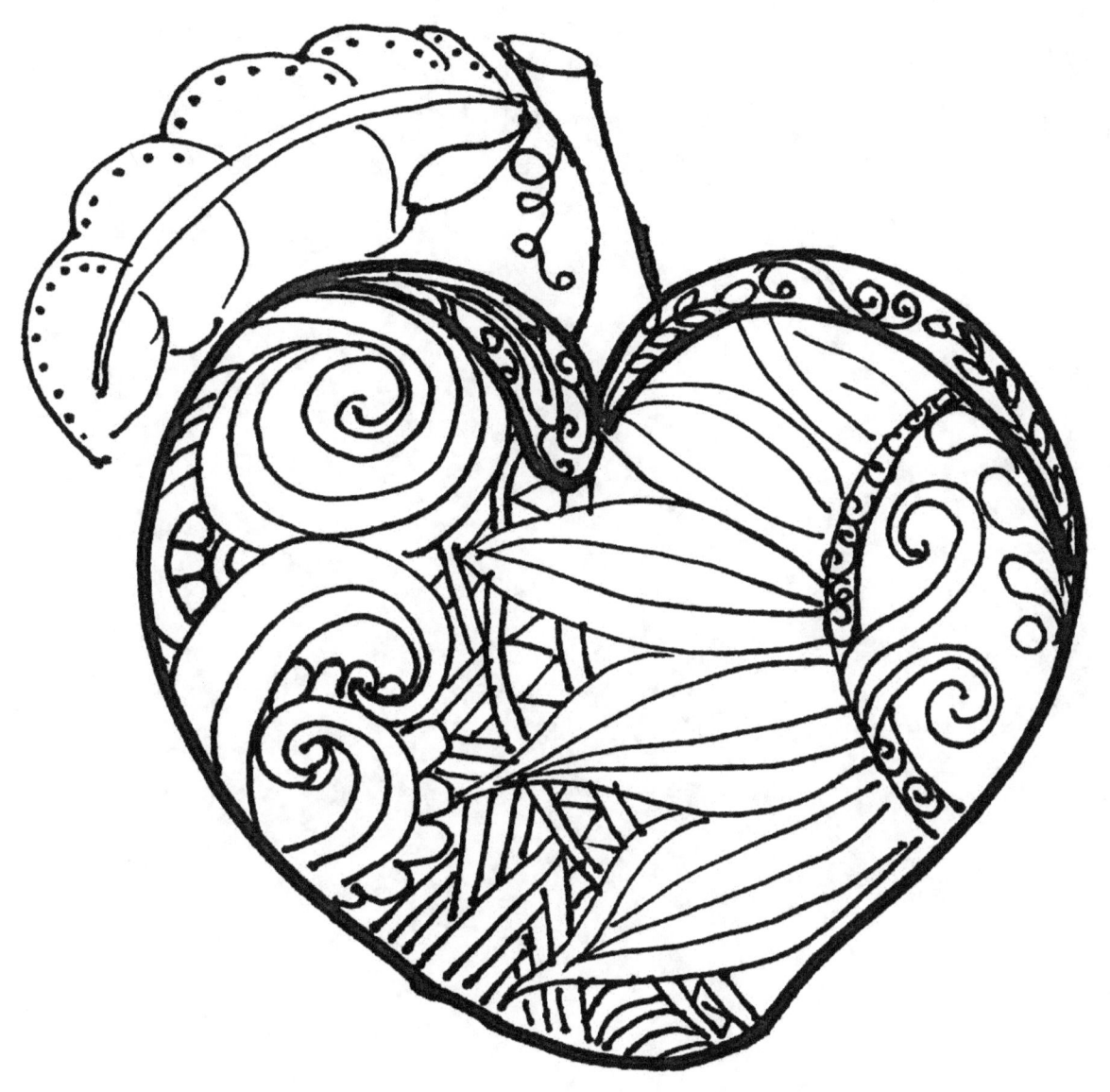

"But the fruit of the Spirit is love, joy, peace, forbearance, kindness, goodness, faithfulness, gentleness, and self-control. Against such things there is no law." Galatians 5:22-23

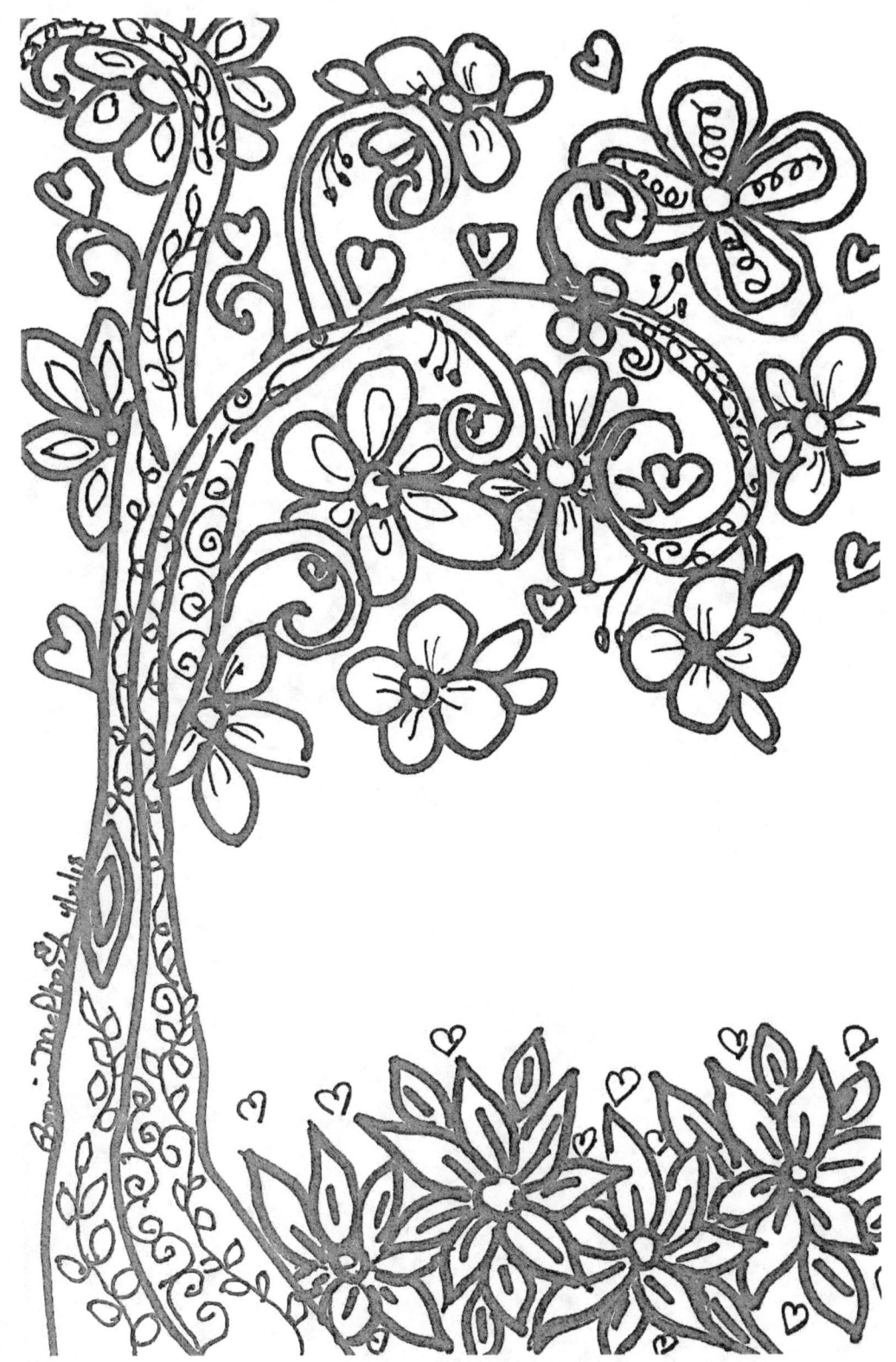

"And this same GOD who takes care of me will supply all your needs from his glorious riches, which have been given to us in Christ Jesus." Philippians 4:19

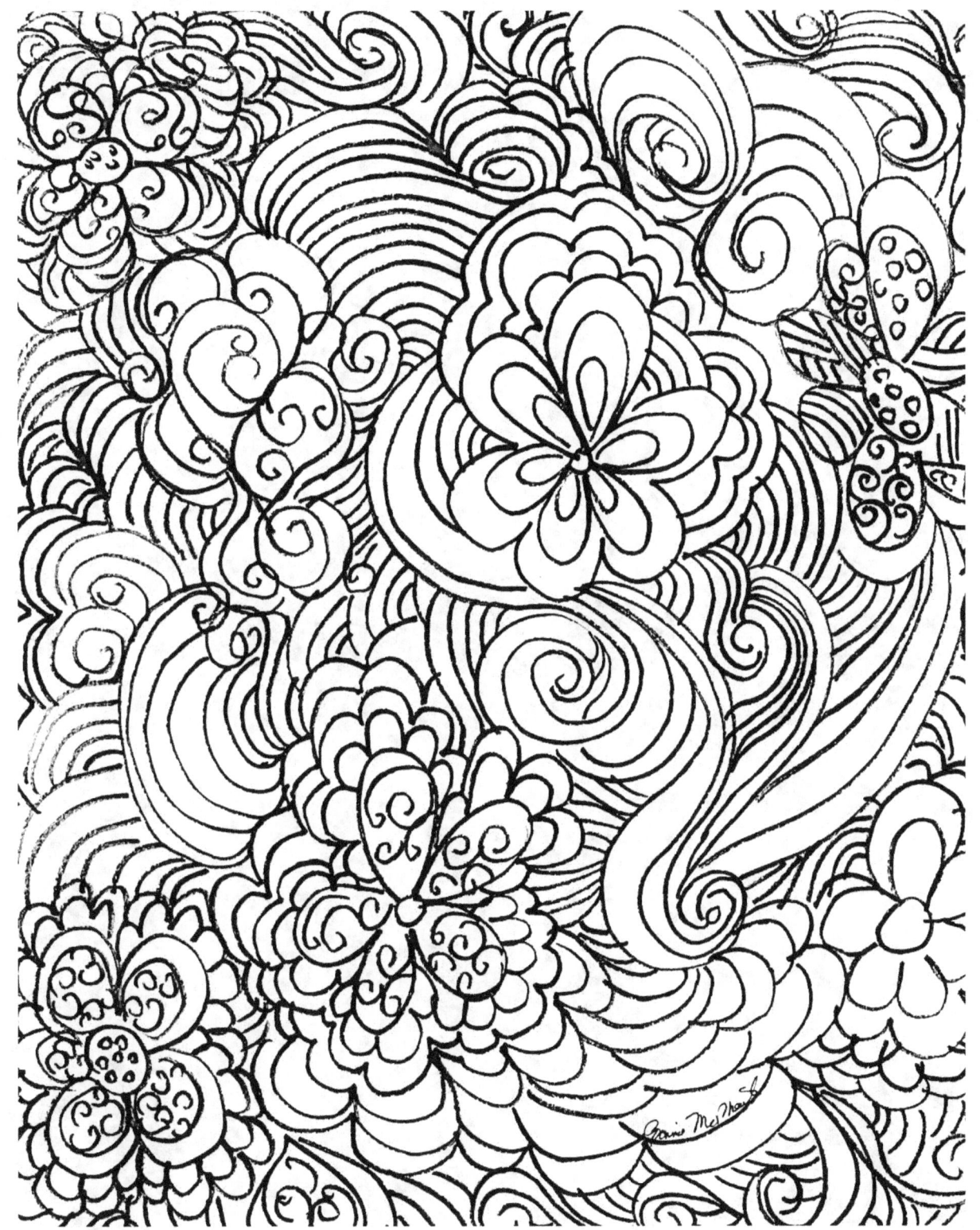

"The blessings of the Lord makes a person rich, and he adds not sorrow with it." Proverbs 10:22

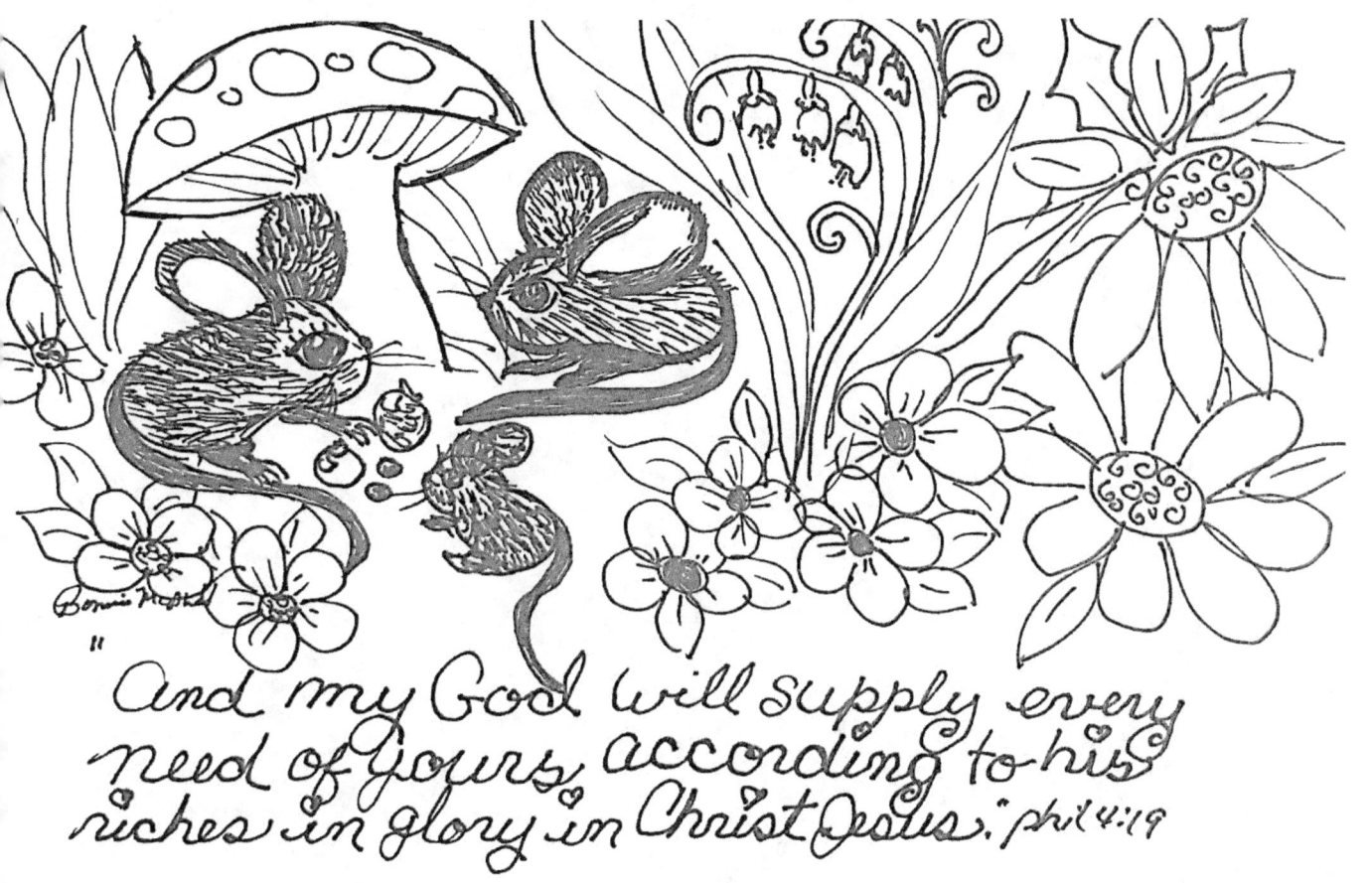

"And my God will supply every
need of yours, according to his
riches in glory in Christ Jesus." phil 4:19

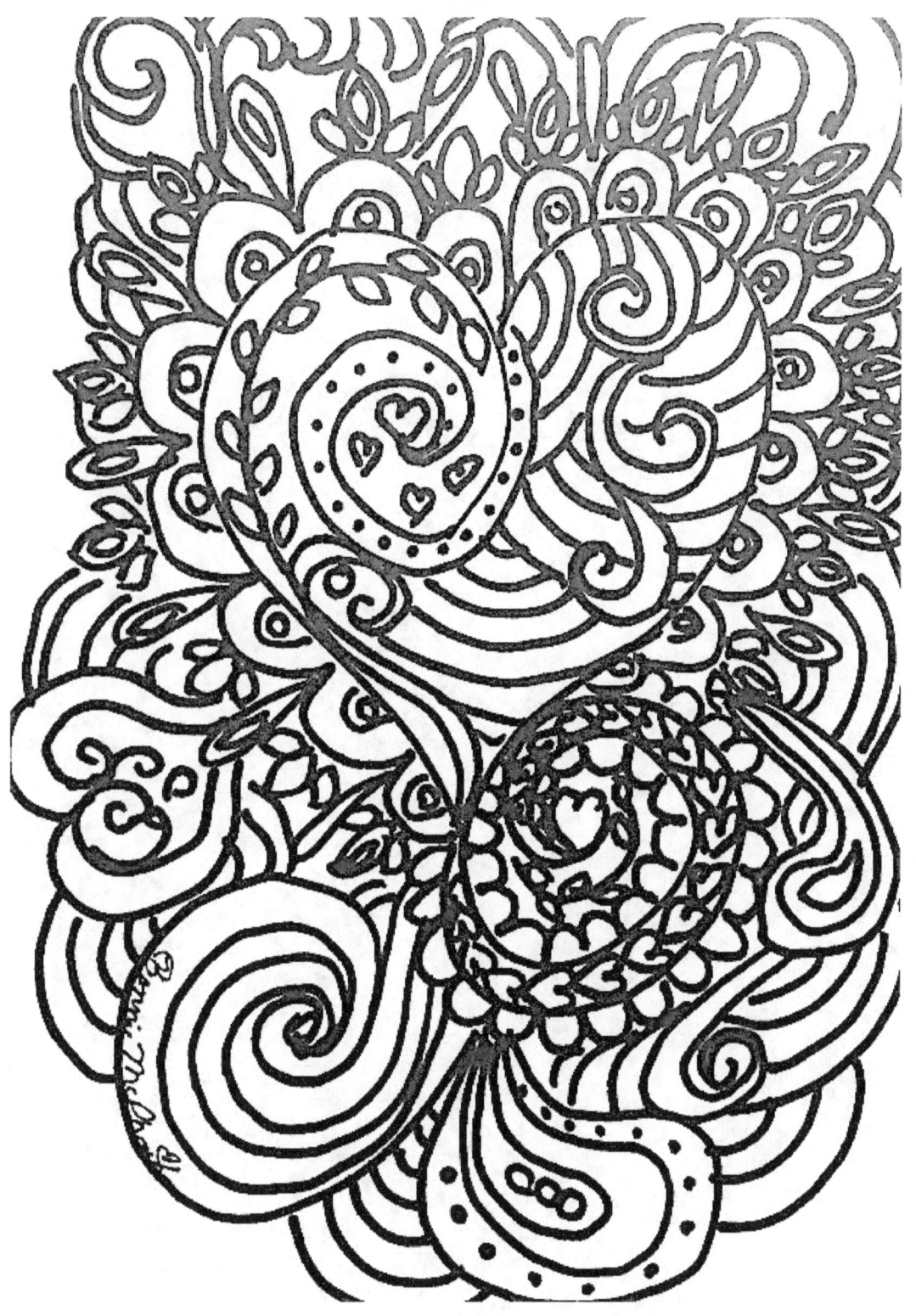

"And God will generously provide all you need. Then you will always have everything you need and plenty left over to share with others." 2 Corinthians 9:8

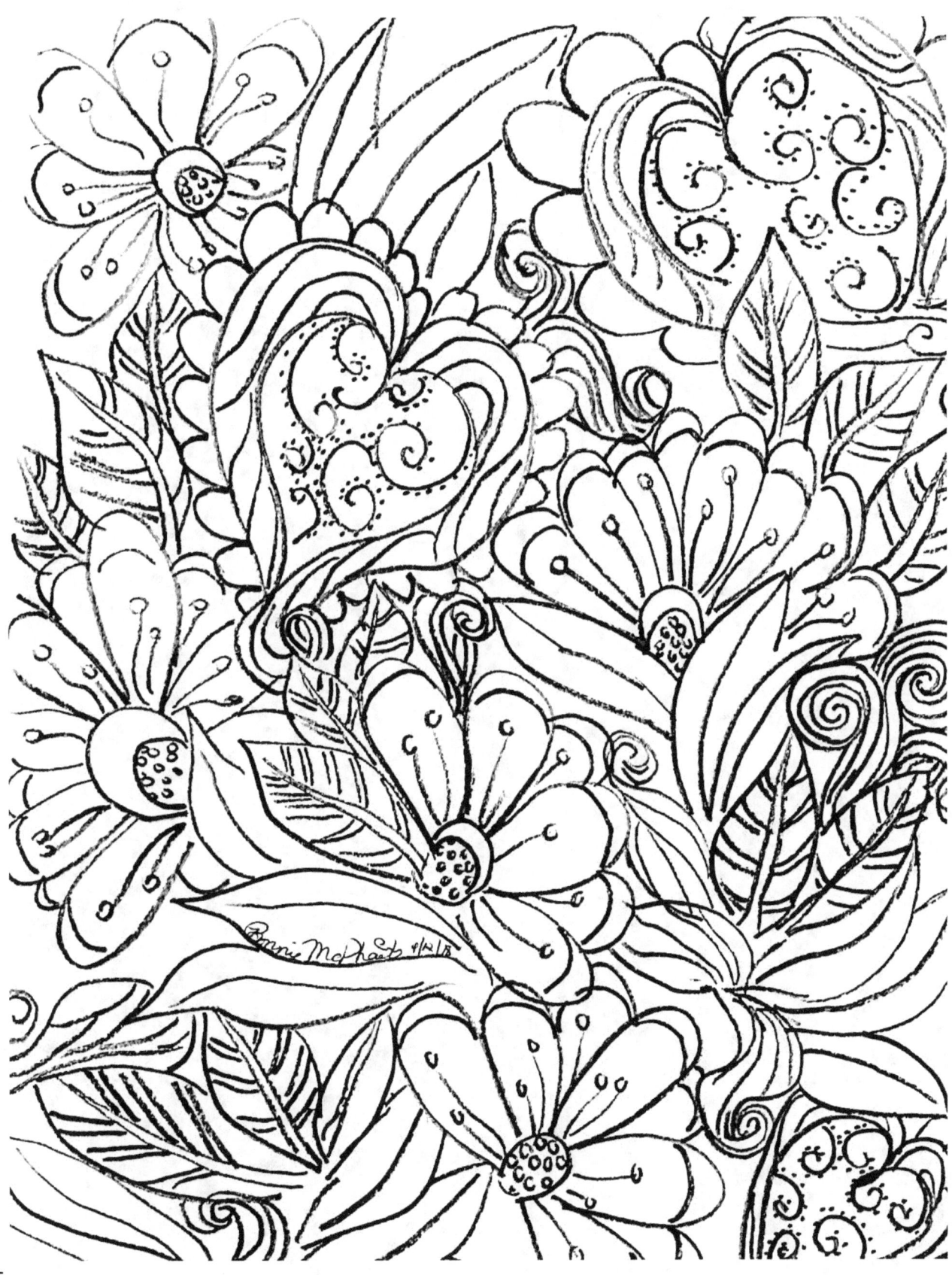

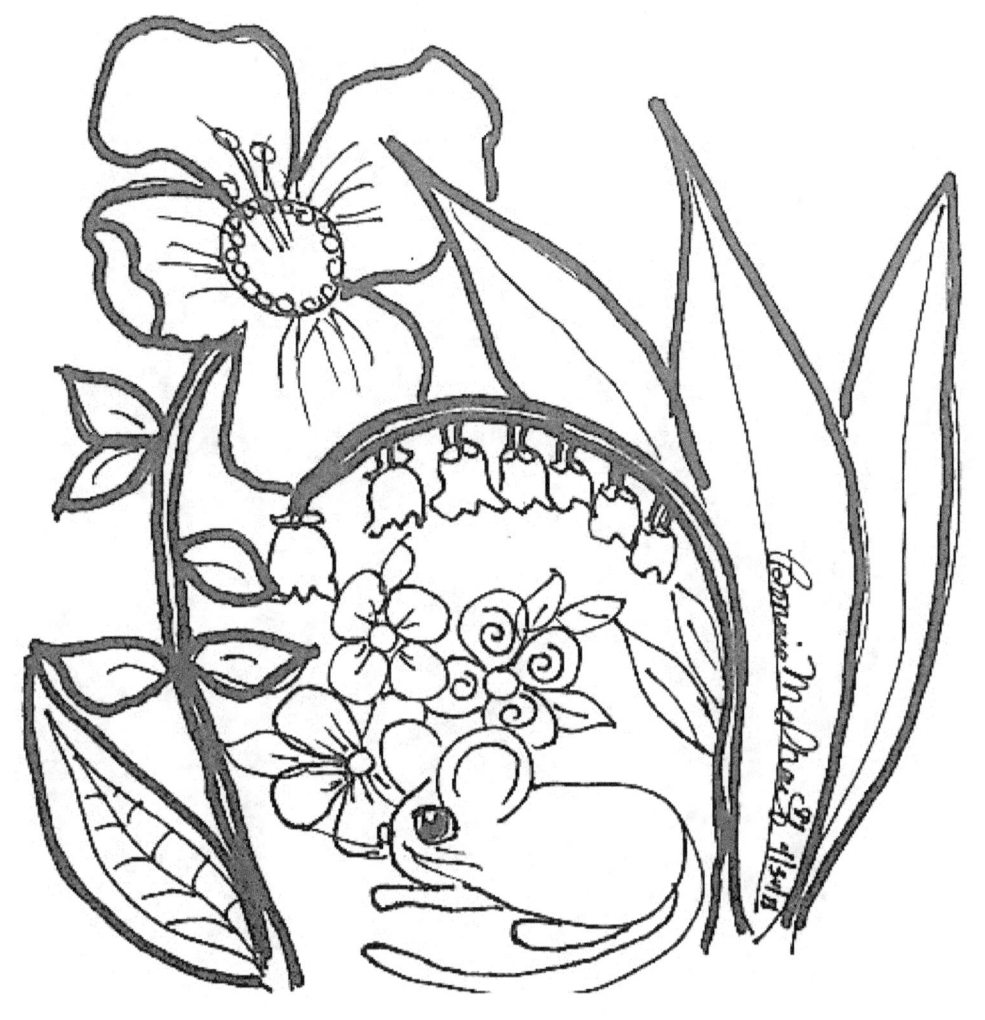

"But blessed are those who trust in the LORD and have made the Lord their hope and confidence. They are like trees planted along a riverbank, with roots that reach deep into the water. Such trees are not bothered by the heat or worried by long months of drought. Their leaves stay green, and they never stop producing fruit."

Jeremiah 17:7-8

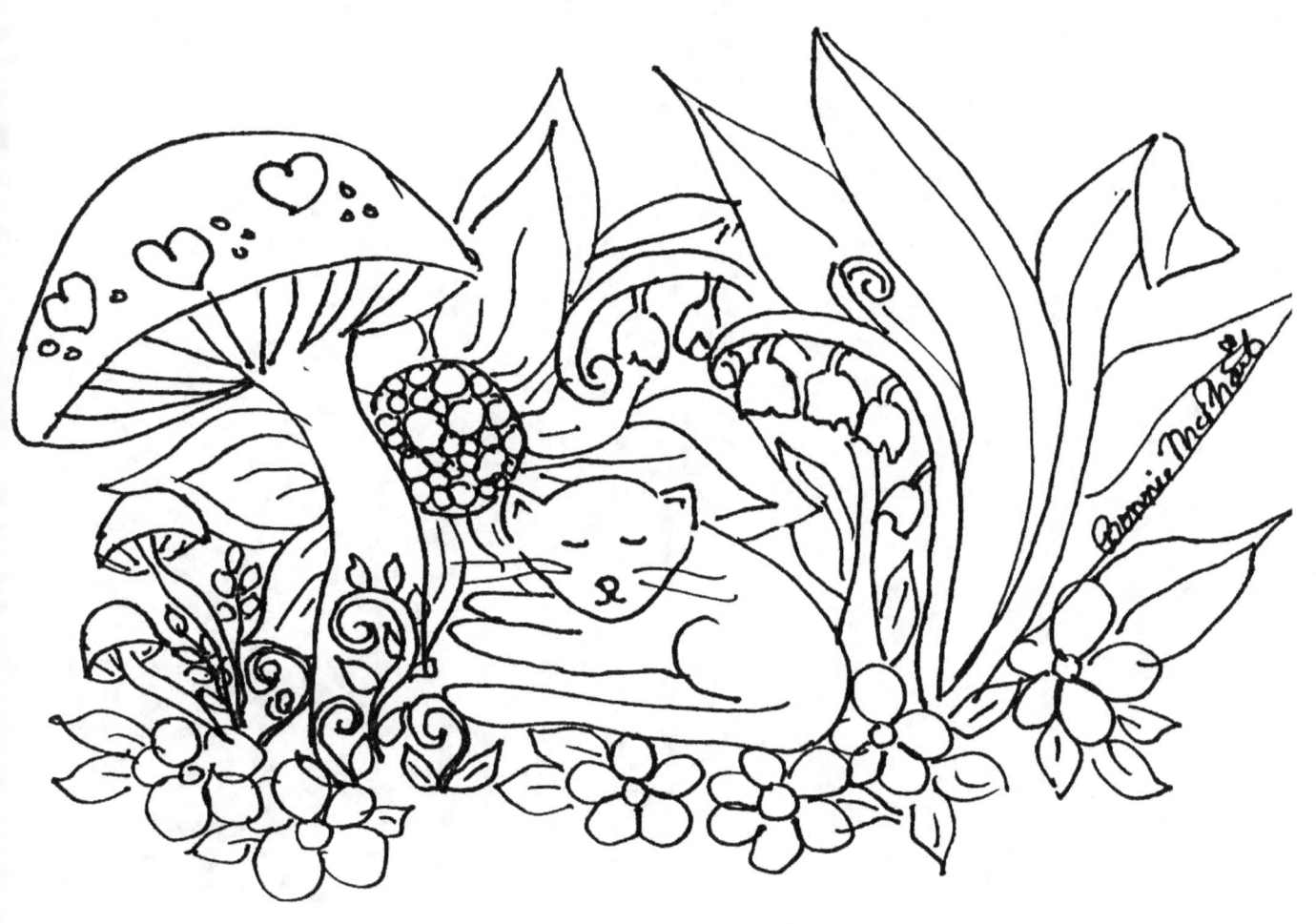

"Trust in the LORD with all your heart and lean not on your own understanding; in all your ways submit to him, and he will make your paths straight." Proverbs 3:5-6

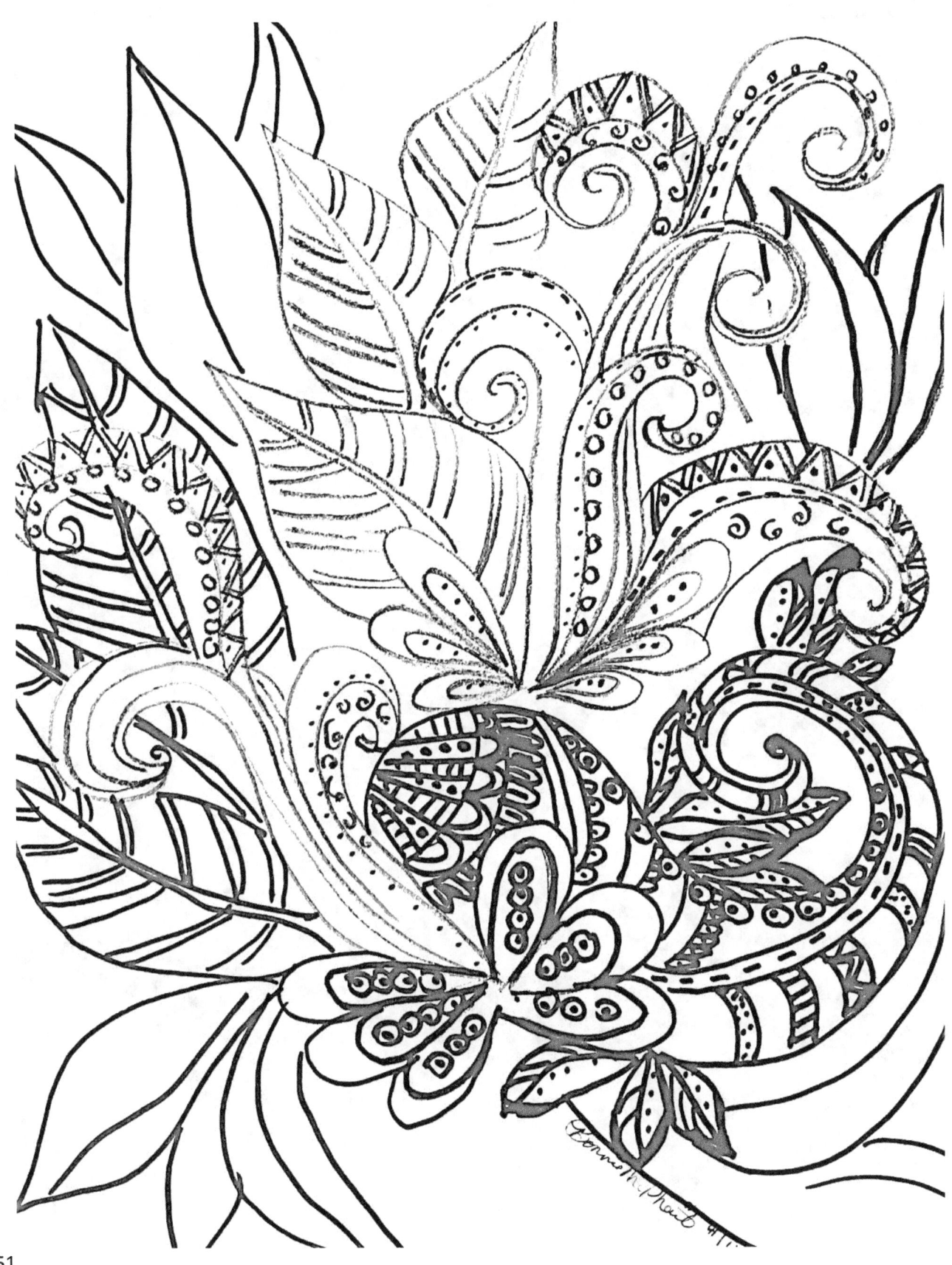

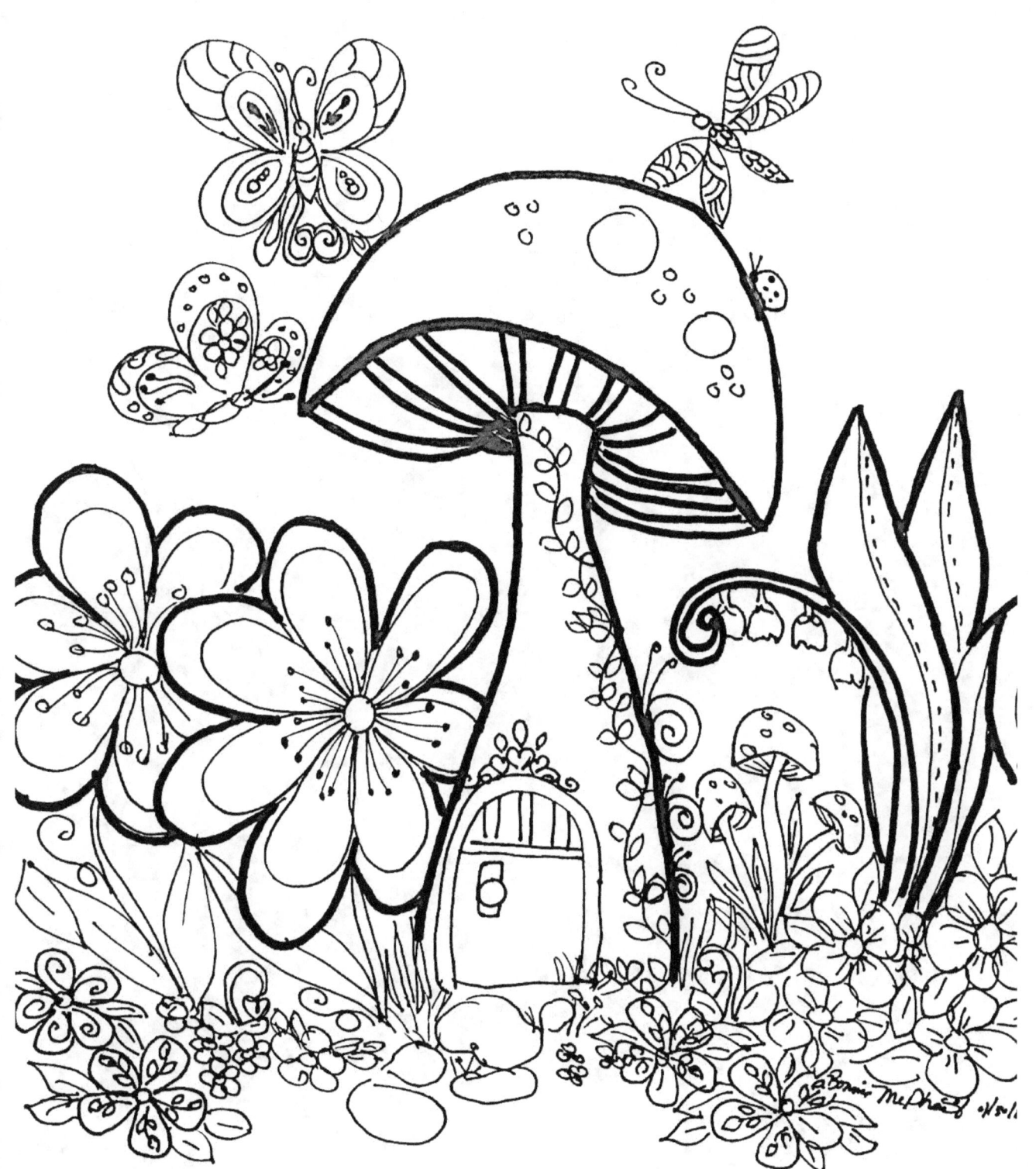

"Don't love money; be satisfied with what you have. For God has said, "I will never fail you. I will never abandon you." Hebrews 13:5

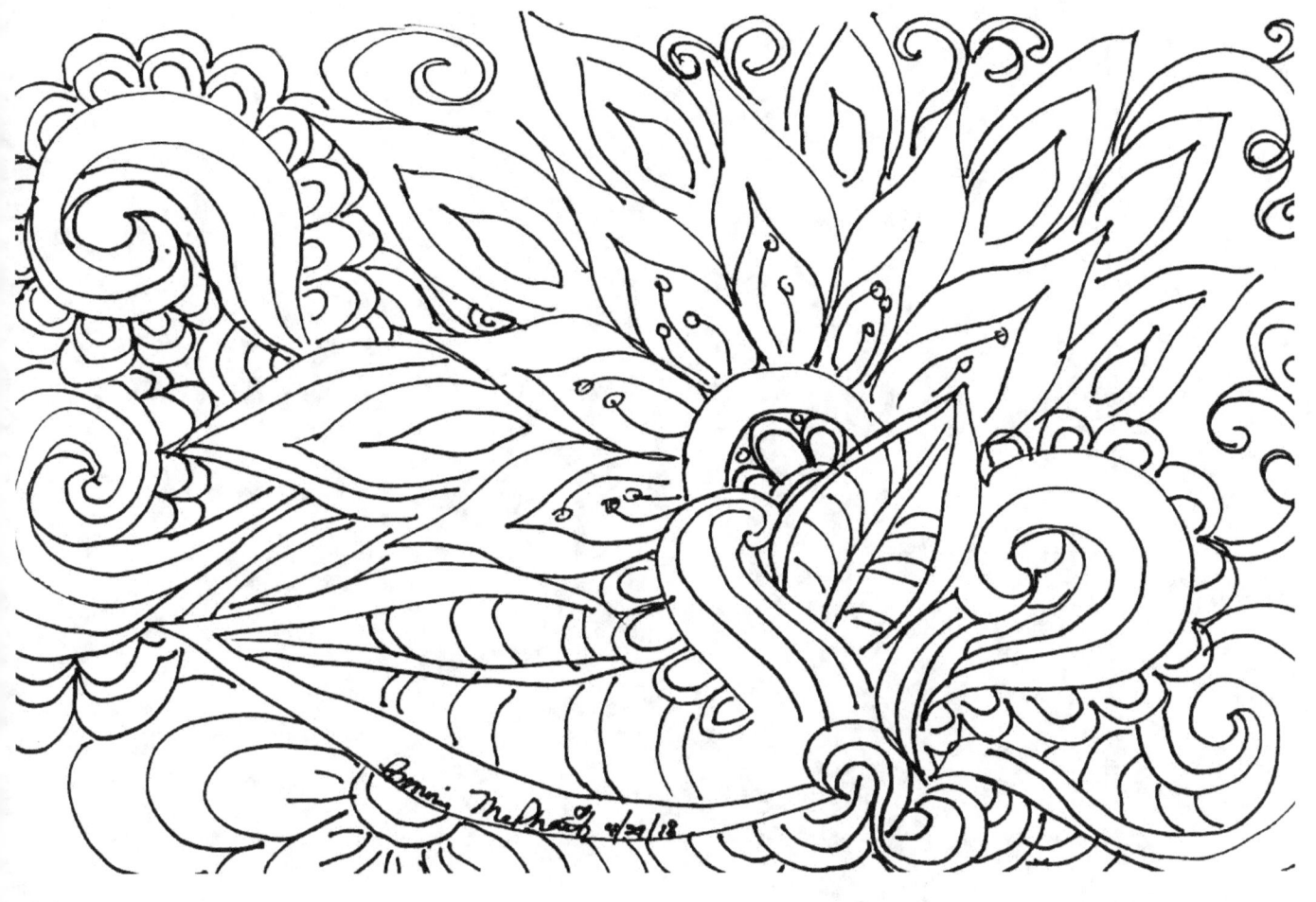

"Do not be anxious about anything, but in every situation, by prayer and petition, with thanksgiving, present your requests to God."

Philippians 4:6

156

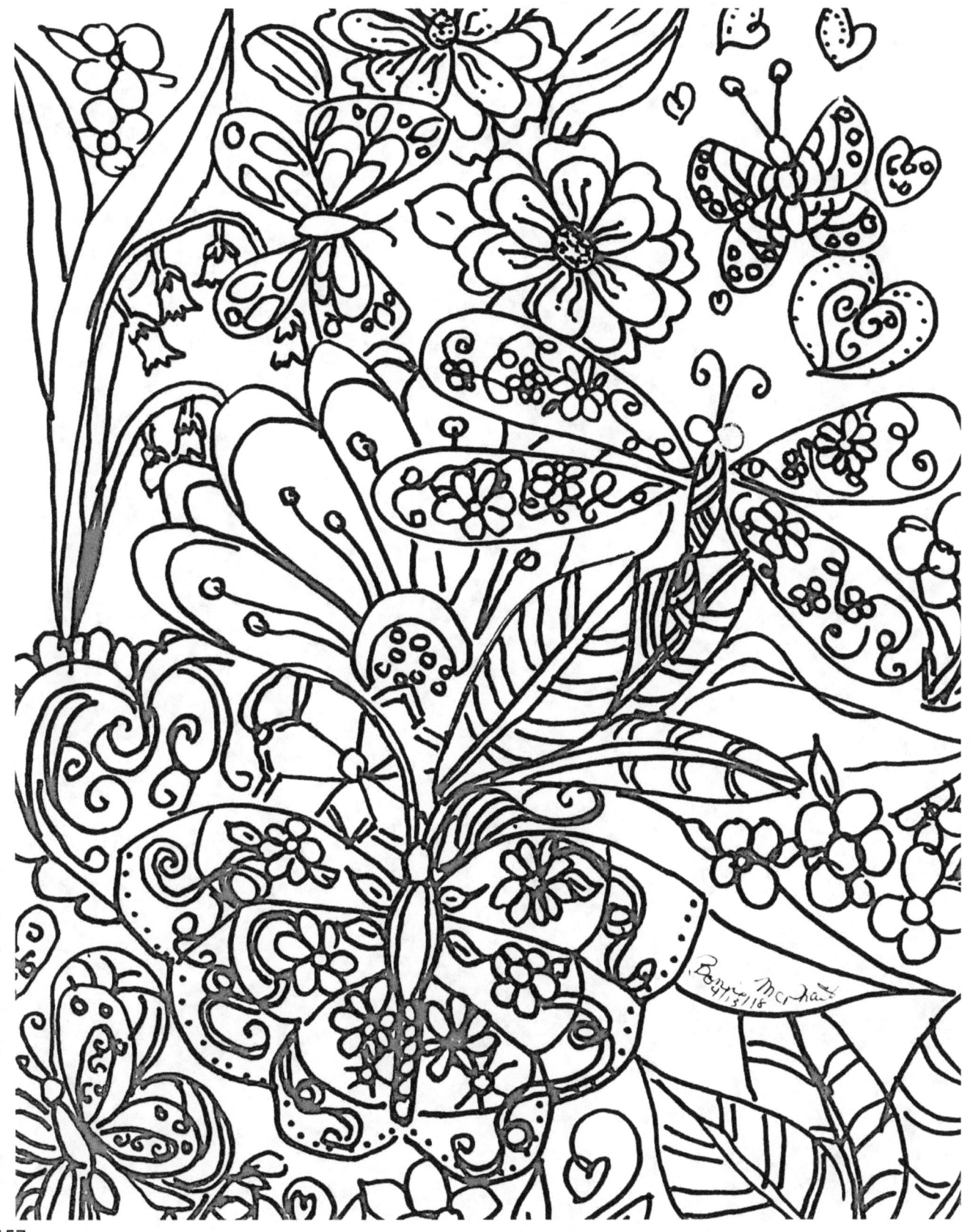

"Trust in the LORD with all your heart and lean not on your own understanding. In all your ways submit to him, and he will make your paths straight." Proverbs 3:5-6

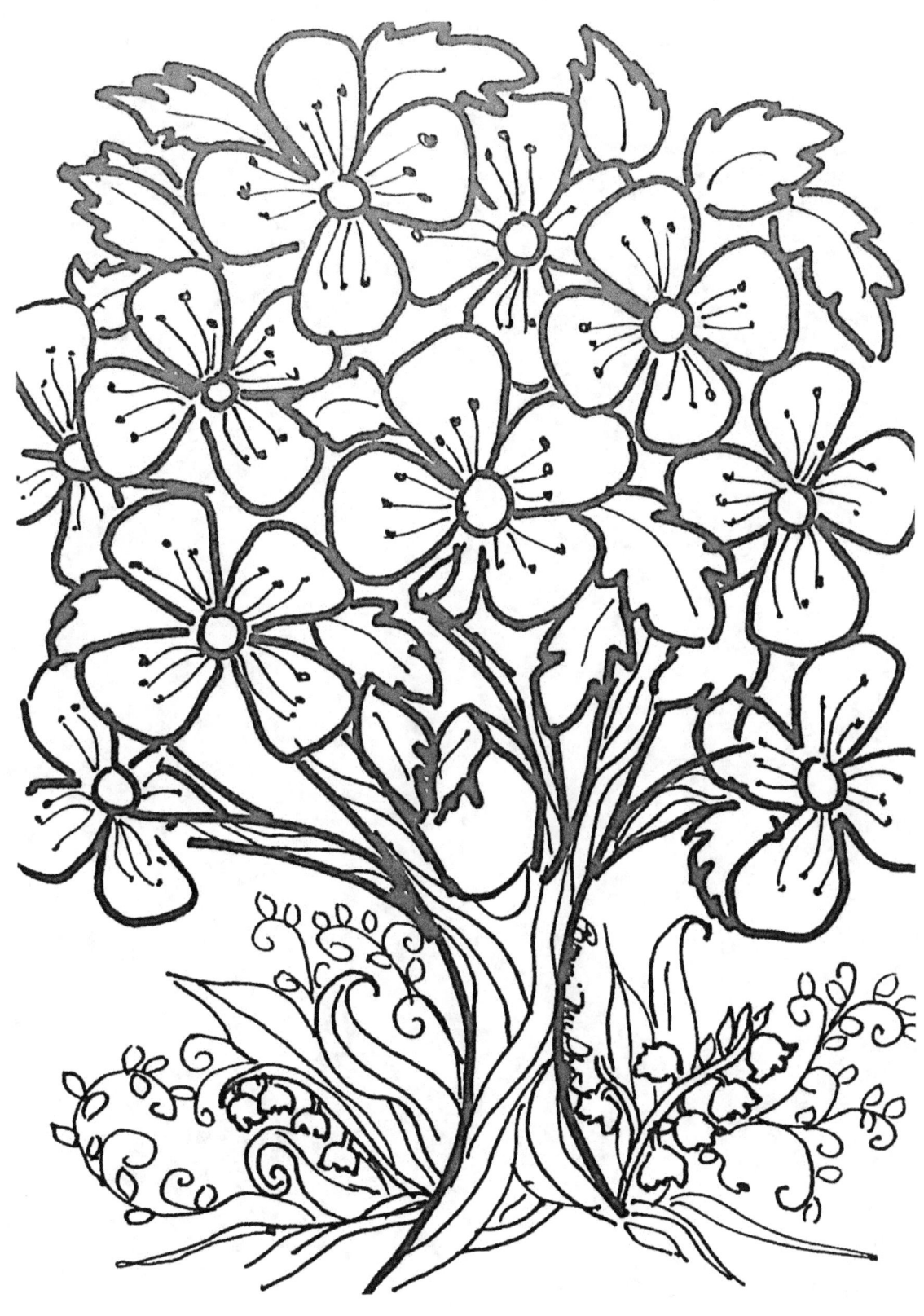

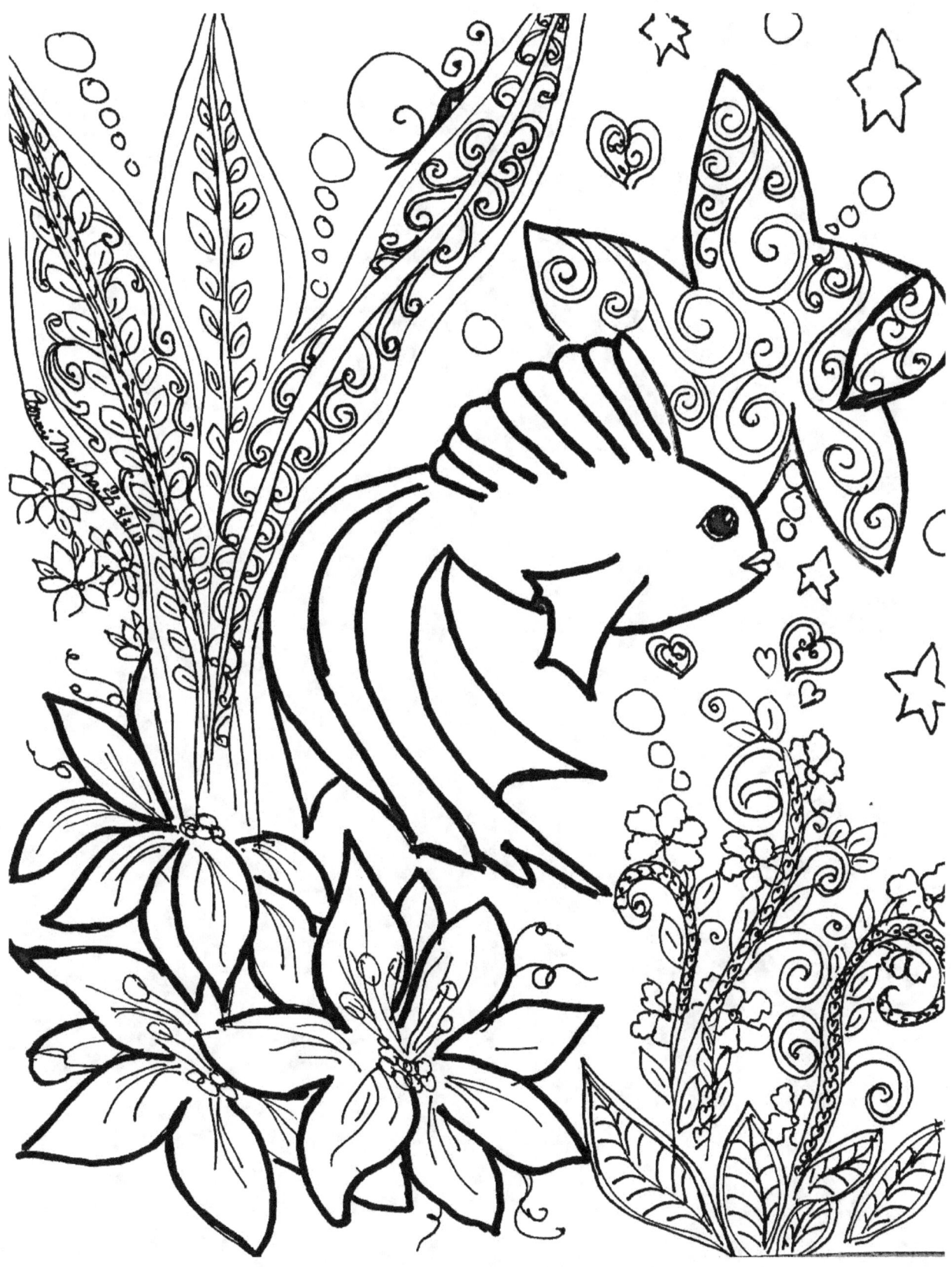

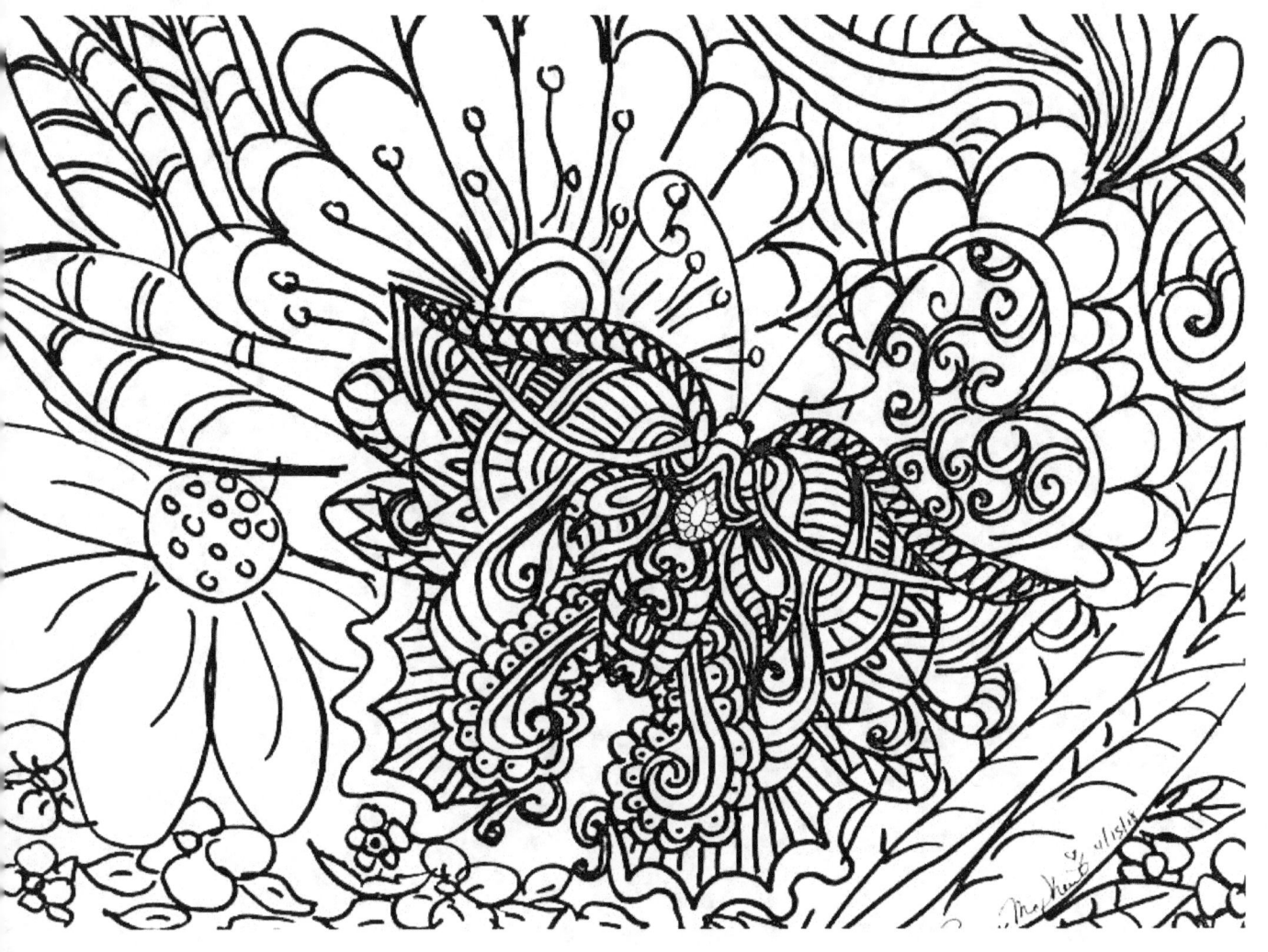

"Now Faith is the confidence in what we hope for and assurance about what we do not see." Hebrews 11:1

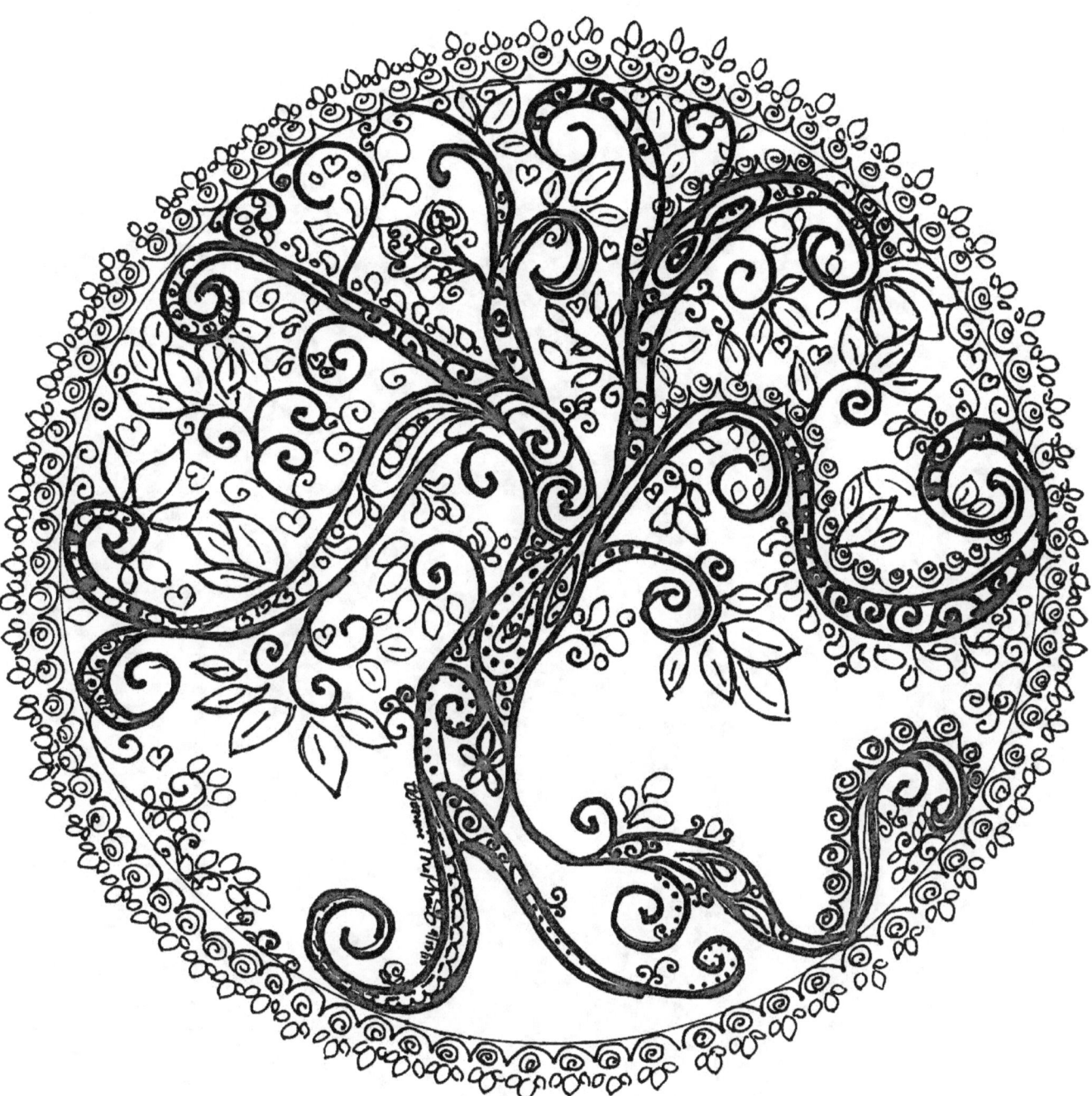

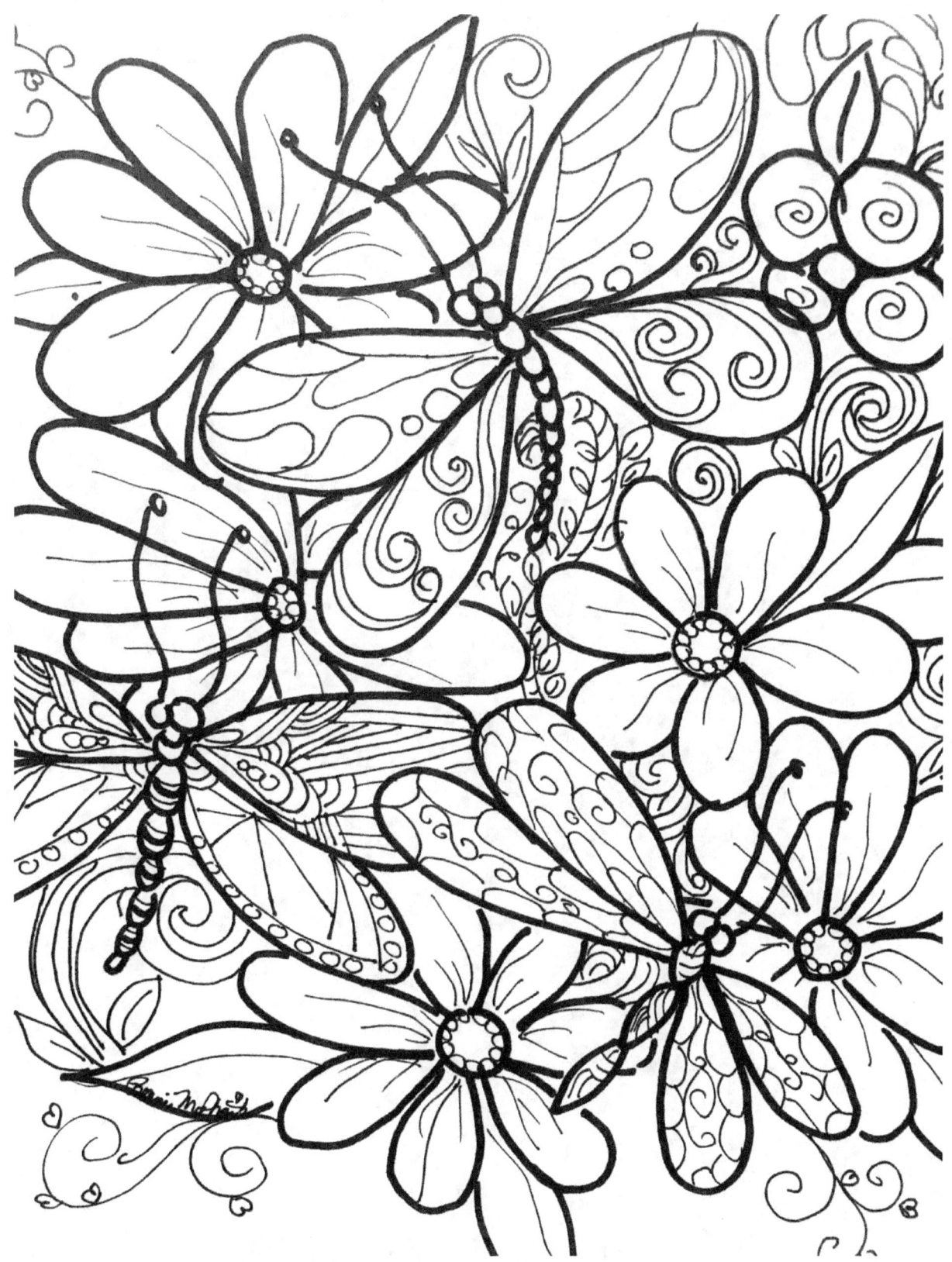

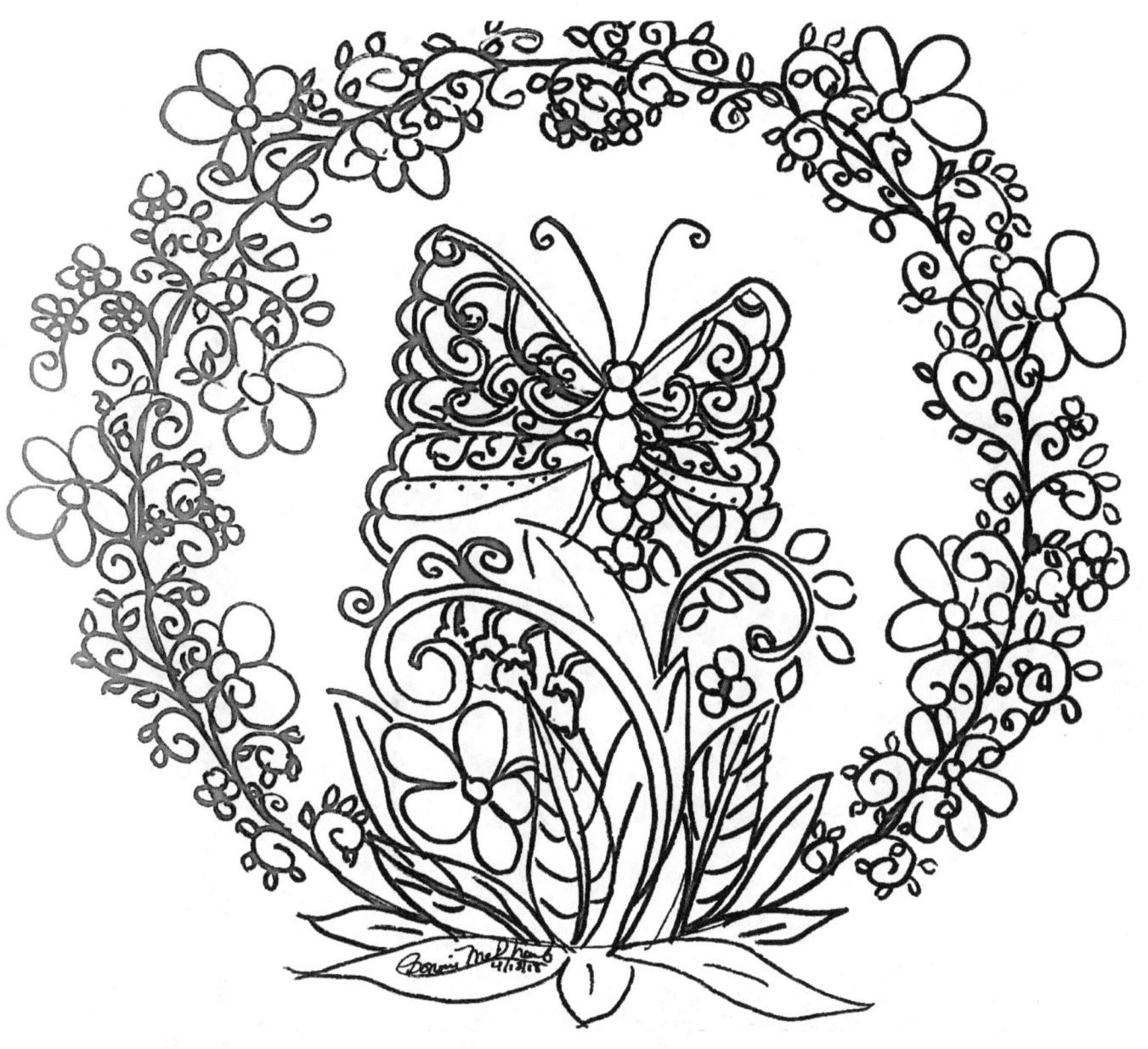

"The LORD your God is with you, the Mighty Warrior who saves.
He will take great delight in you..."
Zephania 3:17

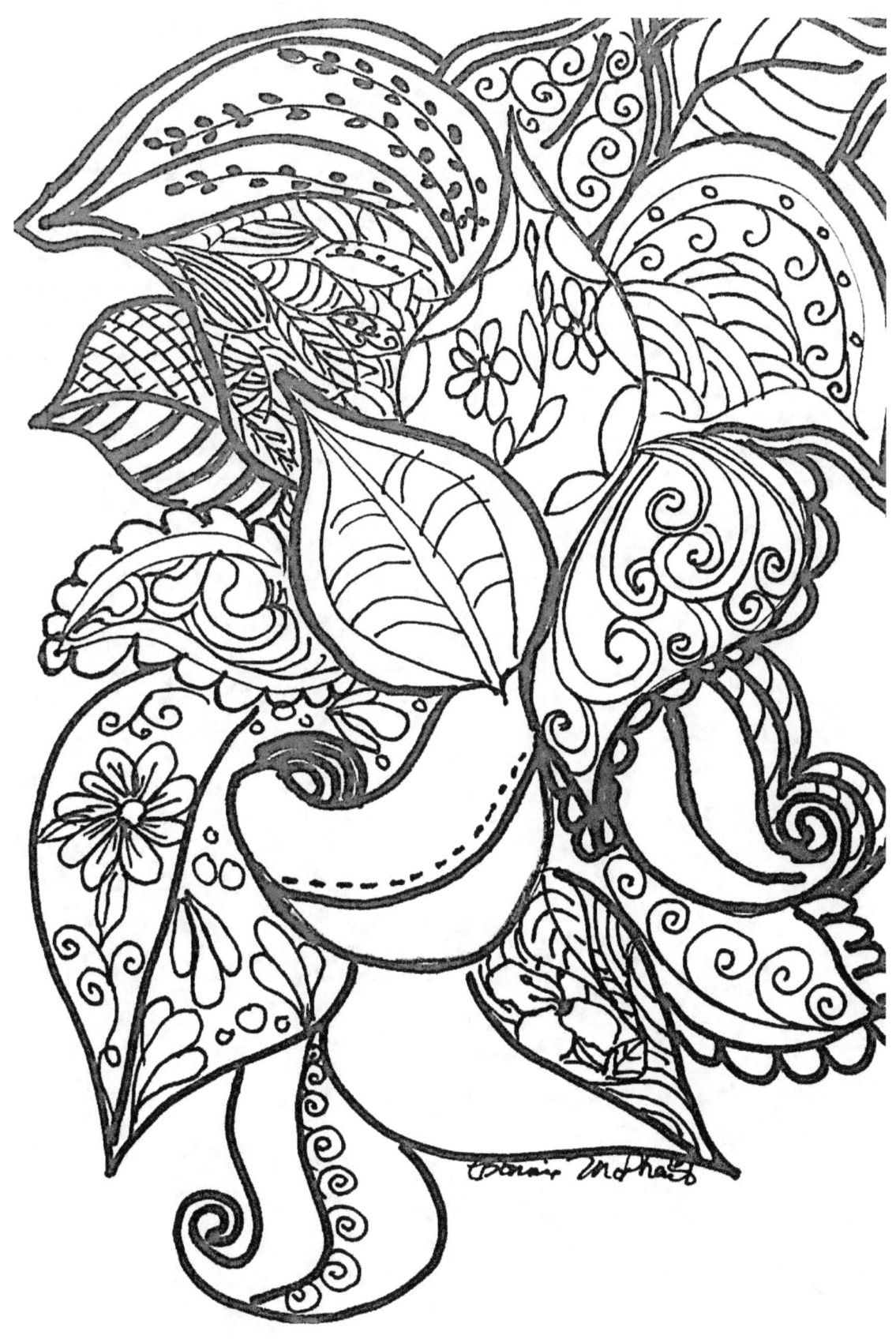

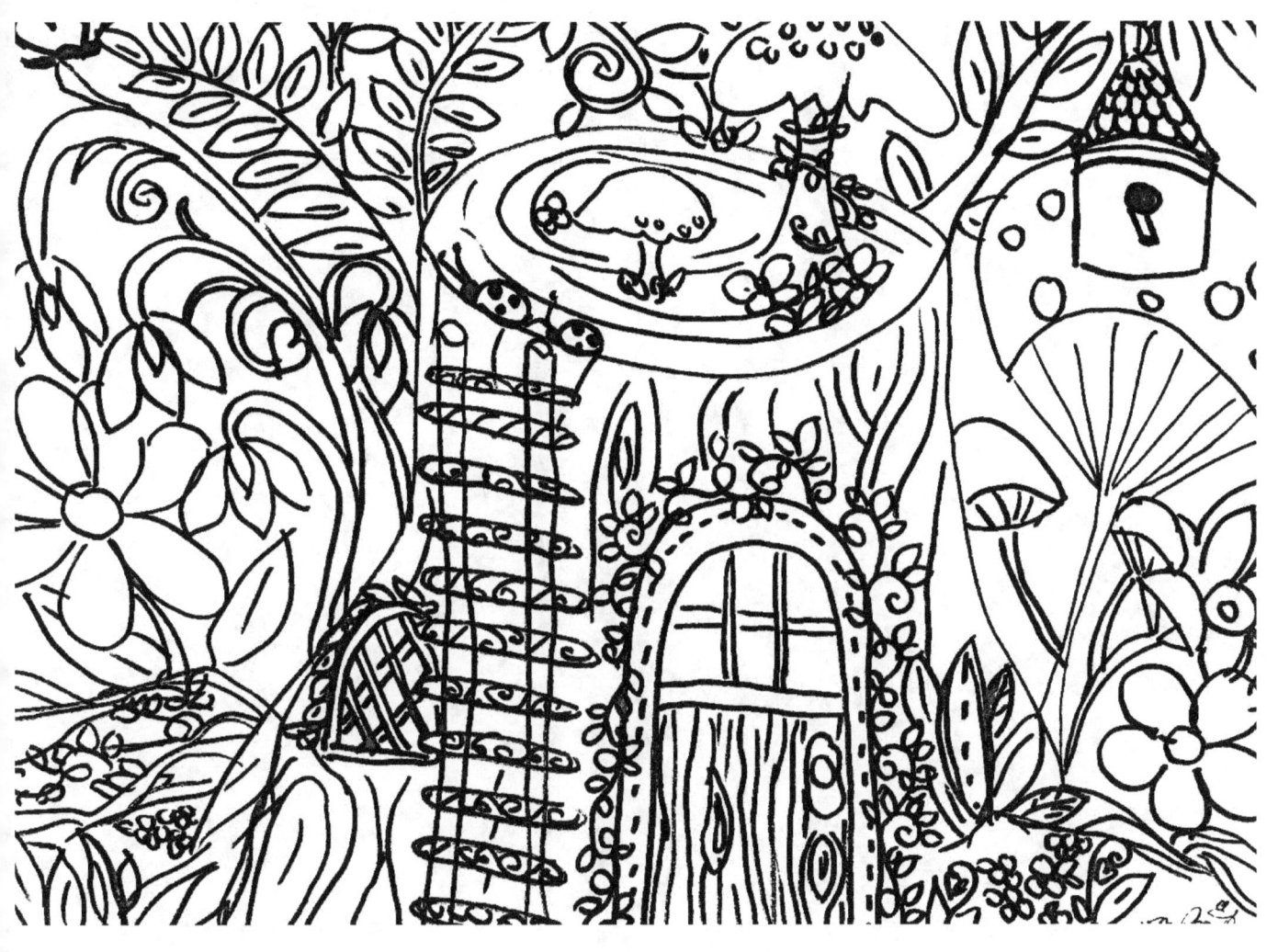

"Surely your goodness and love will follow me all the days of my life,

And I will dwell in the house of the Lord forever."

Psalm 23:6

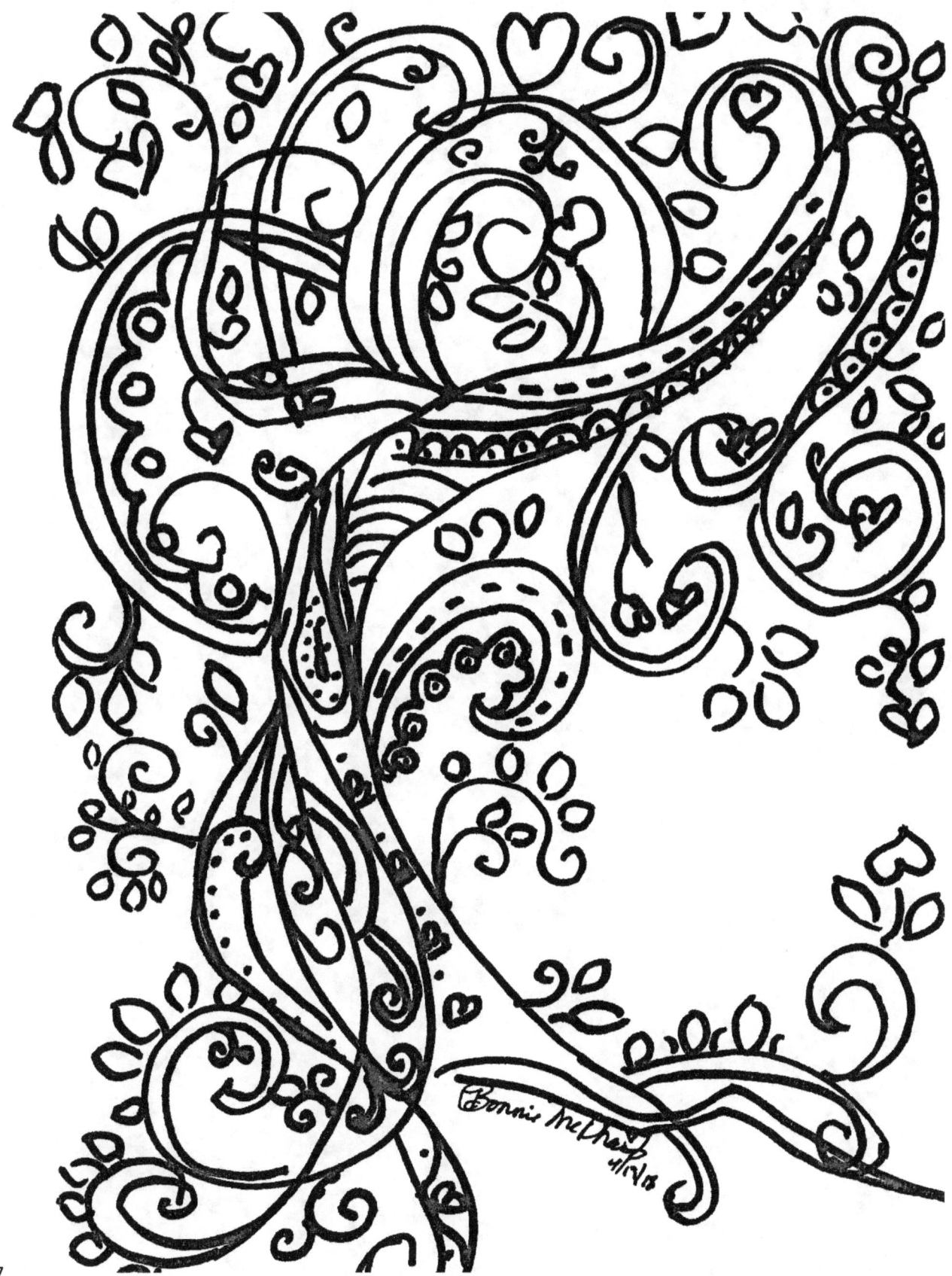

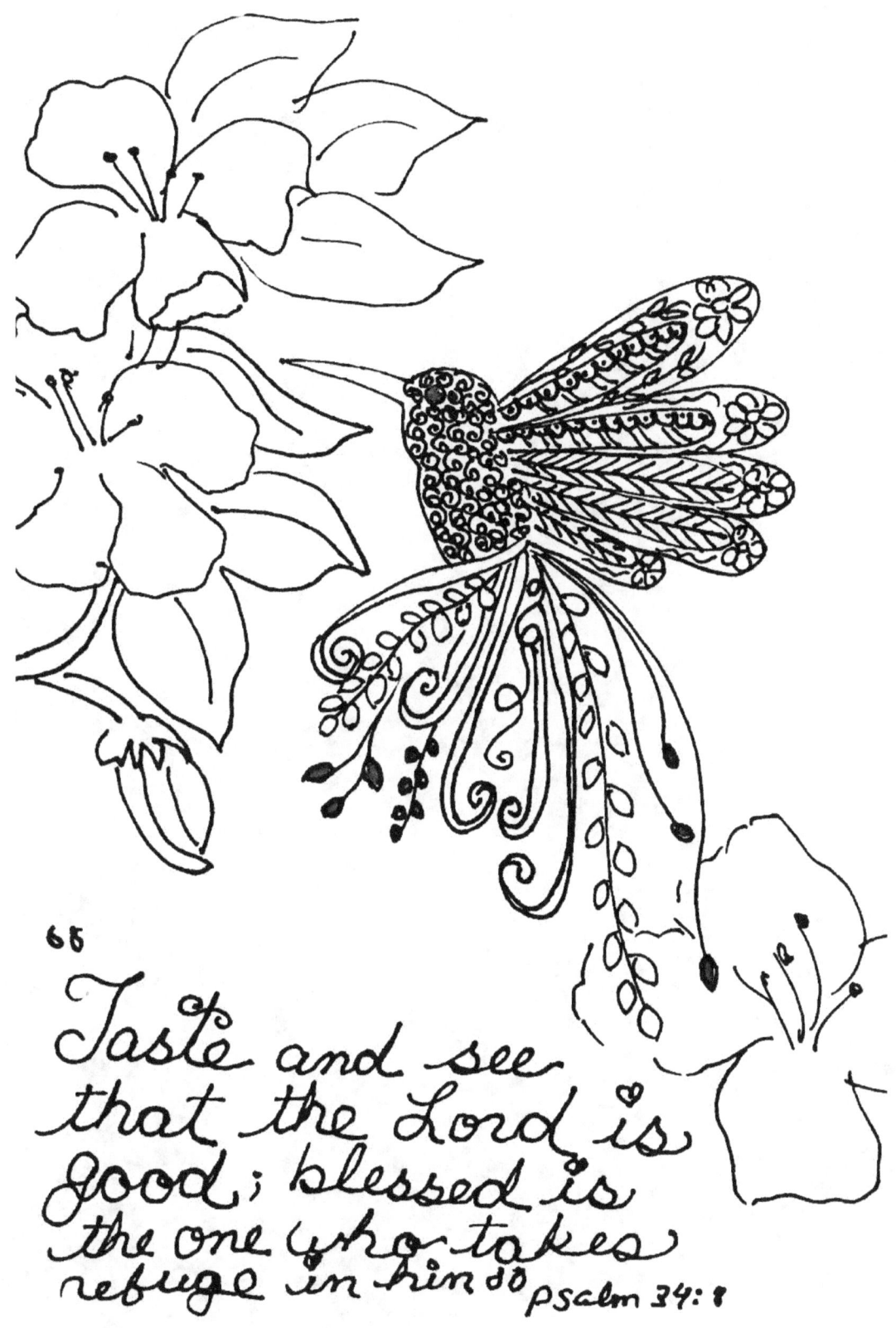

"
Taste and see
that the Lord is
good; blessed is
the one who takes
refuge in him" psalm 34:8

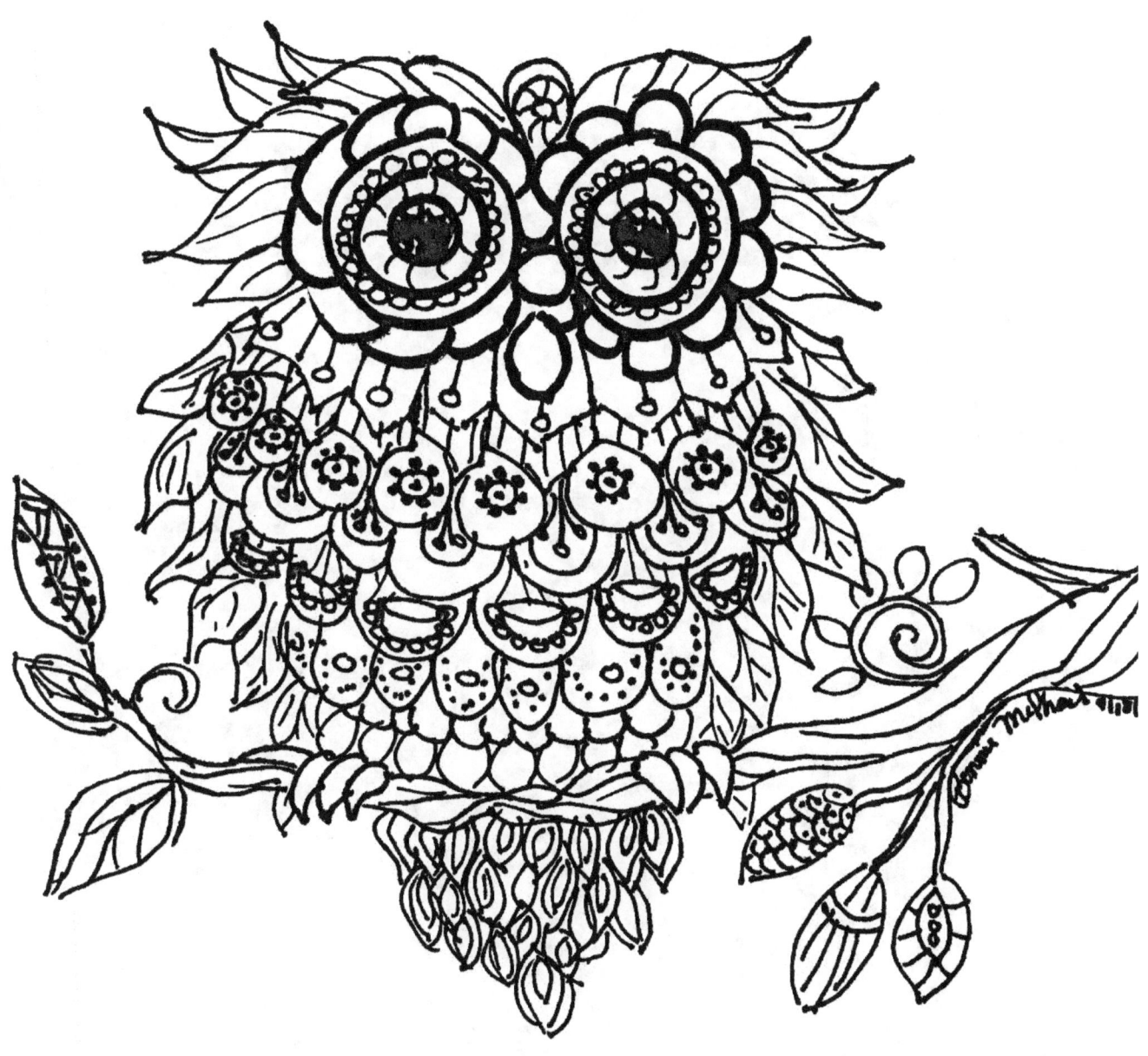

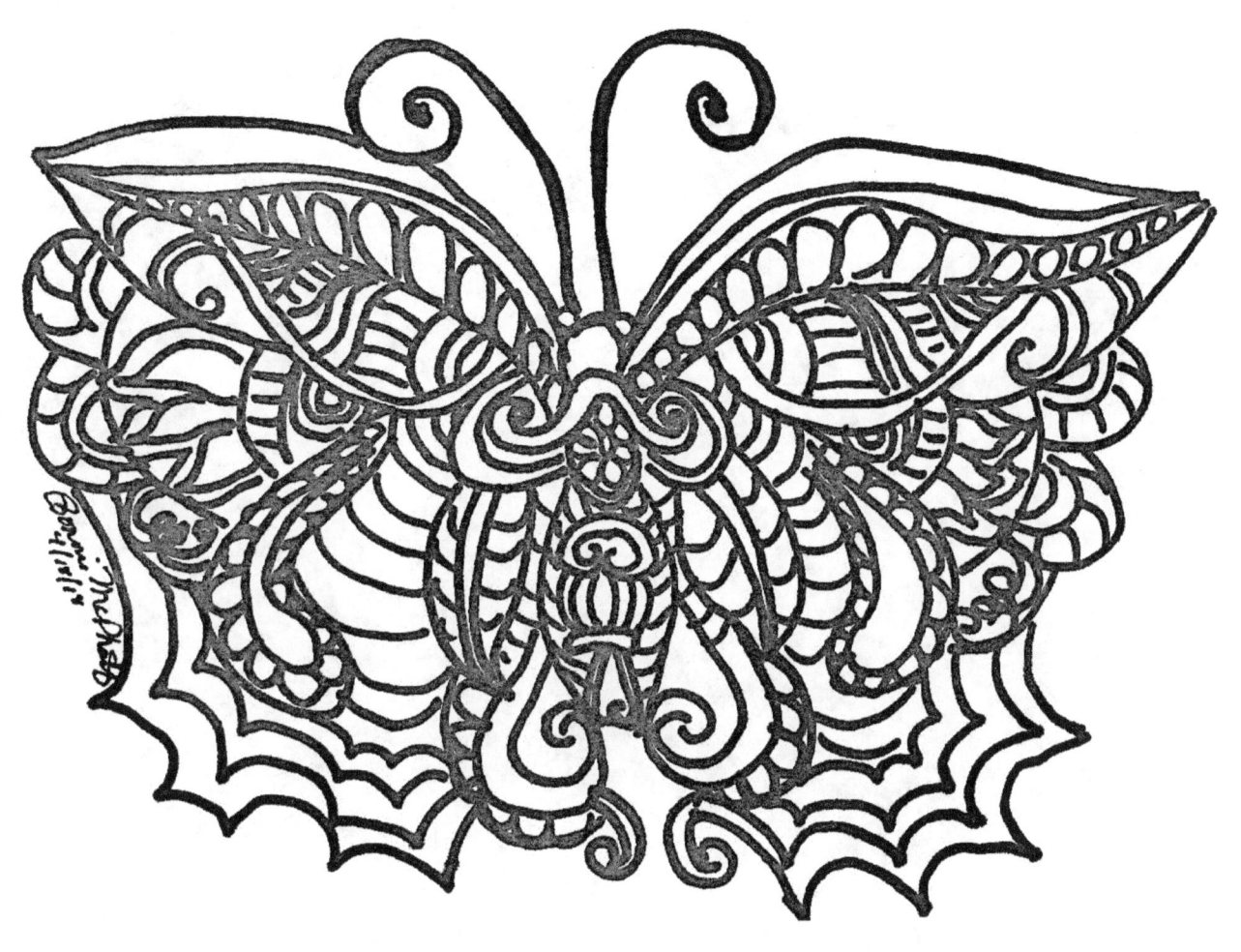

"O LORD, you have searched me and known me!

You know when I sit down and when I rise up;

you discern my thoughts from afar."

Psalm 139: 1-2

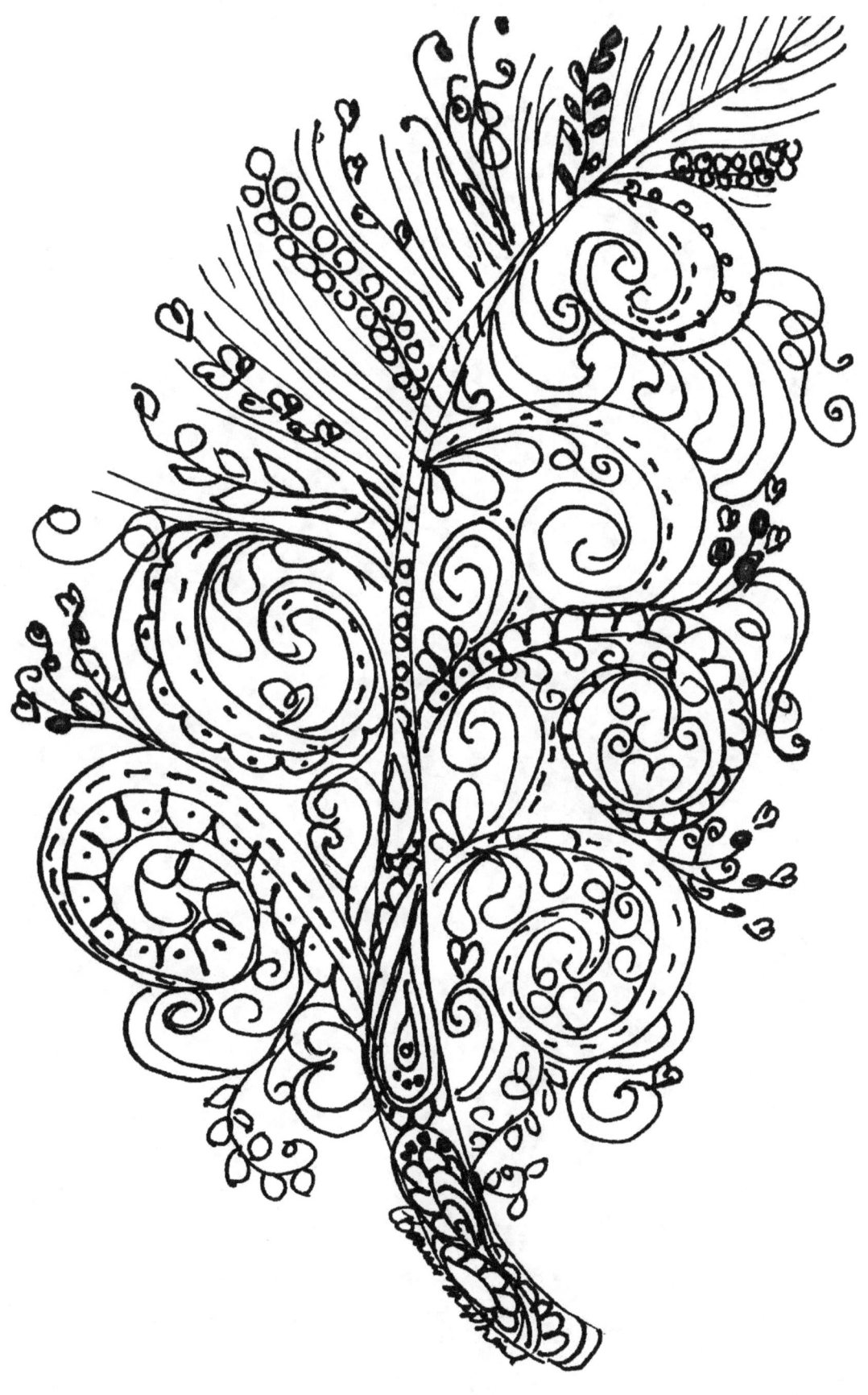

185

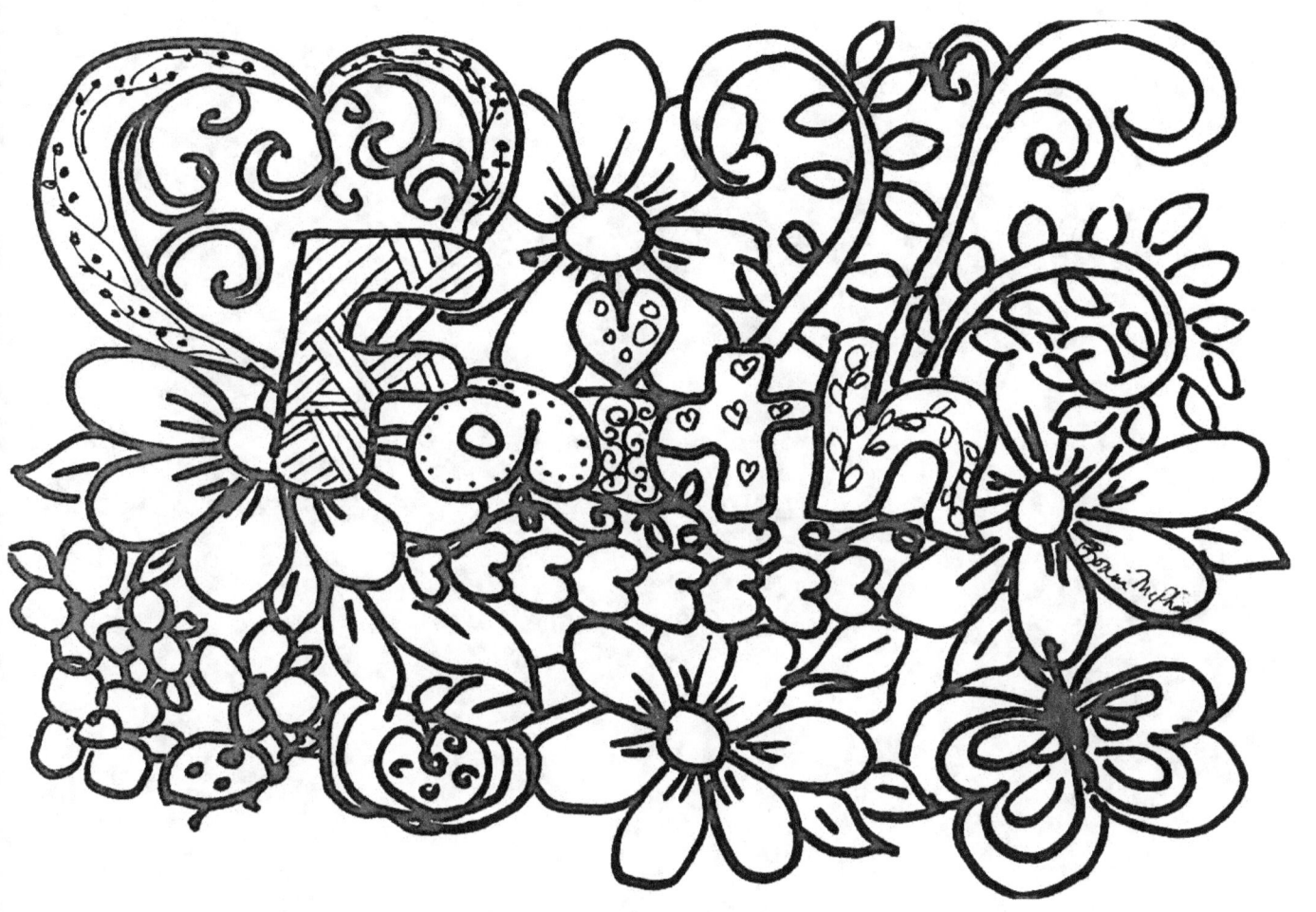

"Therefore I tell you, whatever you ask for in prayer, believe that you have received it, and it will be yours." Mark 11:24

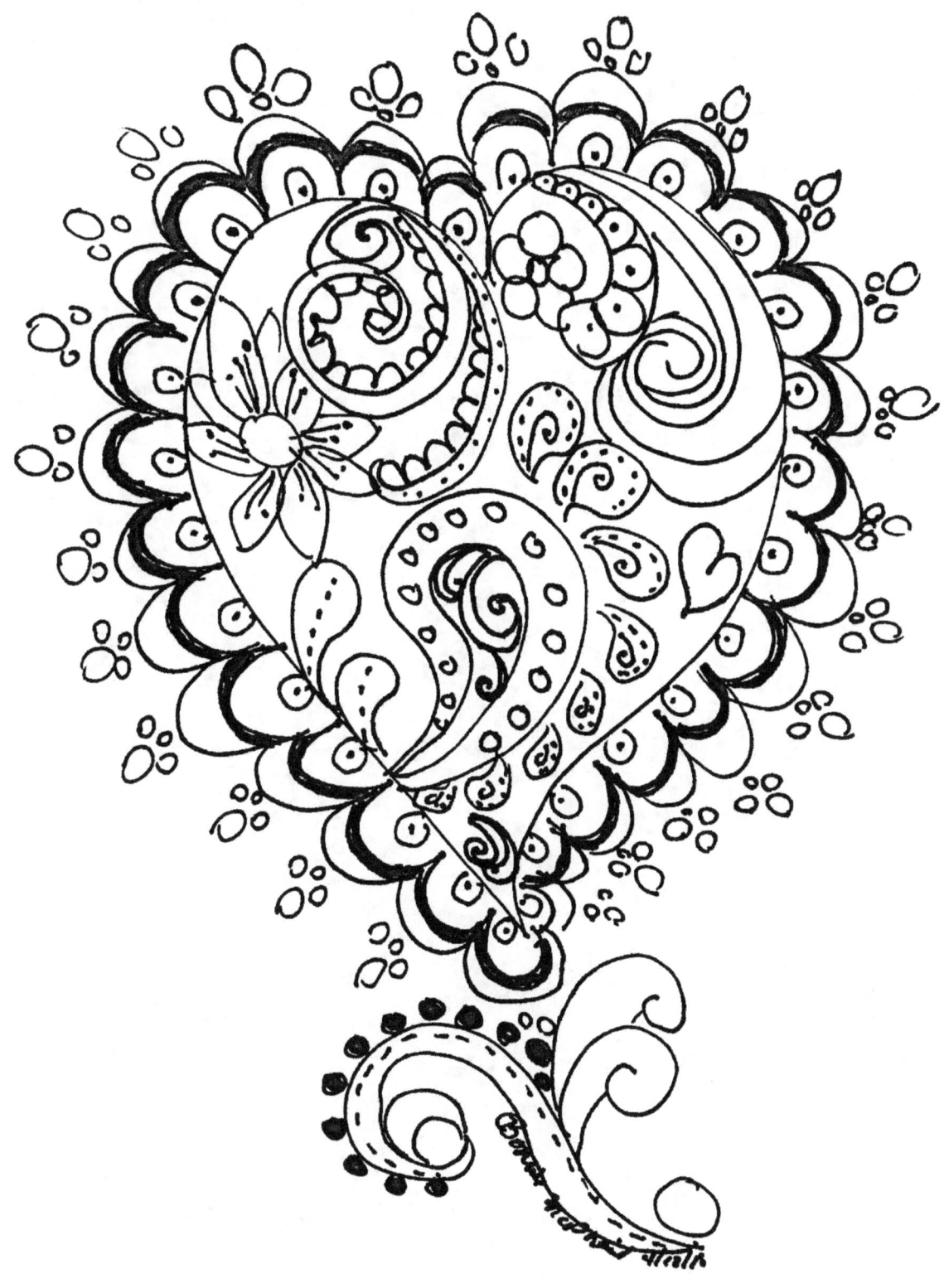

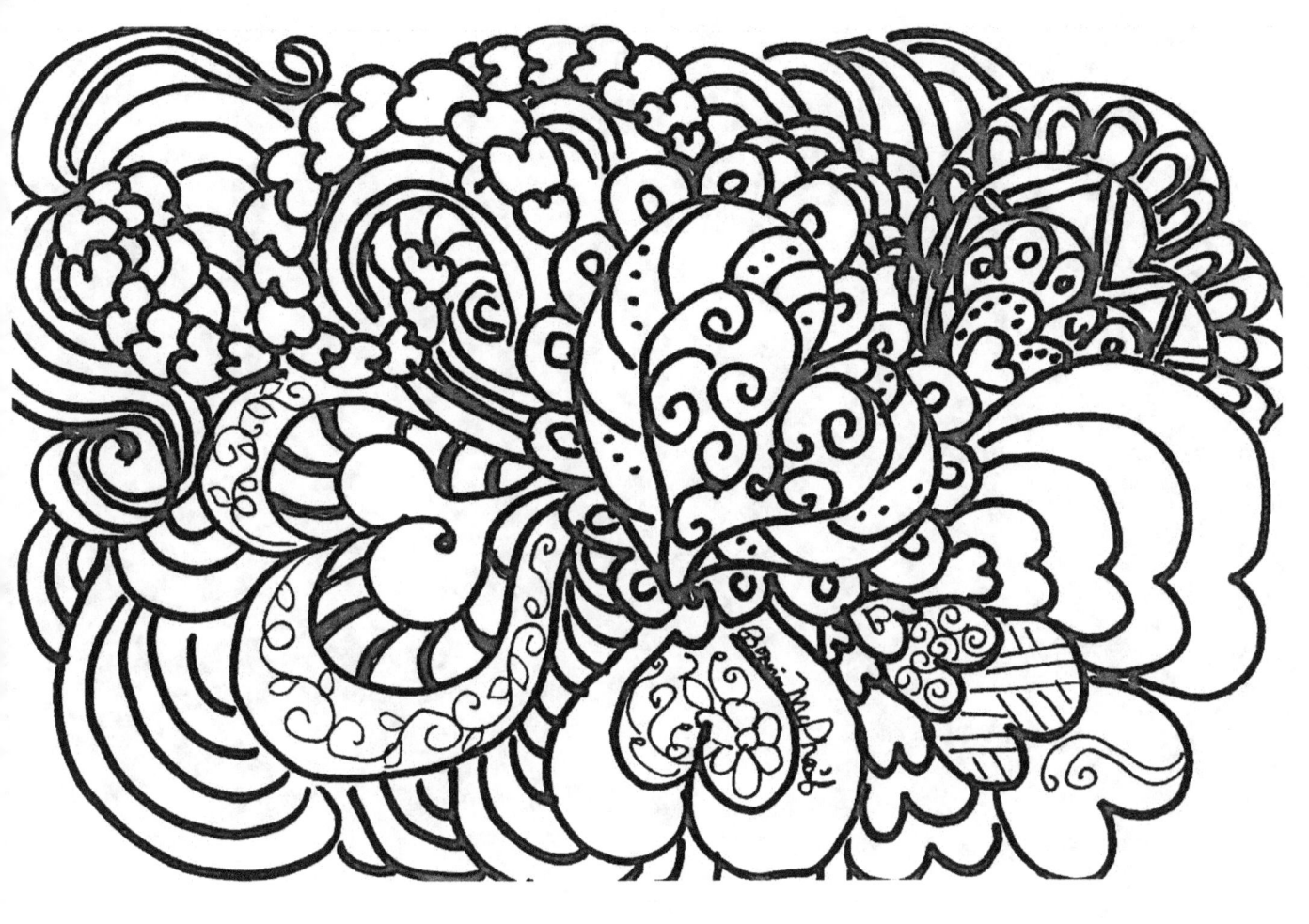

"The LORD is my strength and my shield; my heart trusts in him, and he helps me. My heart leaps for joy, and with my song I praise him."

Psalm 28:7

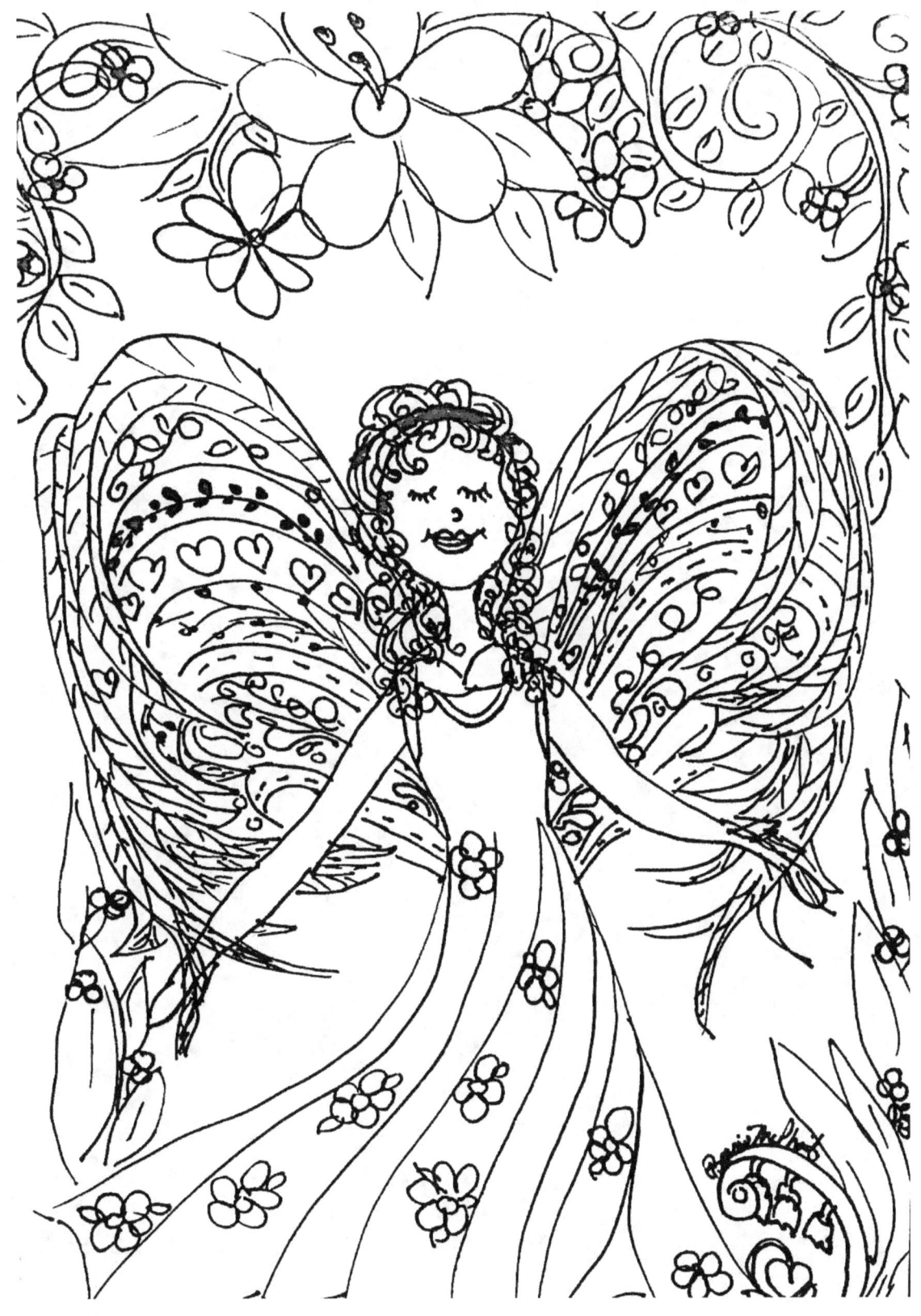

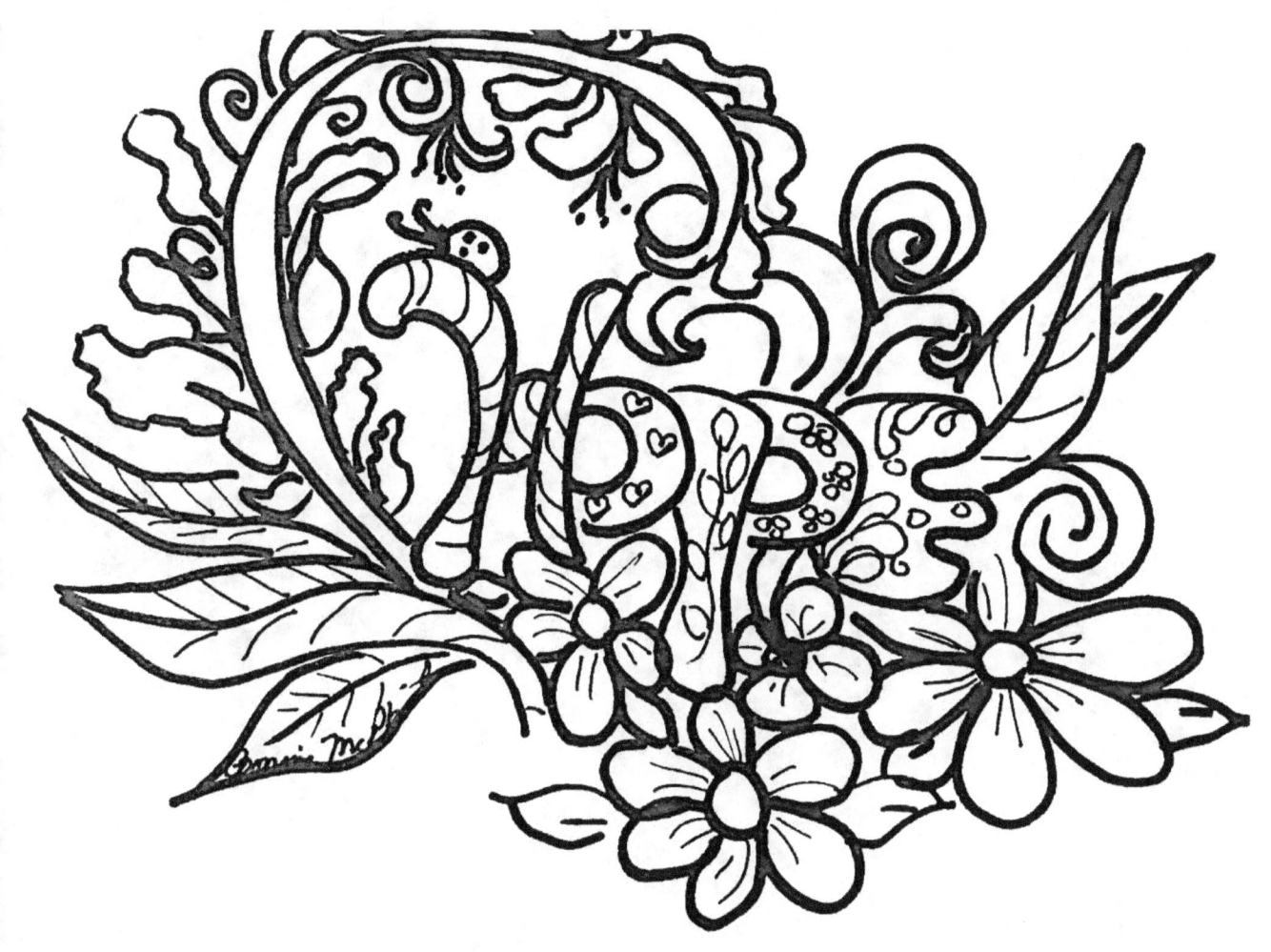

"But those who hope in the Lord will renew their strength. They will soar on wings like eagles; they will run and not grow weary, they will walk and not be faint." Isaiah 40:31

196

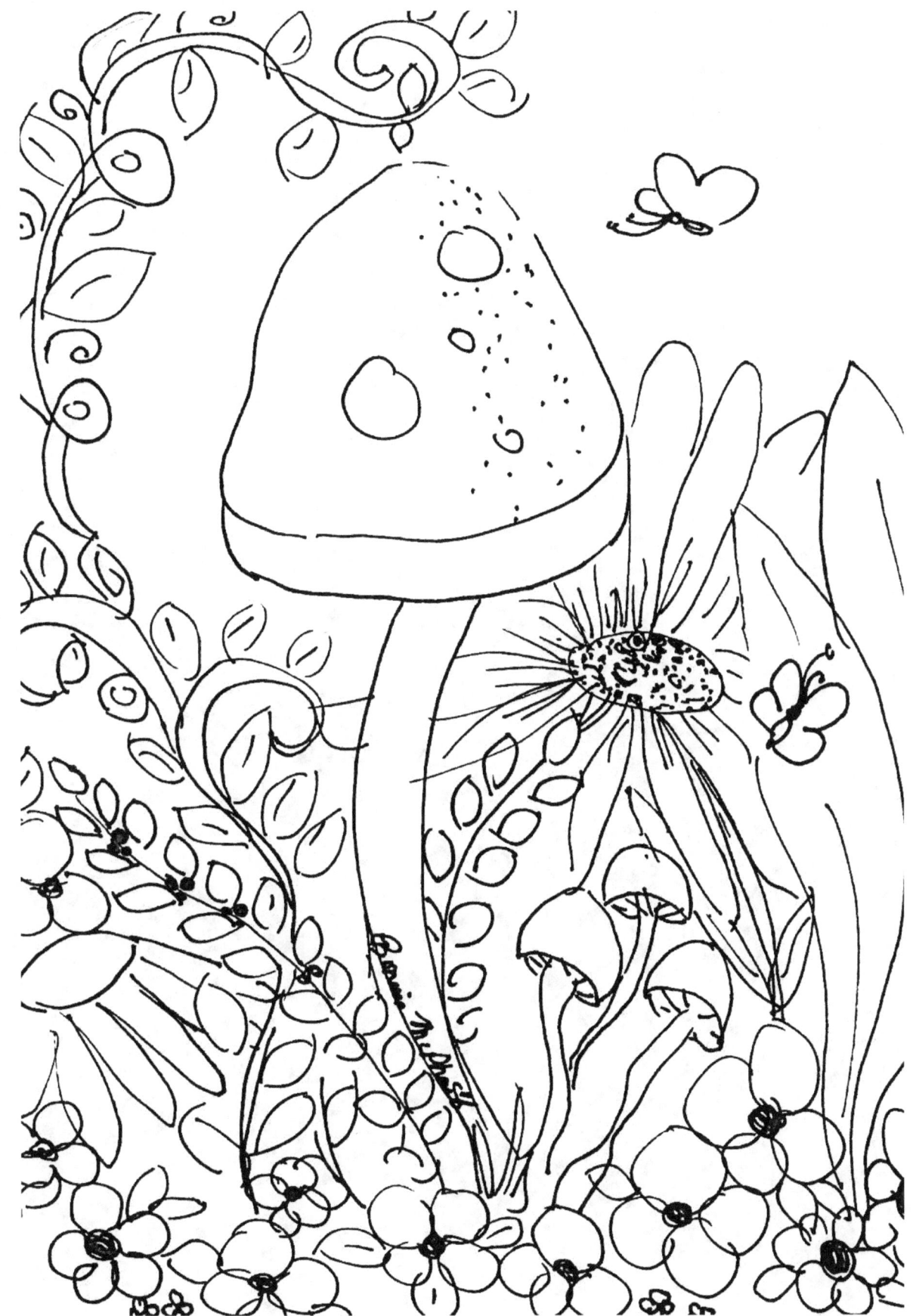

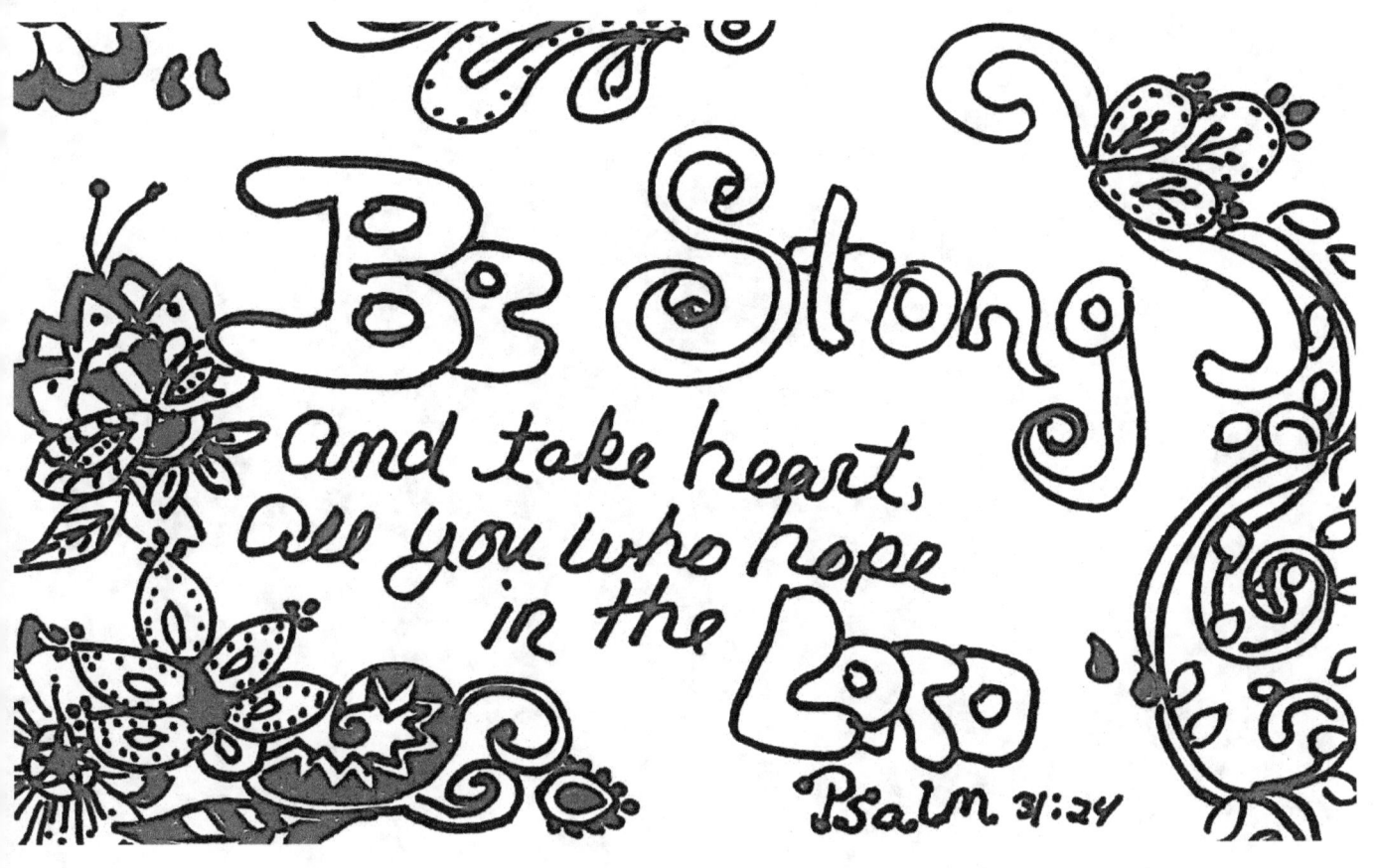

"Be strong and courageous. Do not be afraid or terrified because of them, for the LORD your God goes with you; he will never leave you nor forsake you." Deuteronomy 61:6-8

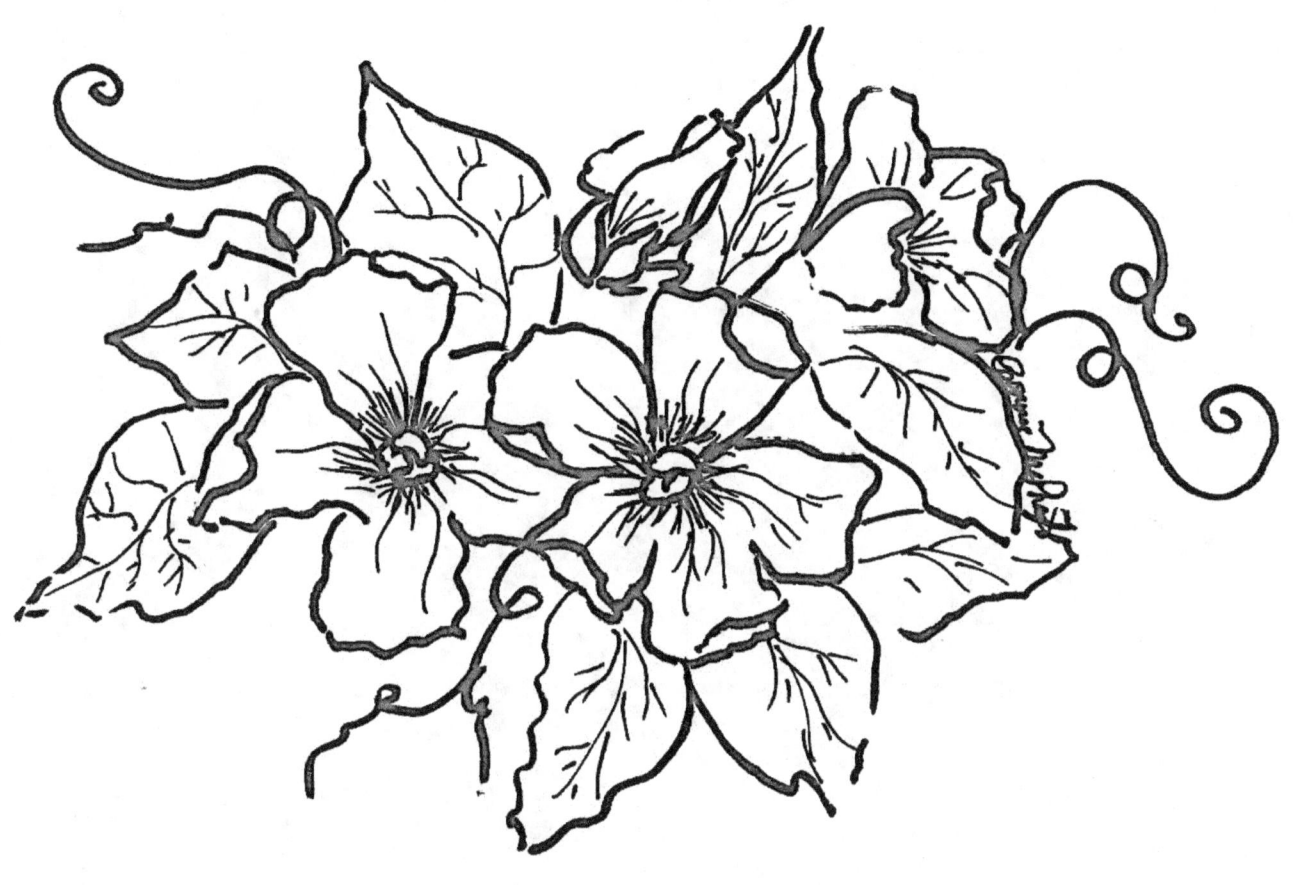

"Be strong and take heart, all you who hope in the Lord."

Psalm 31:24

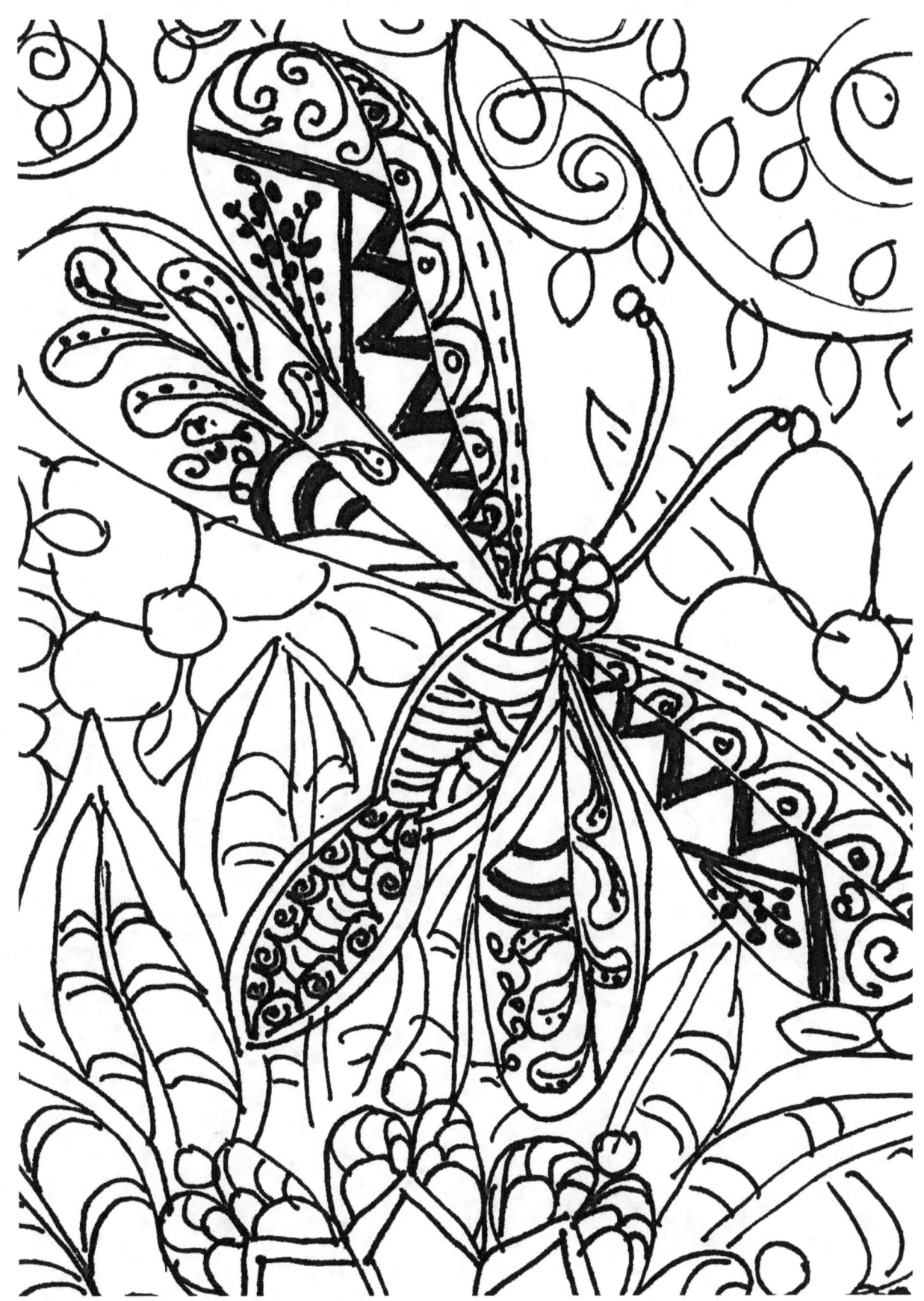

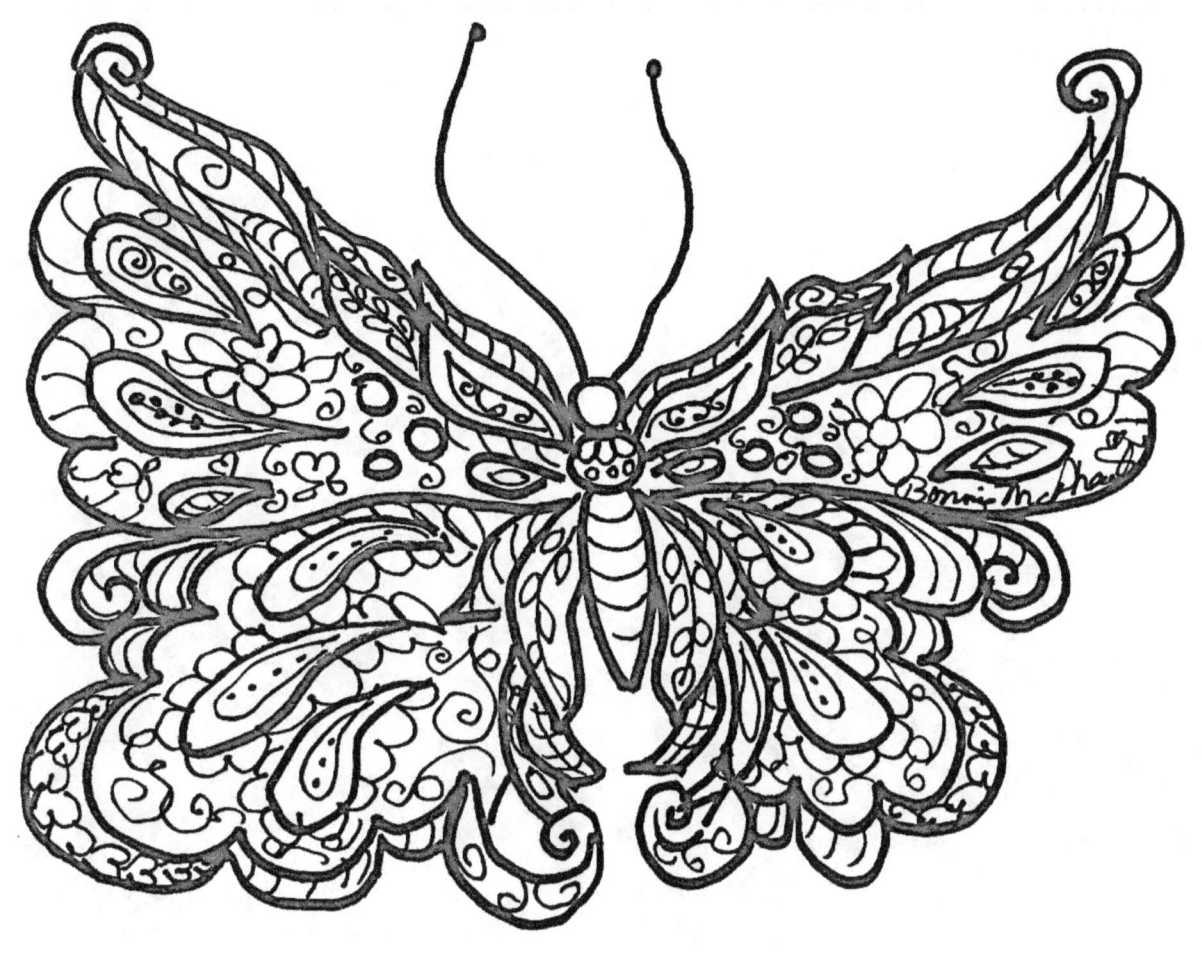

"Trust in the LORD with all your heart and lean not on your own understanding; in all your ways submit to him, and he will make your paths straight." Proverbs 3:5-6

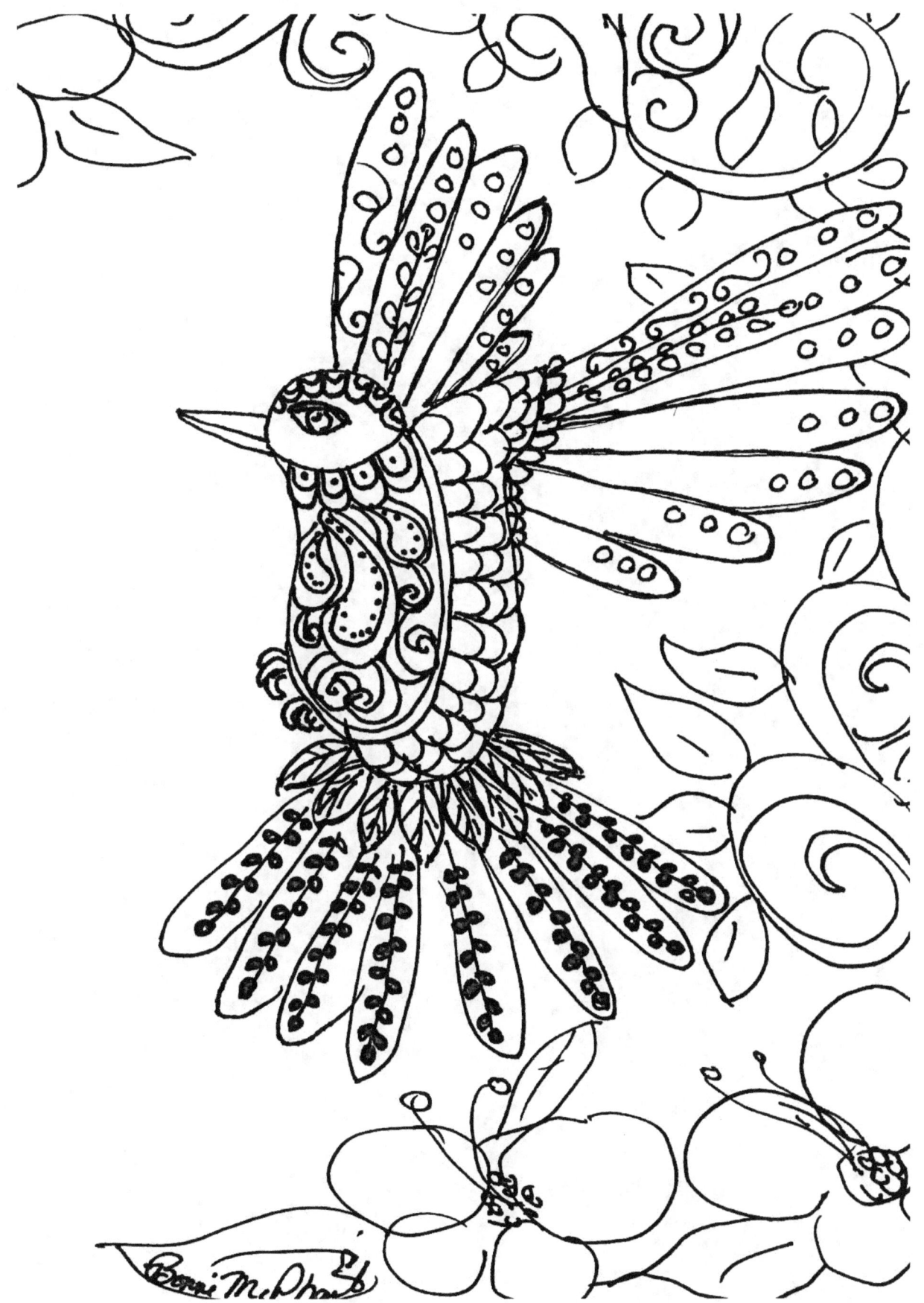

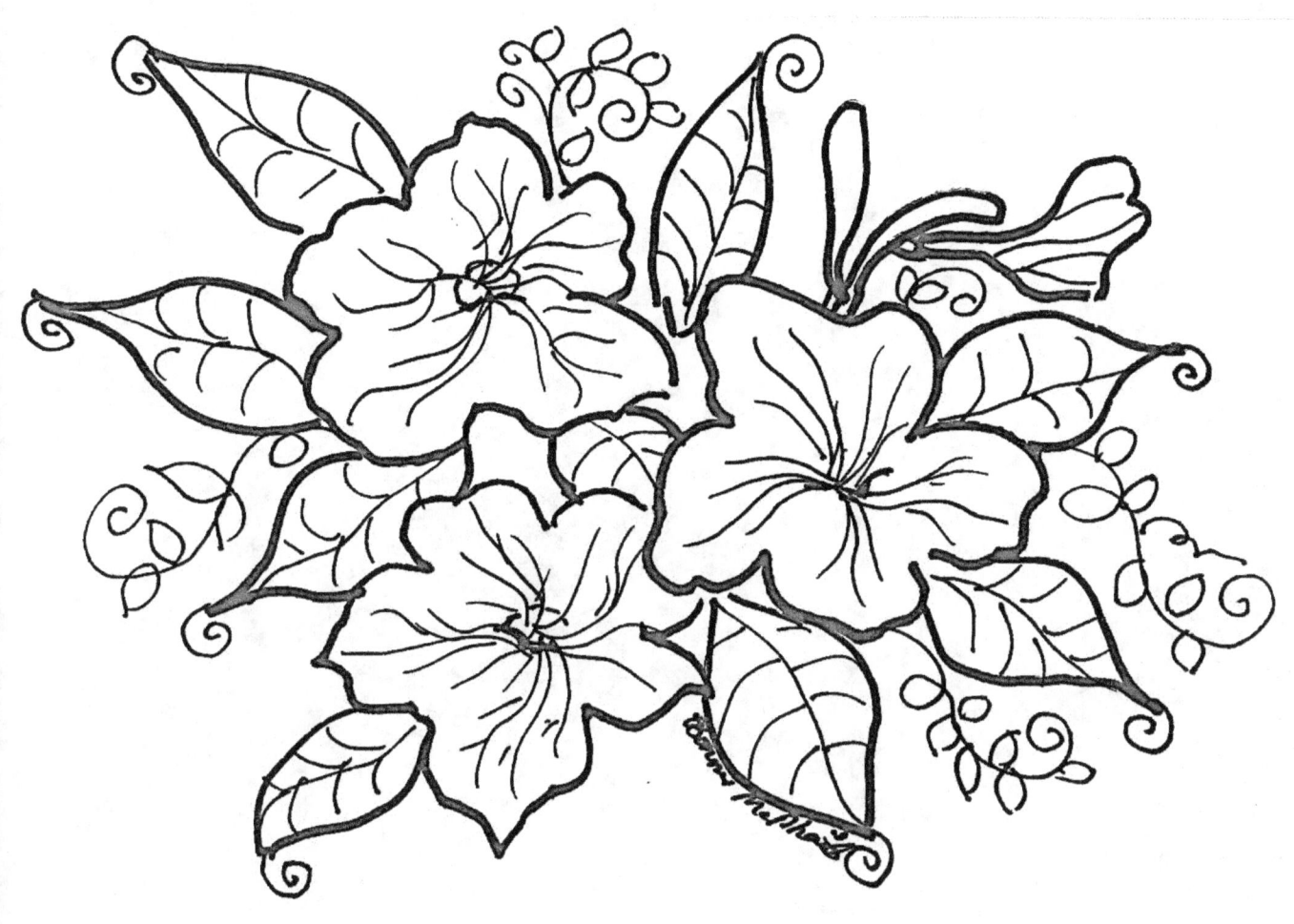

"Praise be to the God and Father of our Lord Jesus Christ, the Father of compassion and the God of all comfort, who comforts us in all our troubles, so that we can comfort those in any trouble with the comfort we ourselves receive from God." 2 Corinthians 1:3-4

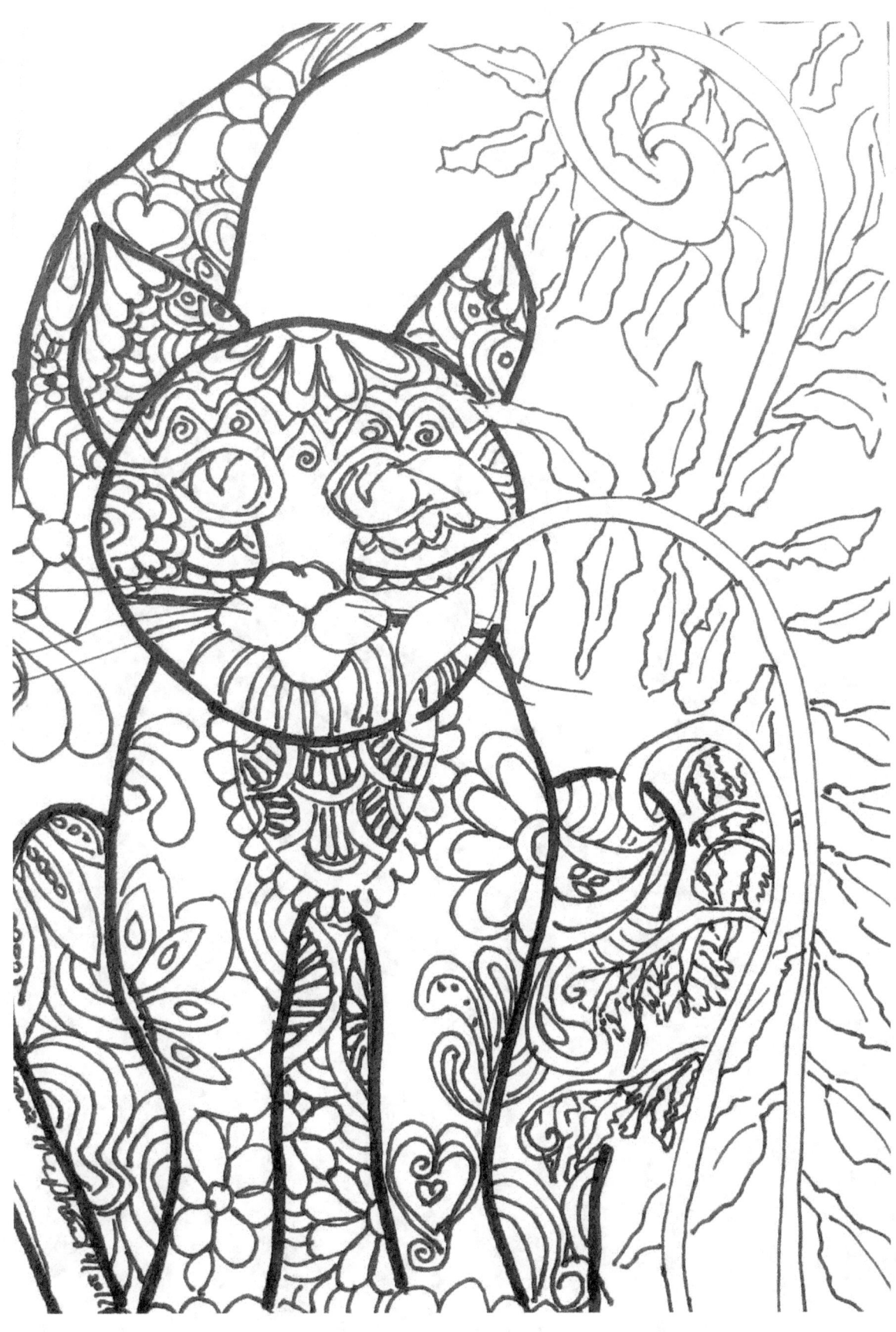

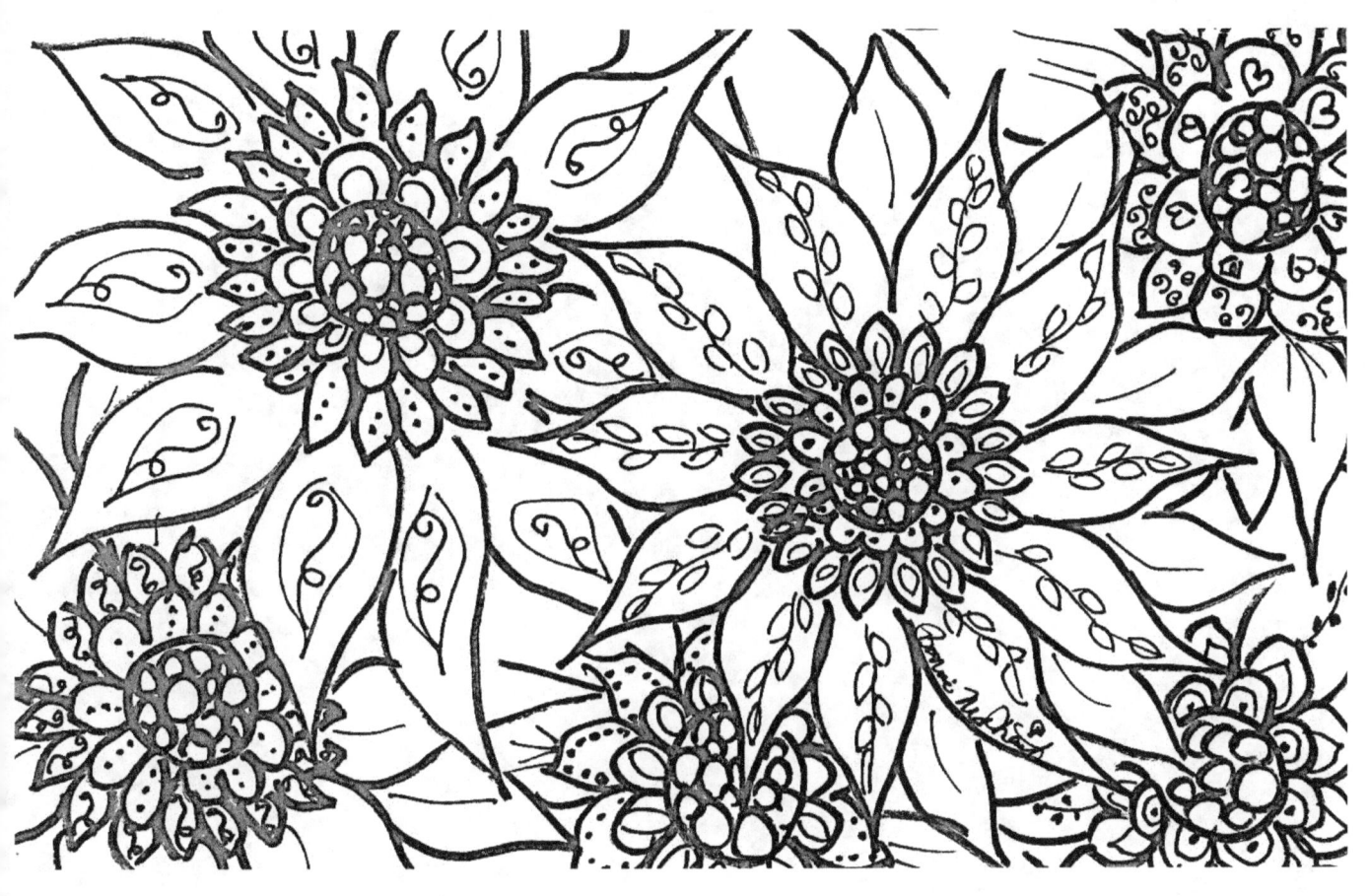

"So do not fear, for I am with you; do not be dismayed, for I am your God. I will strengthen you and help you; I will uphold you with my righteous right hand." Isaiah 41:10

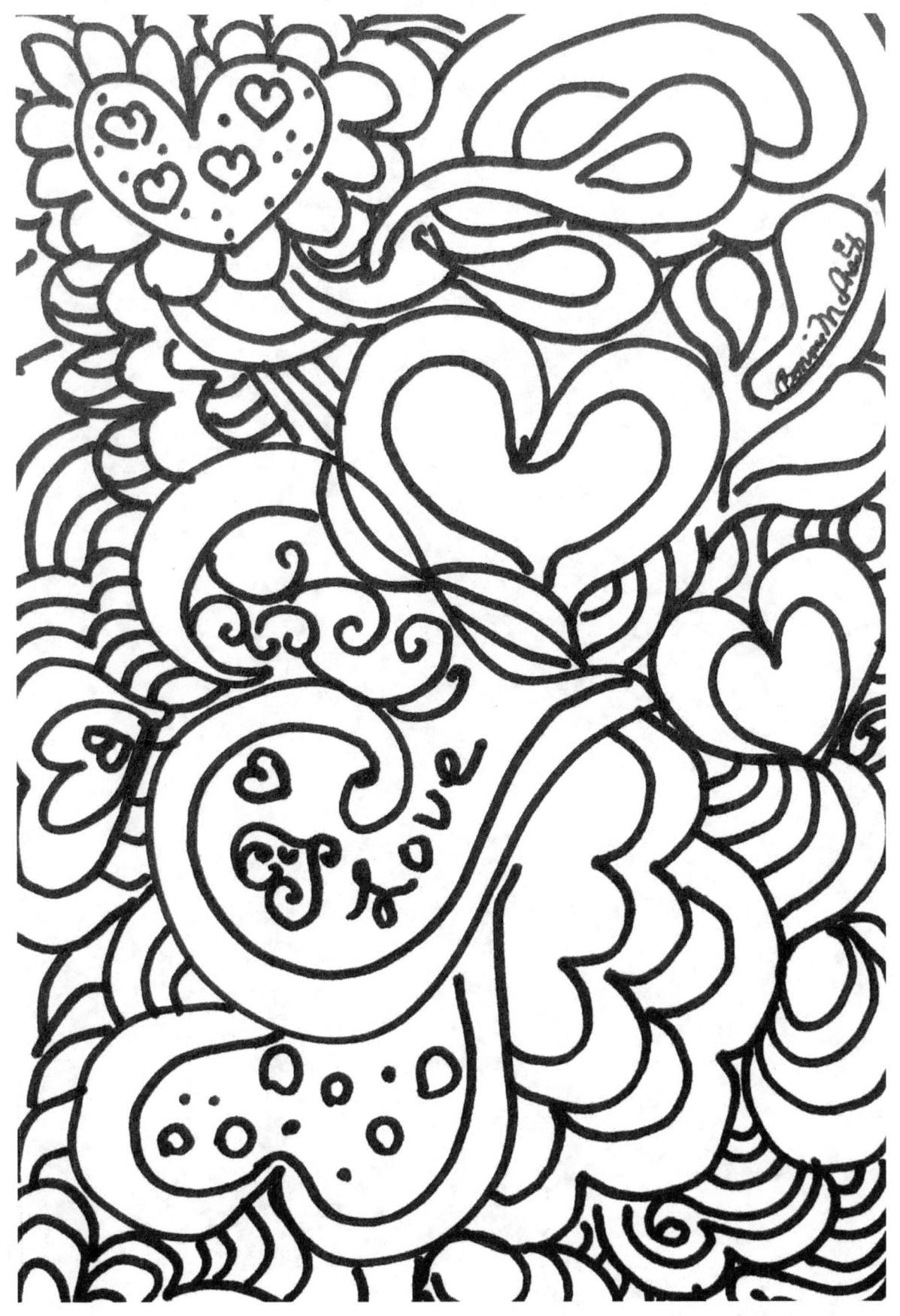

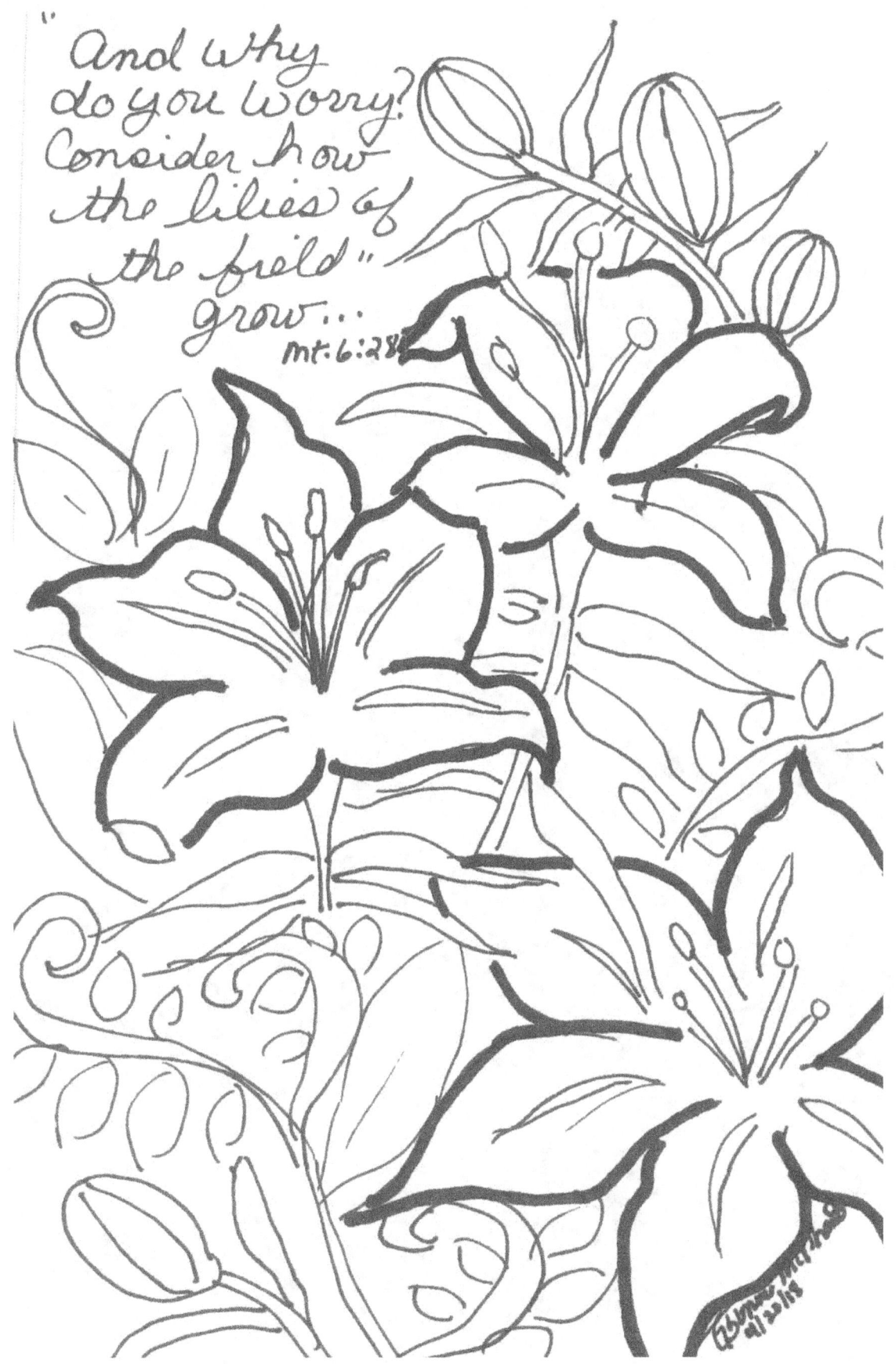

"And why do you worry? Consider how the lilies of the field" grow...
mt. 6:28

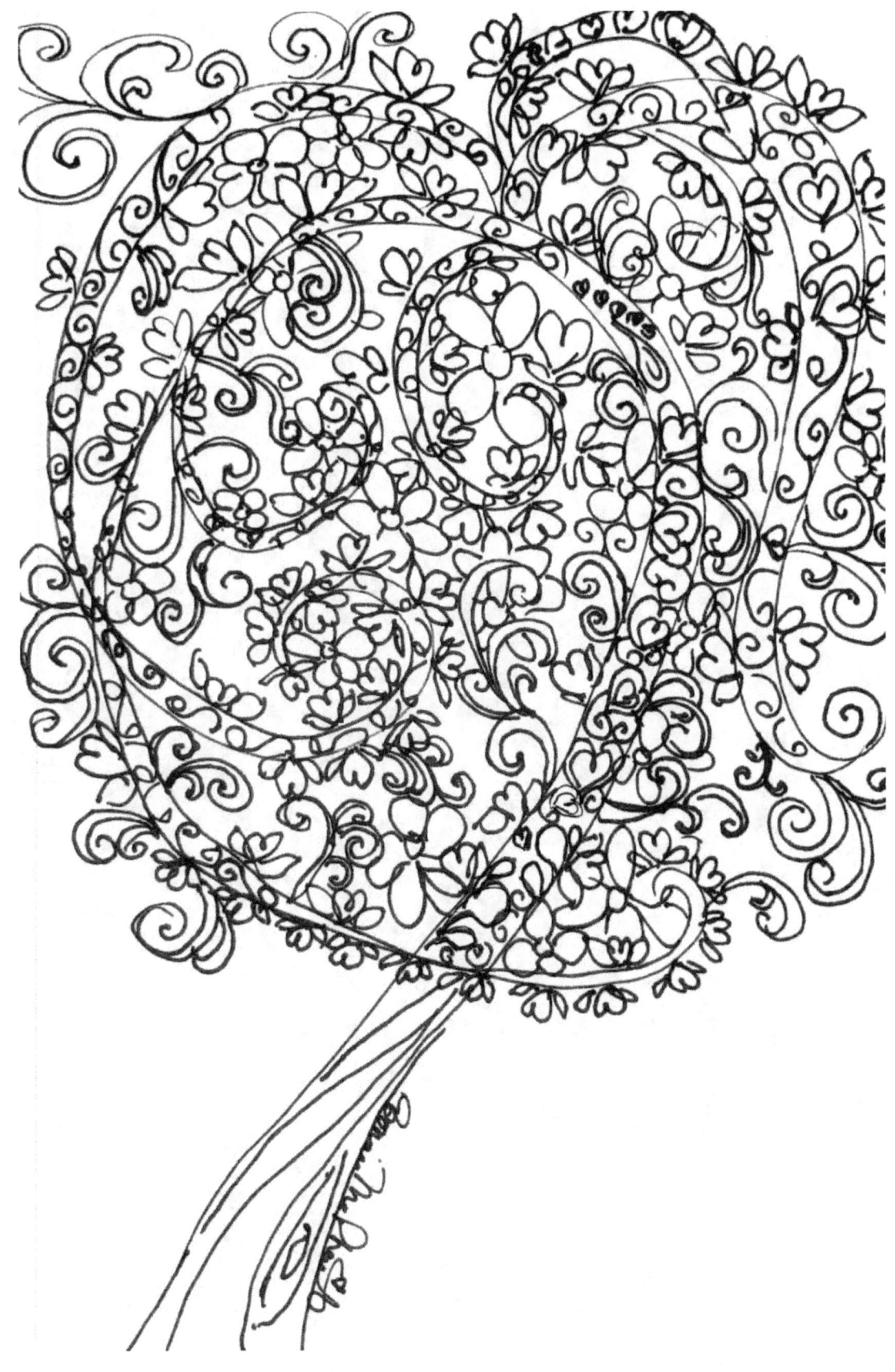

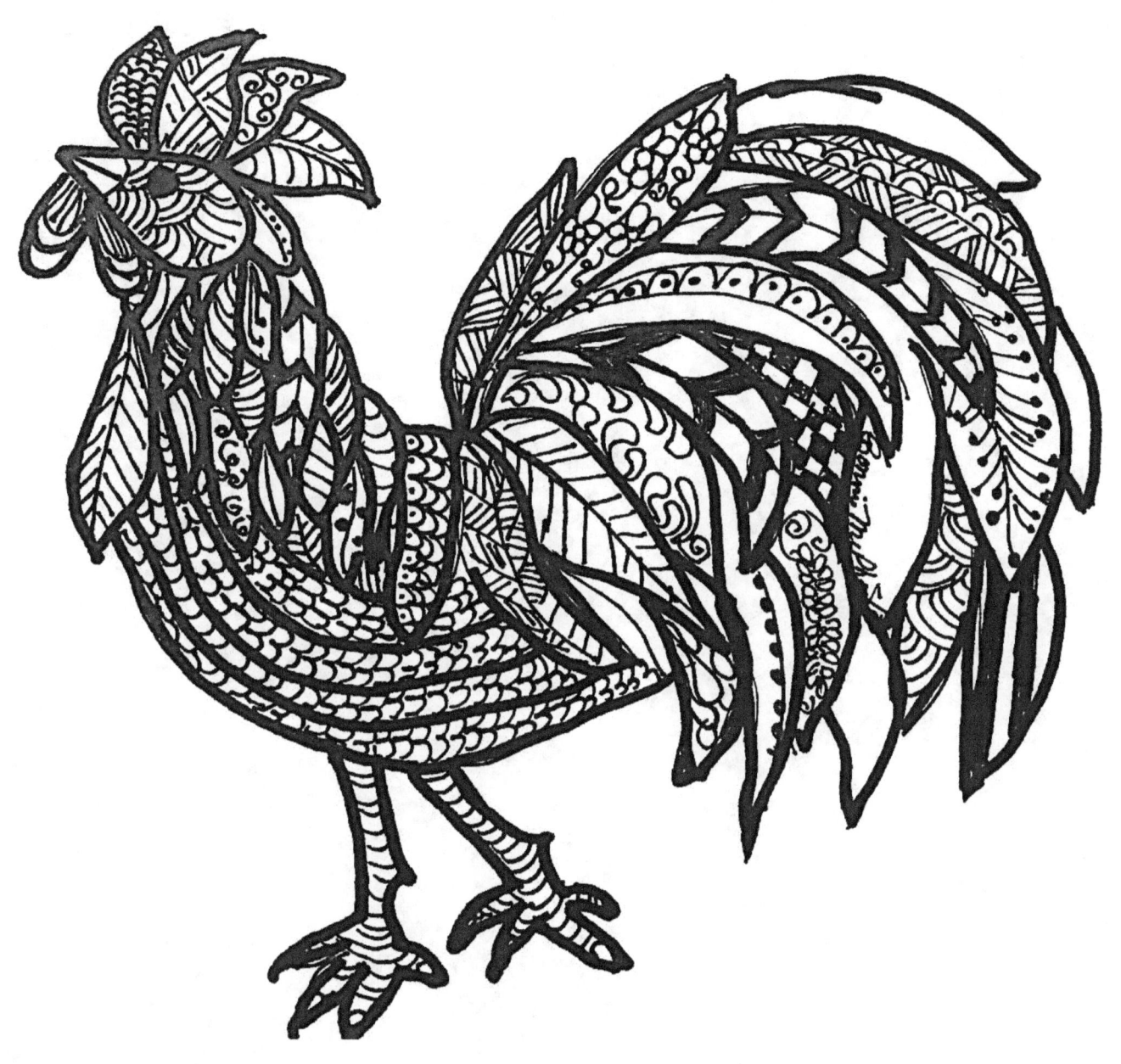

"but those who hope in the LORD will renew their strength. They will soar on wings like eagles; they will run and not grow weary, they will walk and not be faint." Isaiah 40:31

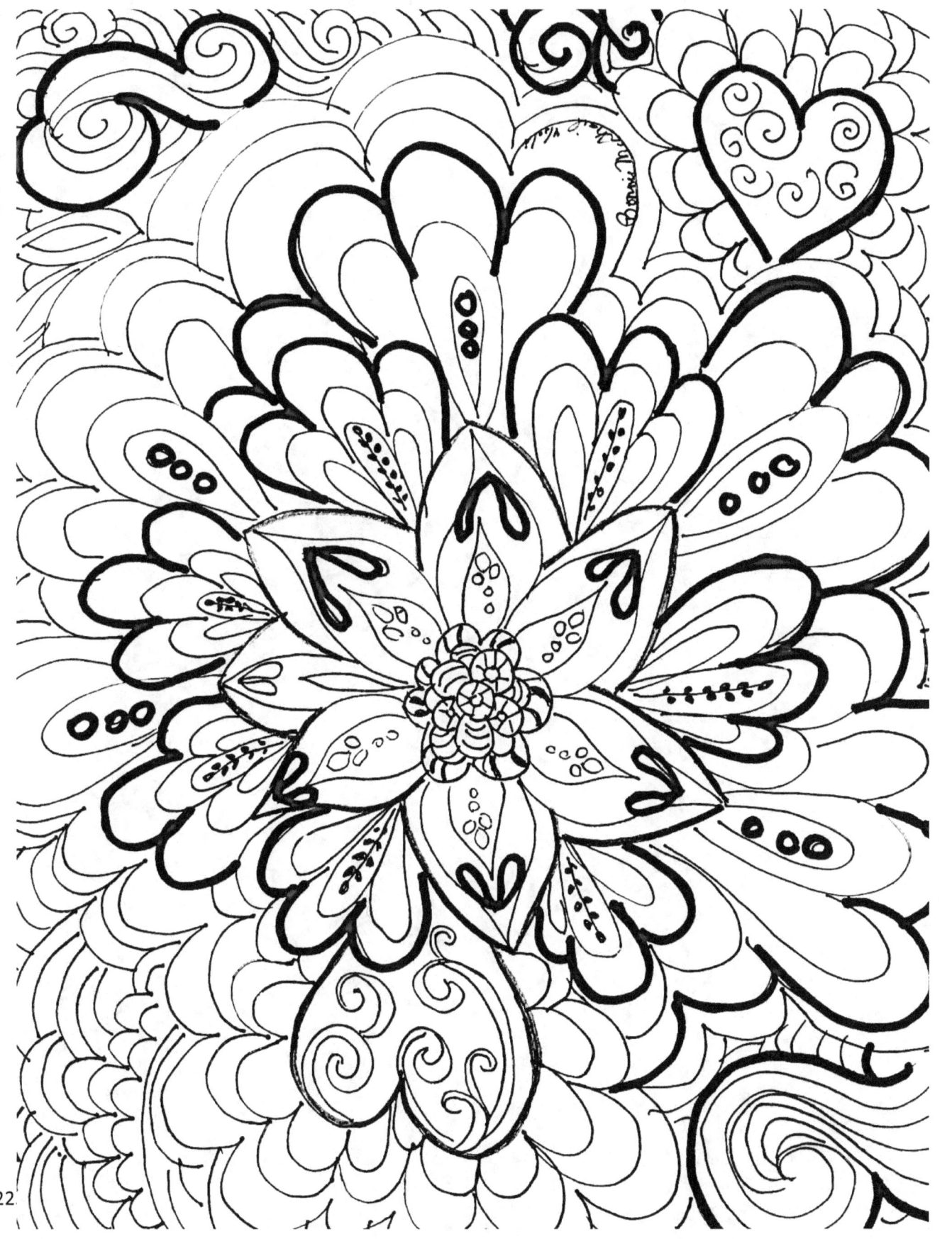

22

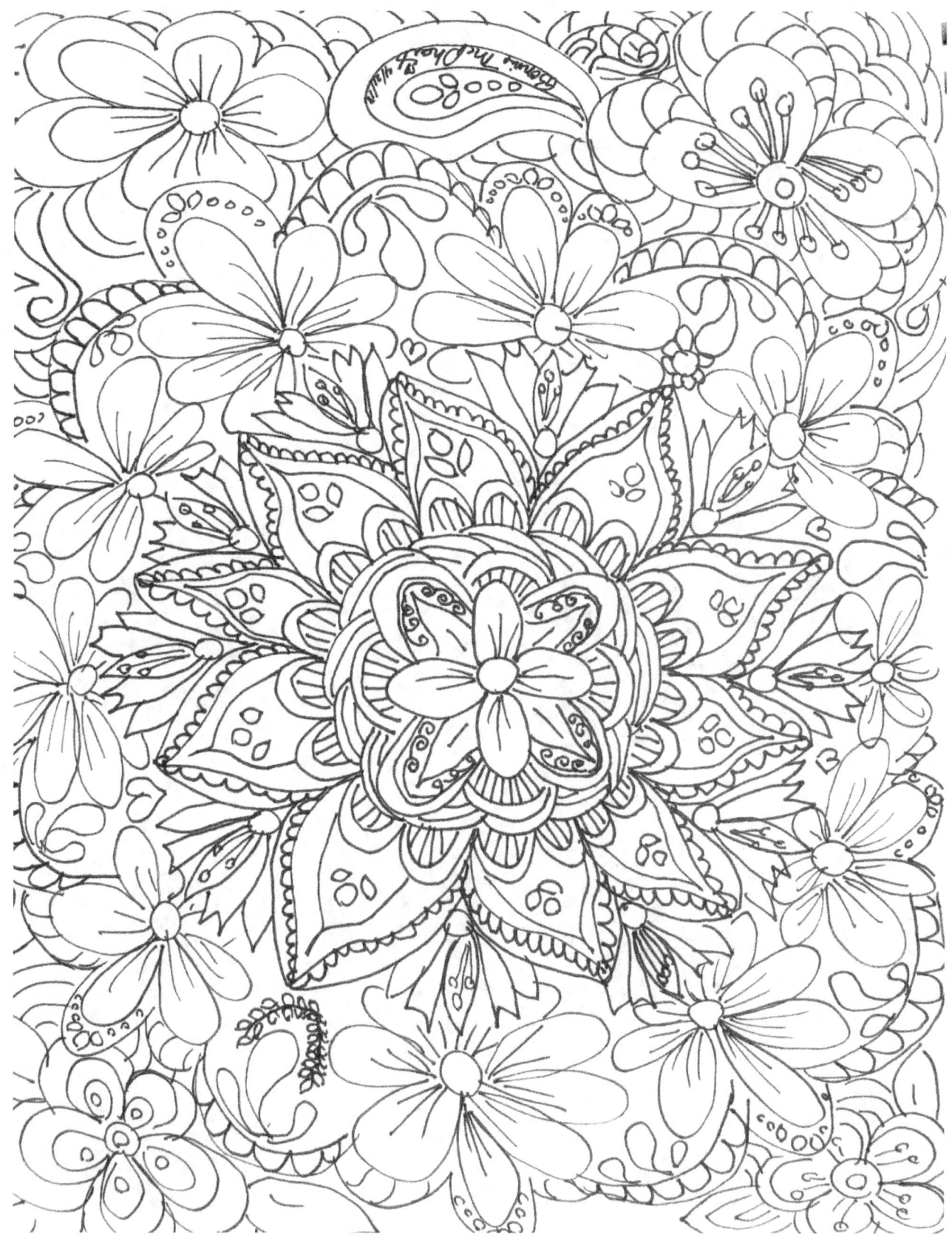

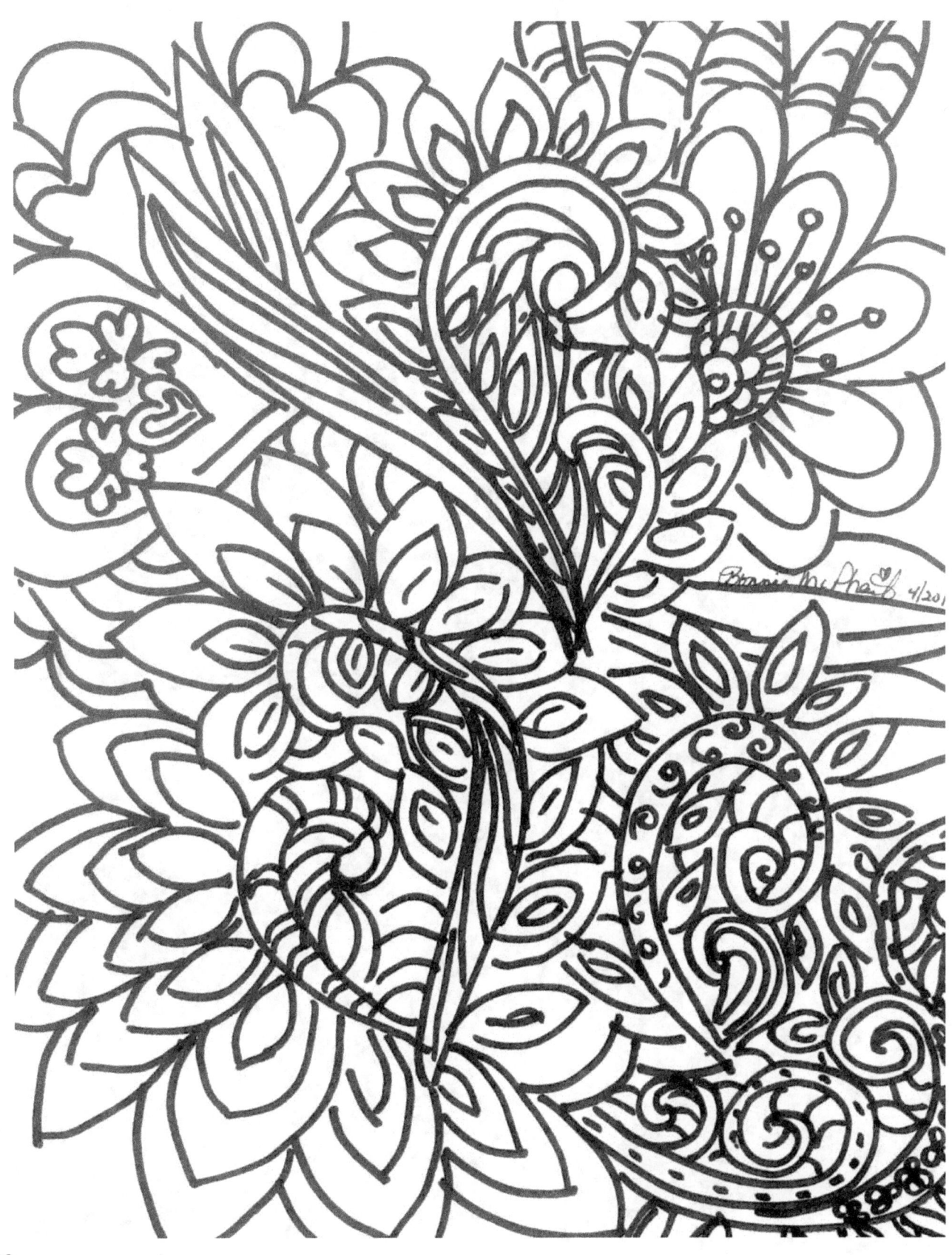

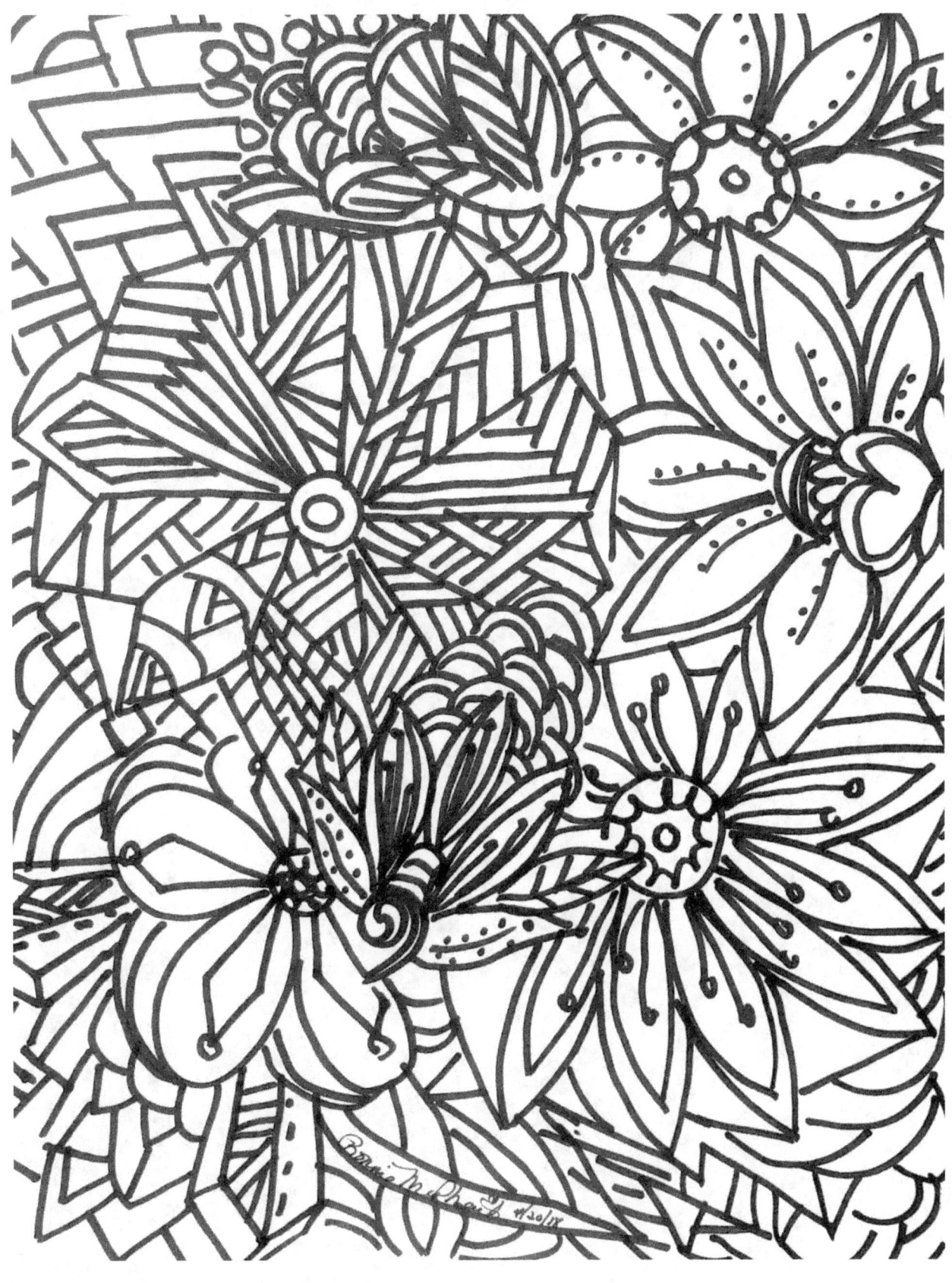

"Bless the Lord, O my Soul, and all that is within me, bless His holy name"

psalm 103:1

"I will sing to the LORD as long as I live; I will sing praise to my God while I have my being."

Psalm 104:33

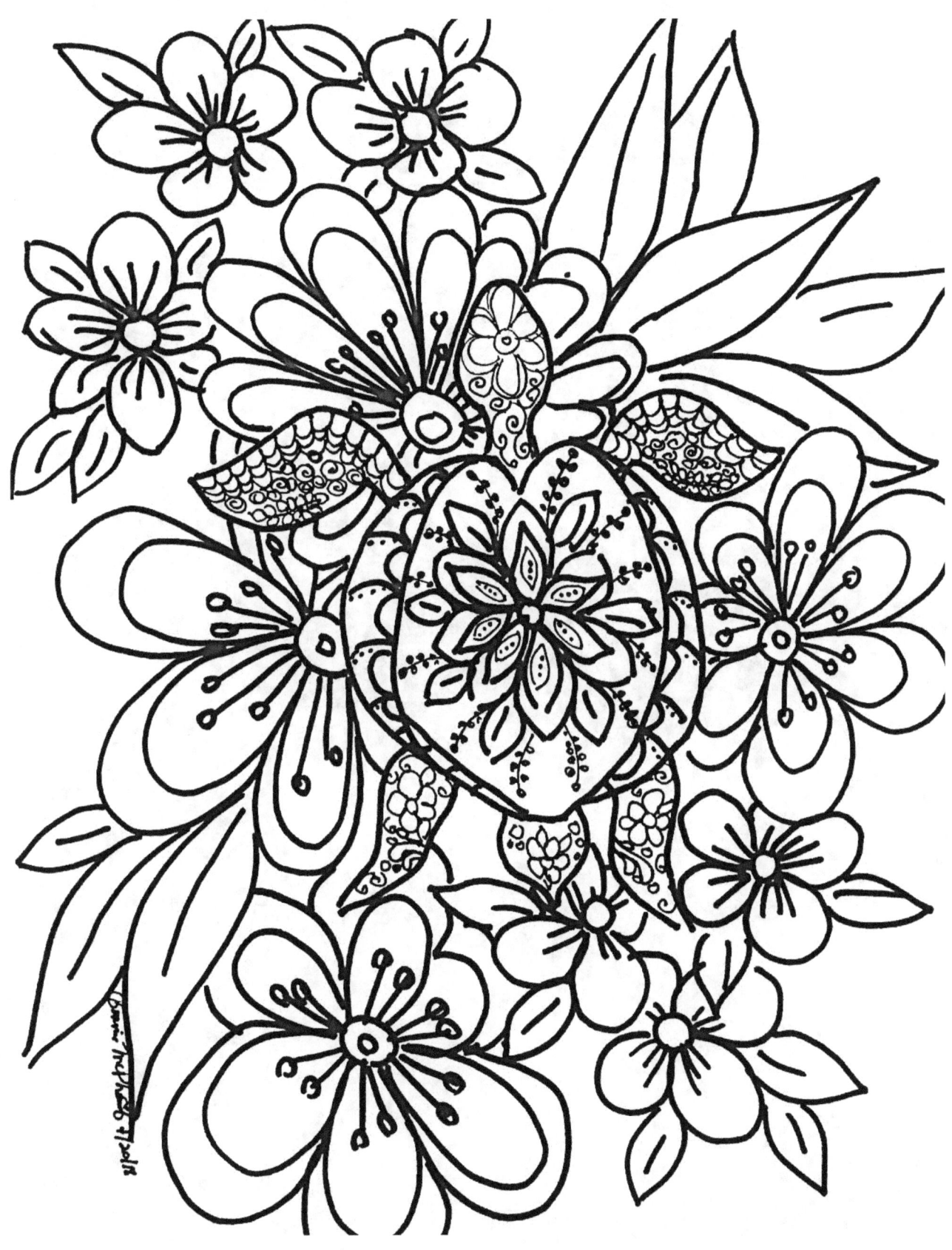

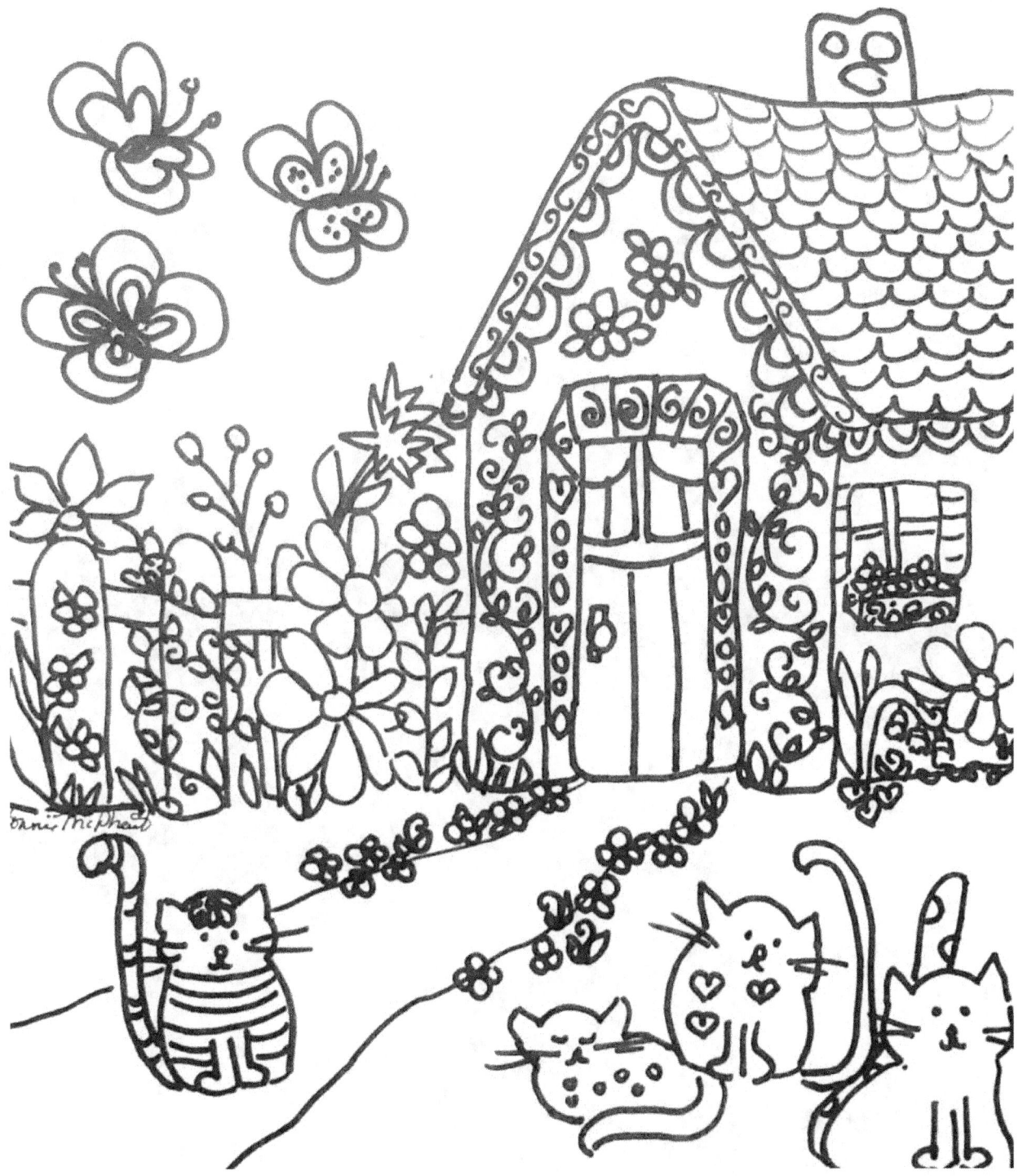

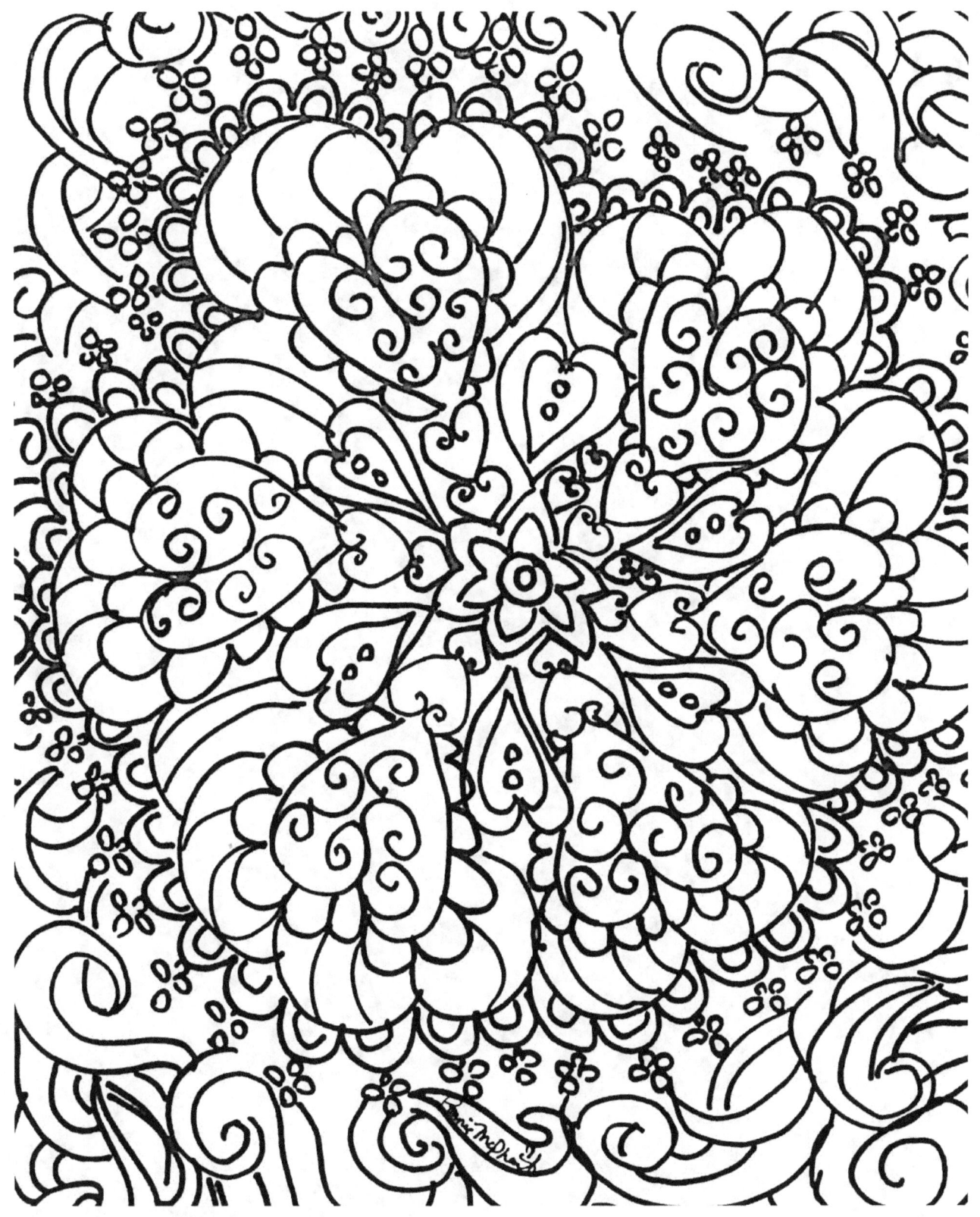

241

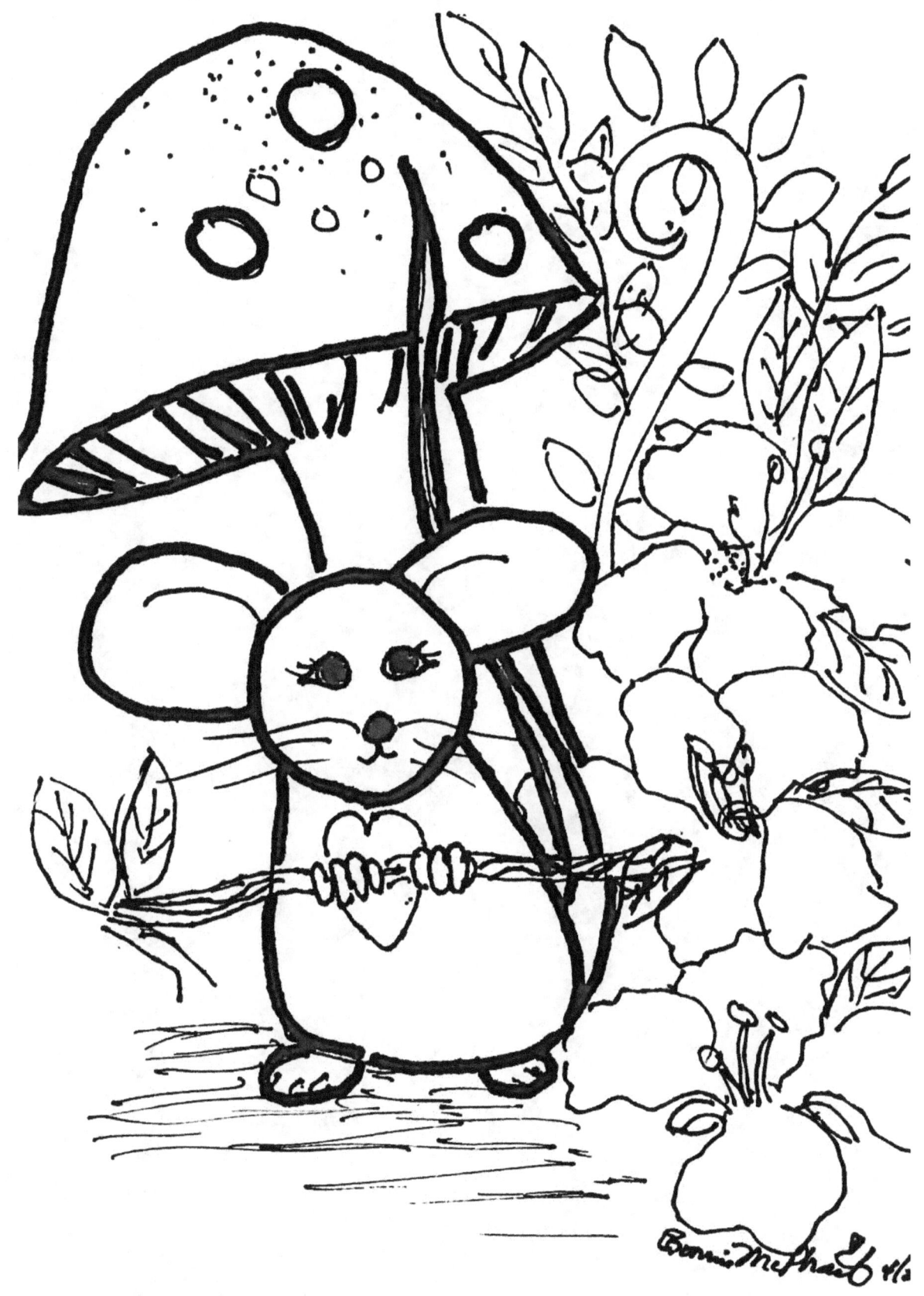

243

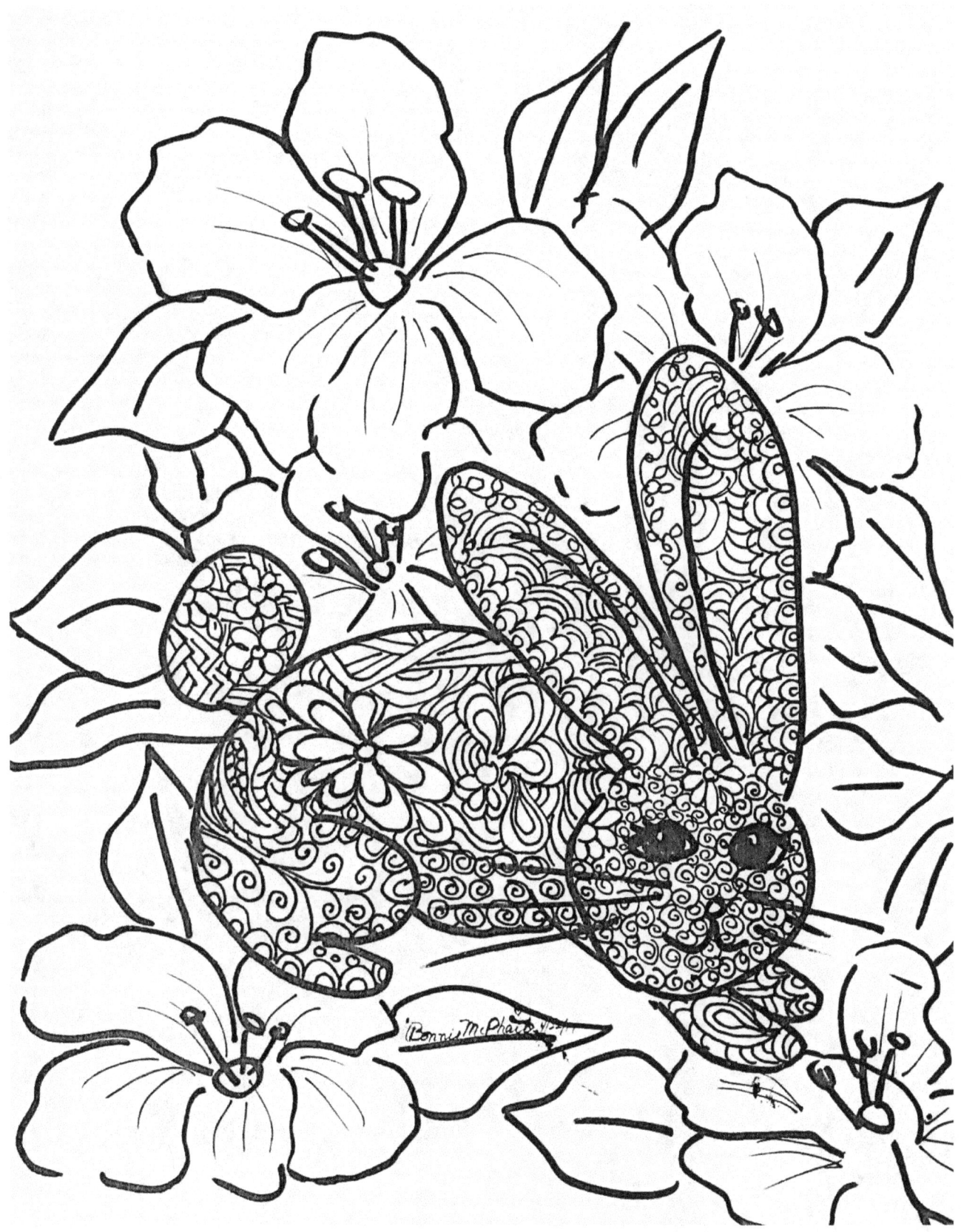

247

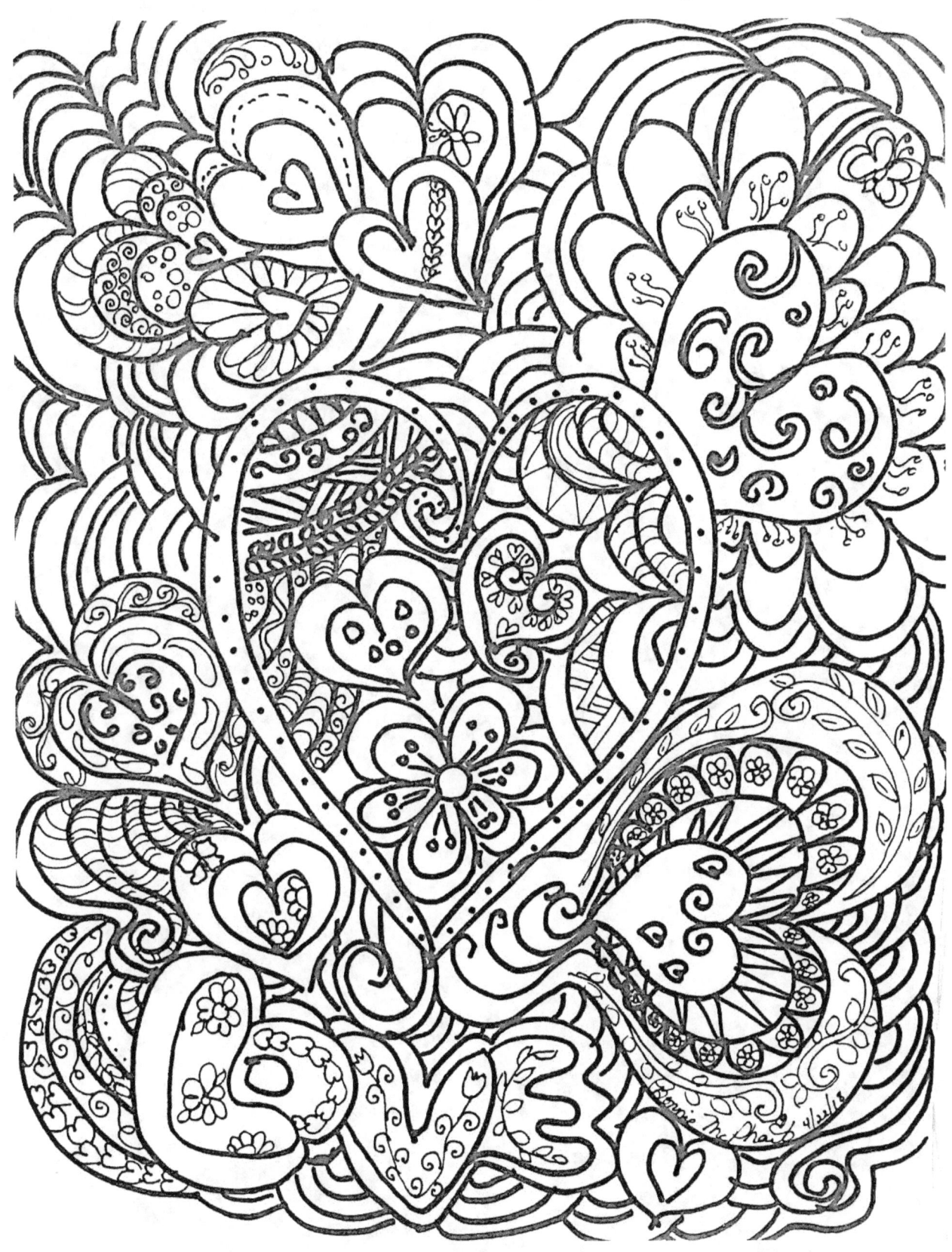

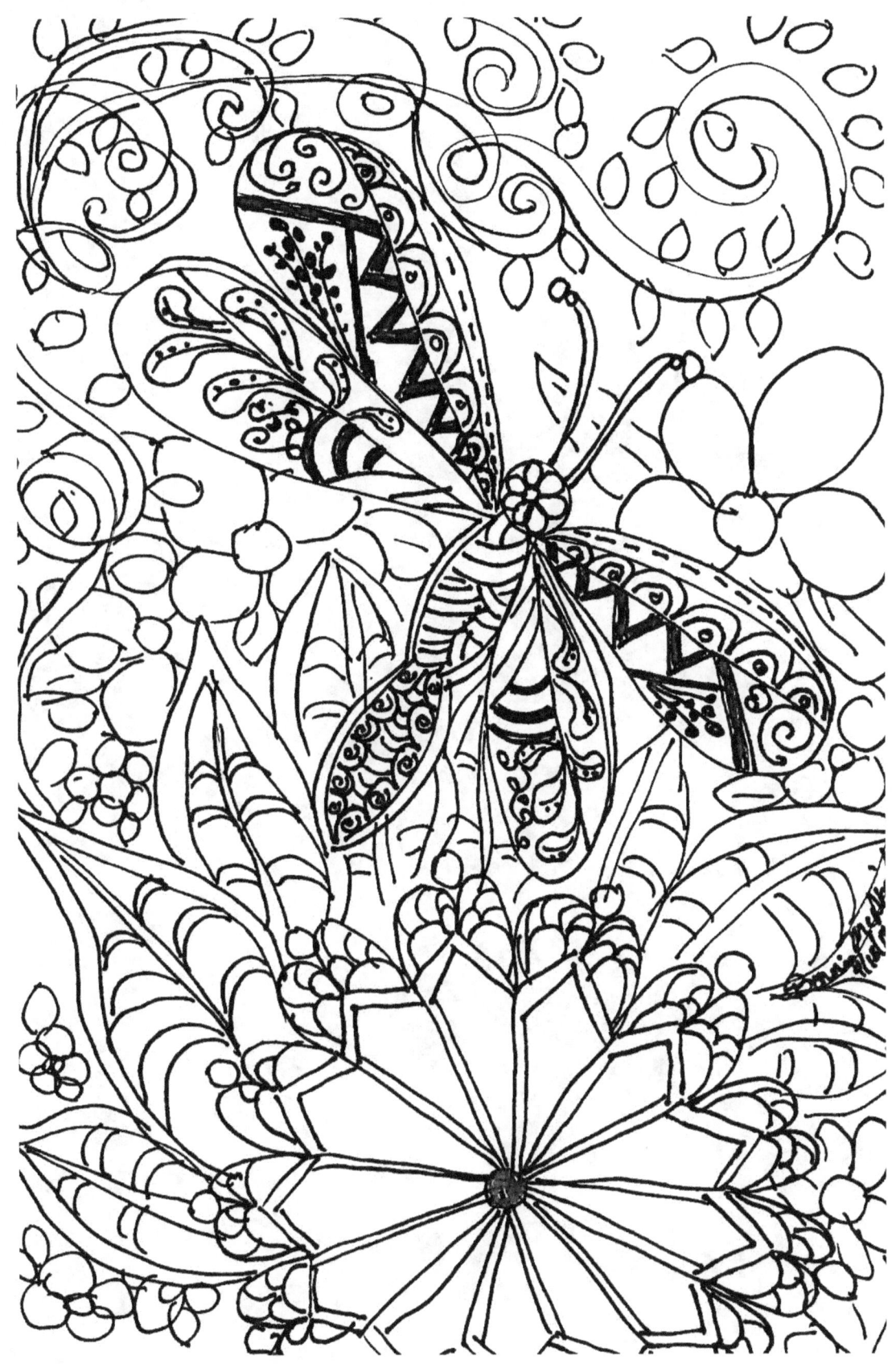

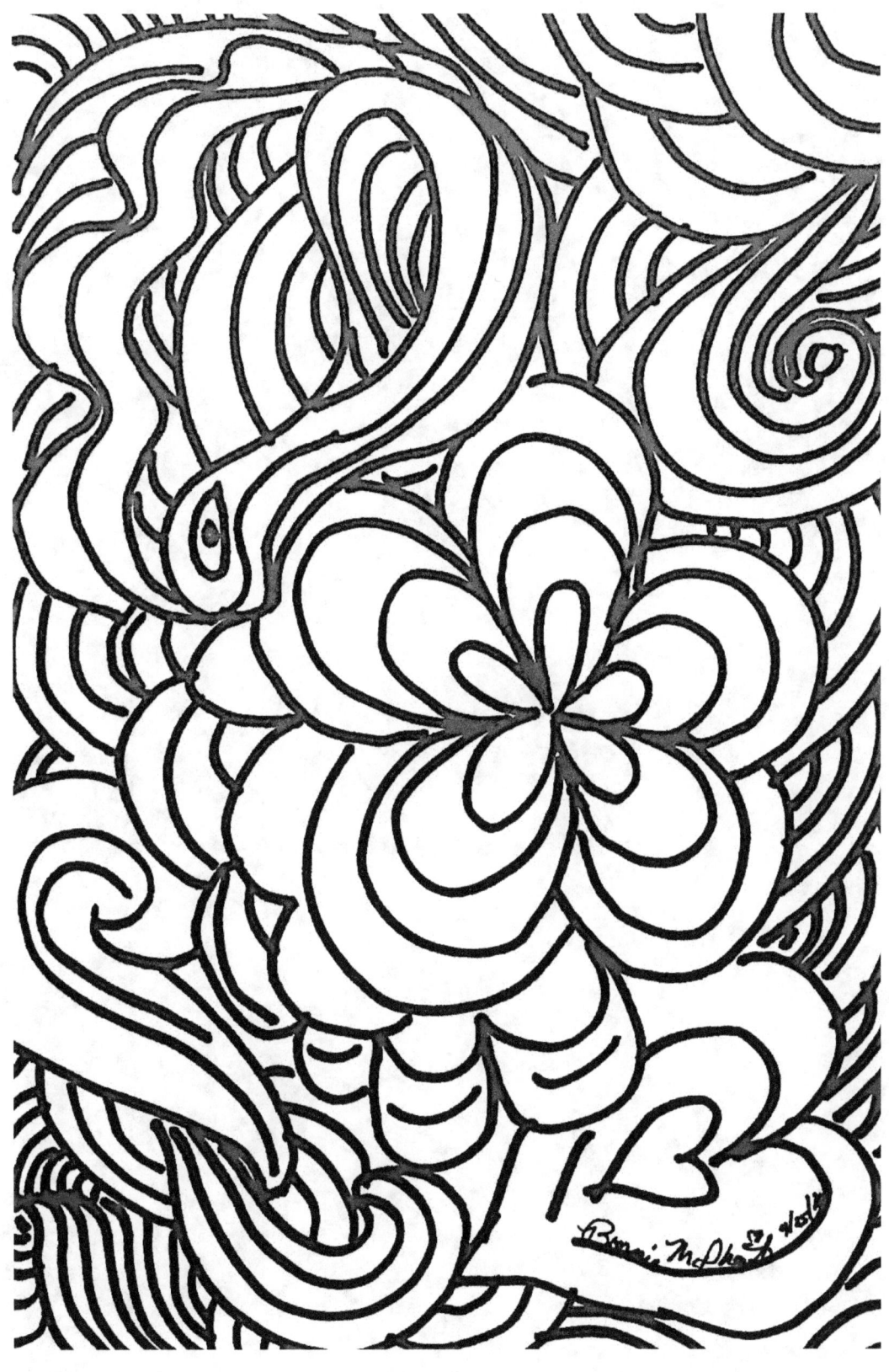

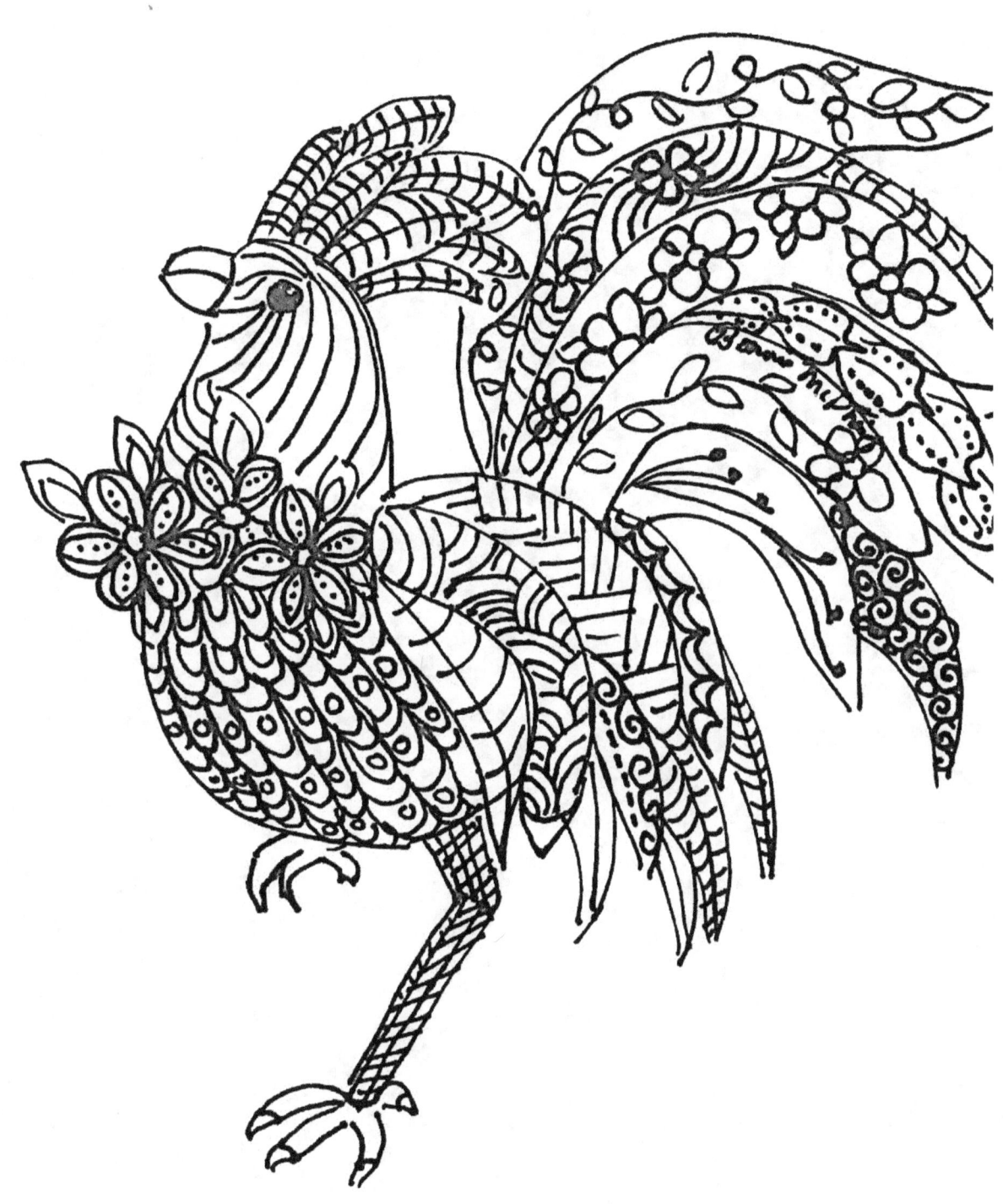

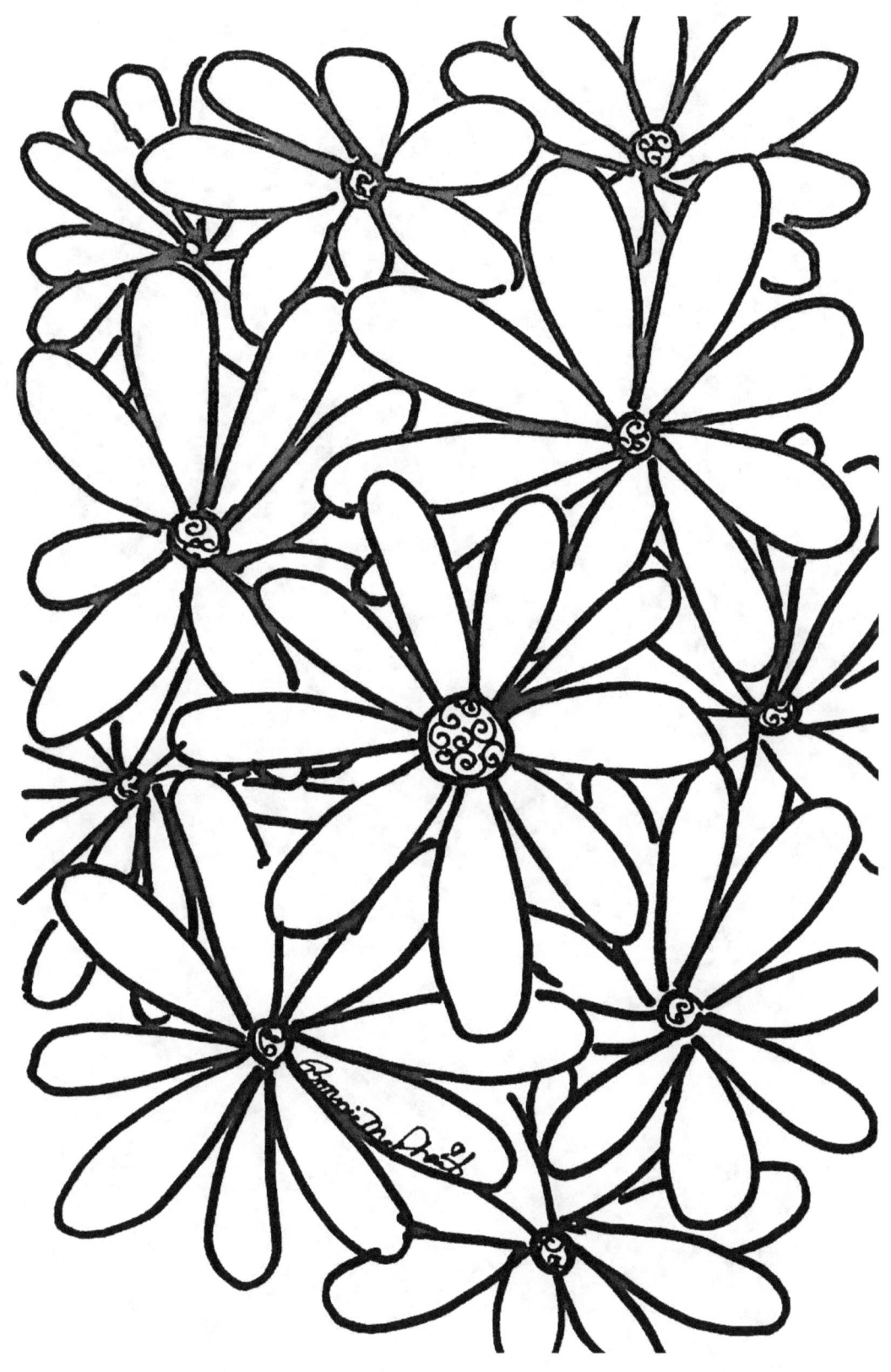

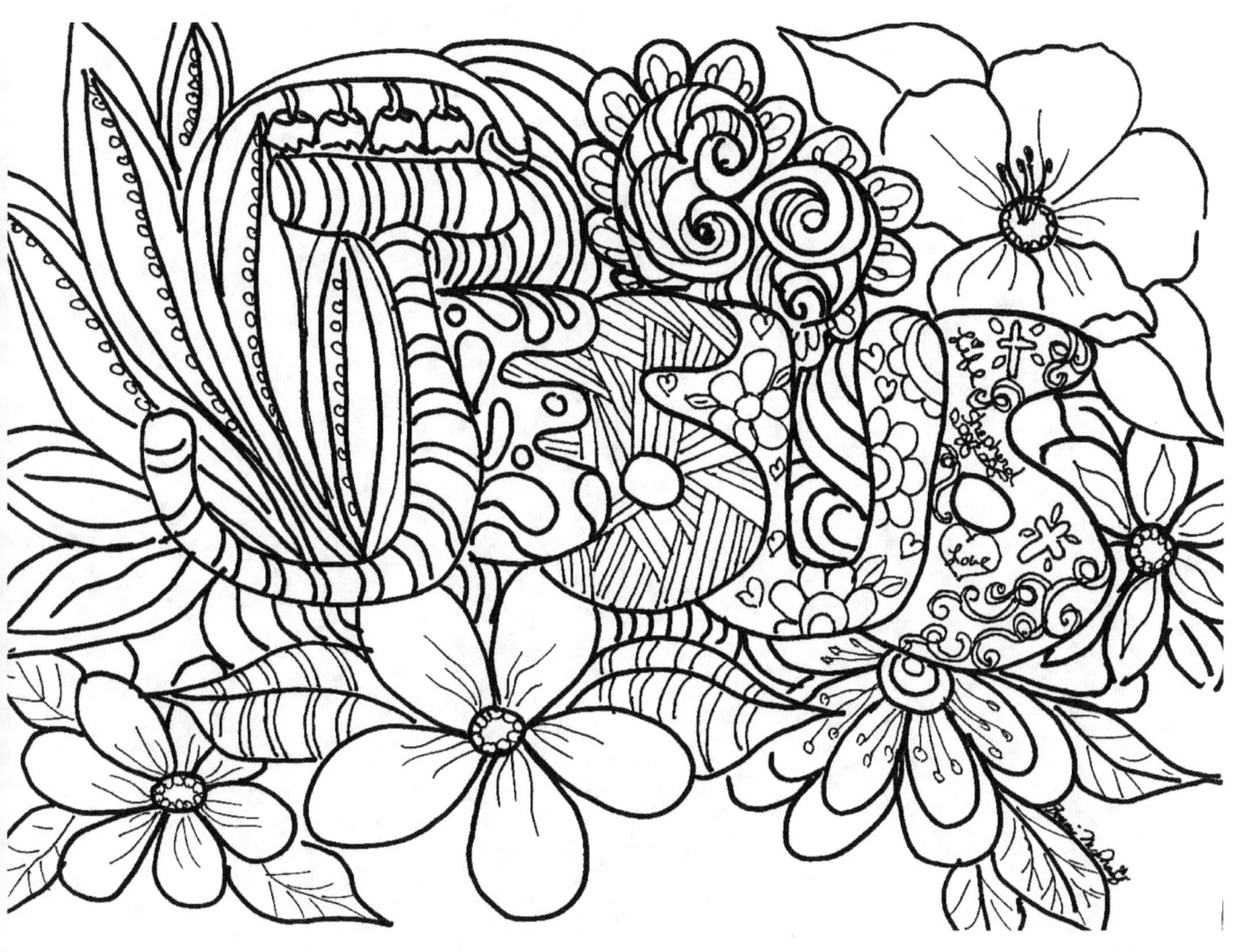

"Jesus looked at them and said, "With man this is impossible, but not with God; all things are possible with God." Mark 1027

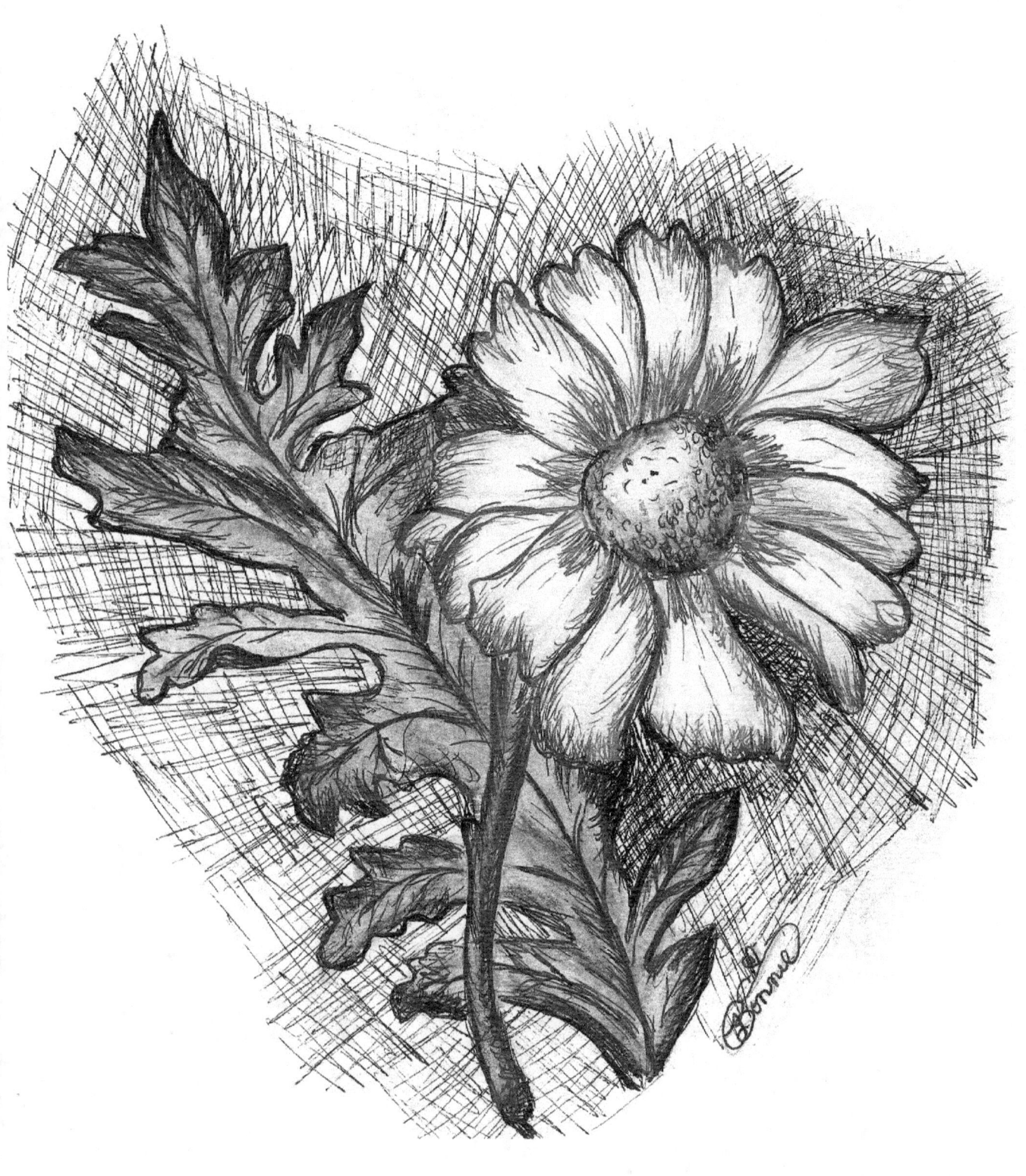

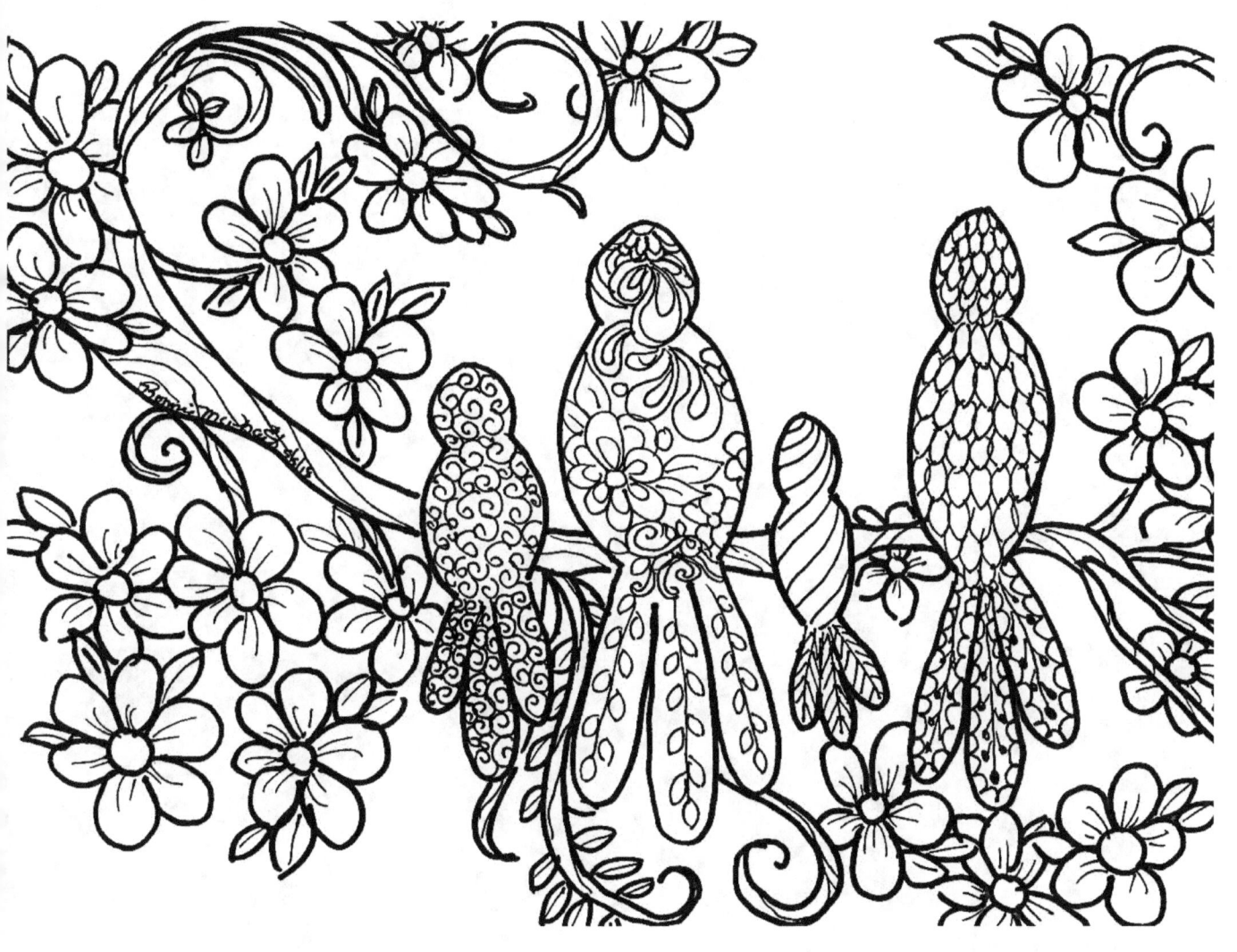

"In your relationships with one another, have the same mind set as Christ Jesus." 1John 4:15

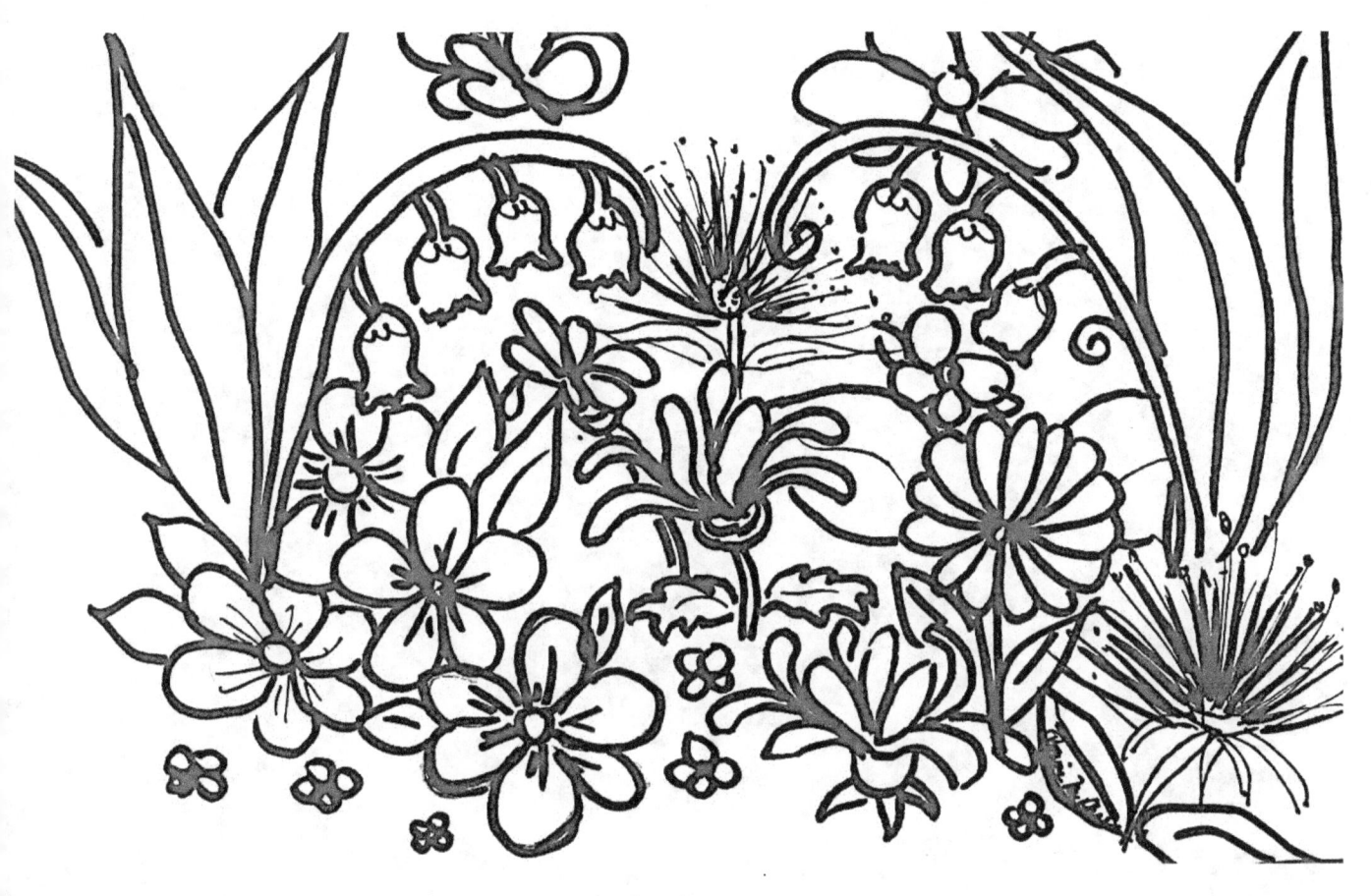

"For where two or three gather in my name, there I am with them."
Matthew 18:20

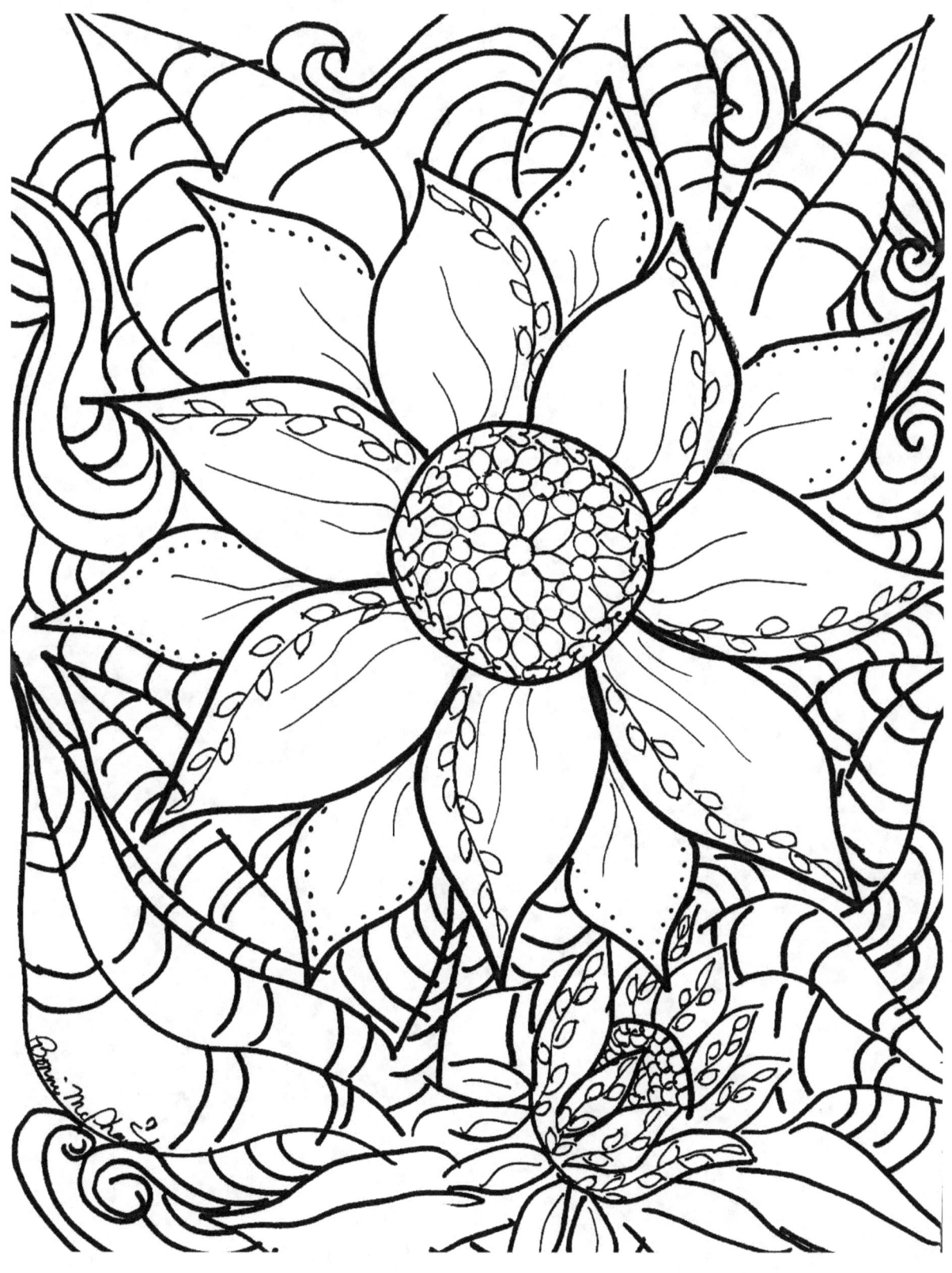

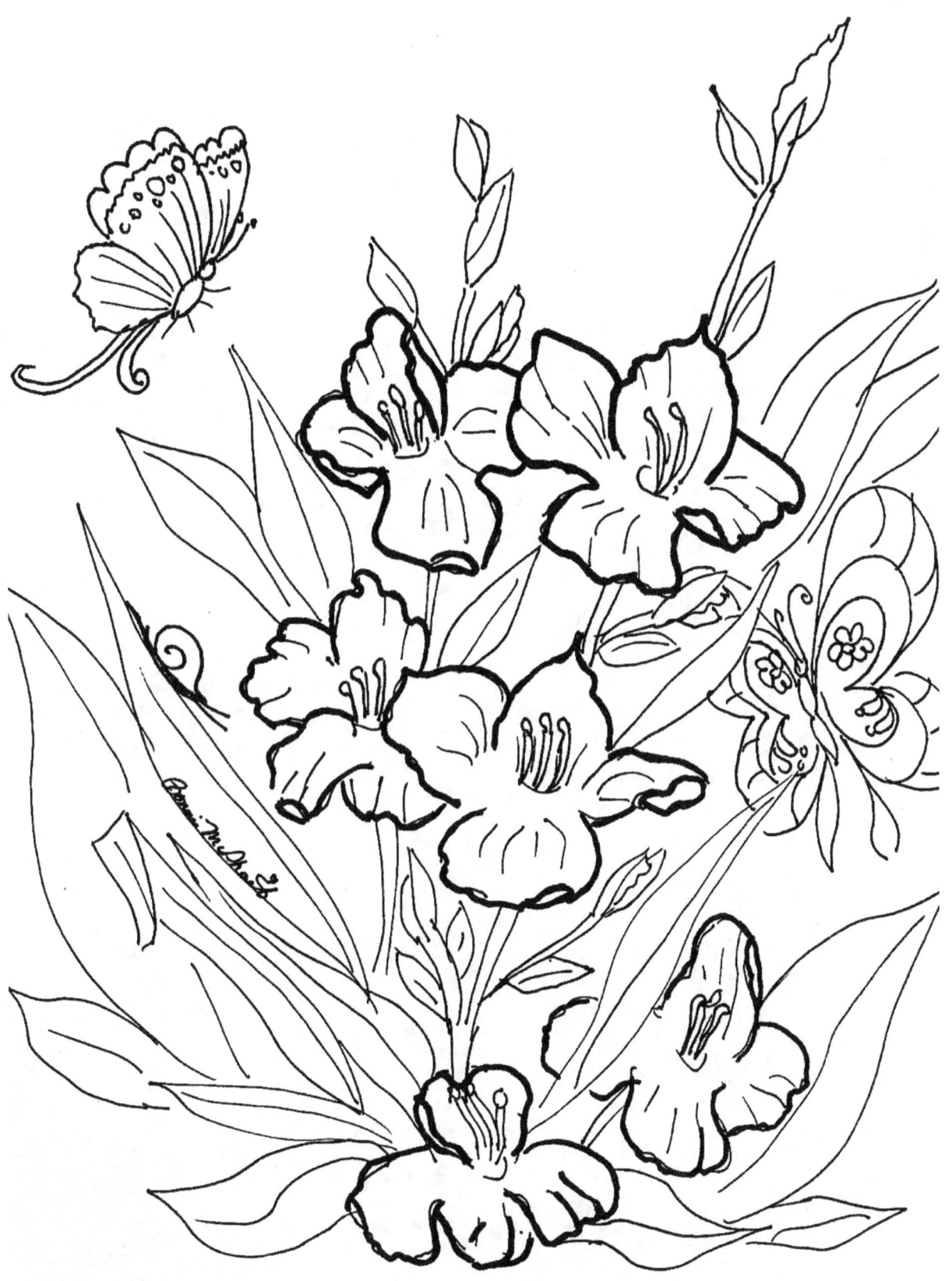

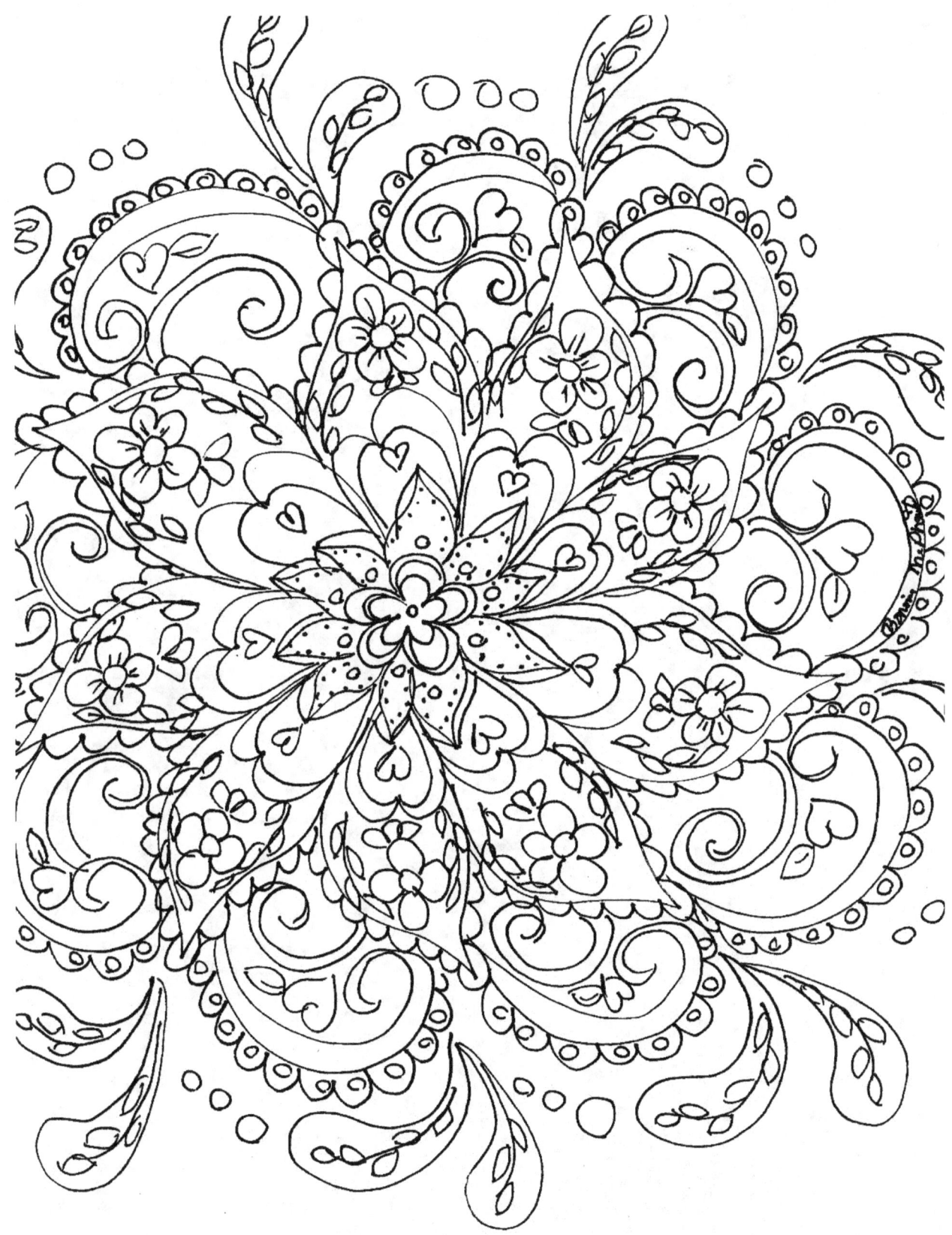

273

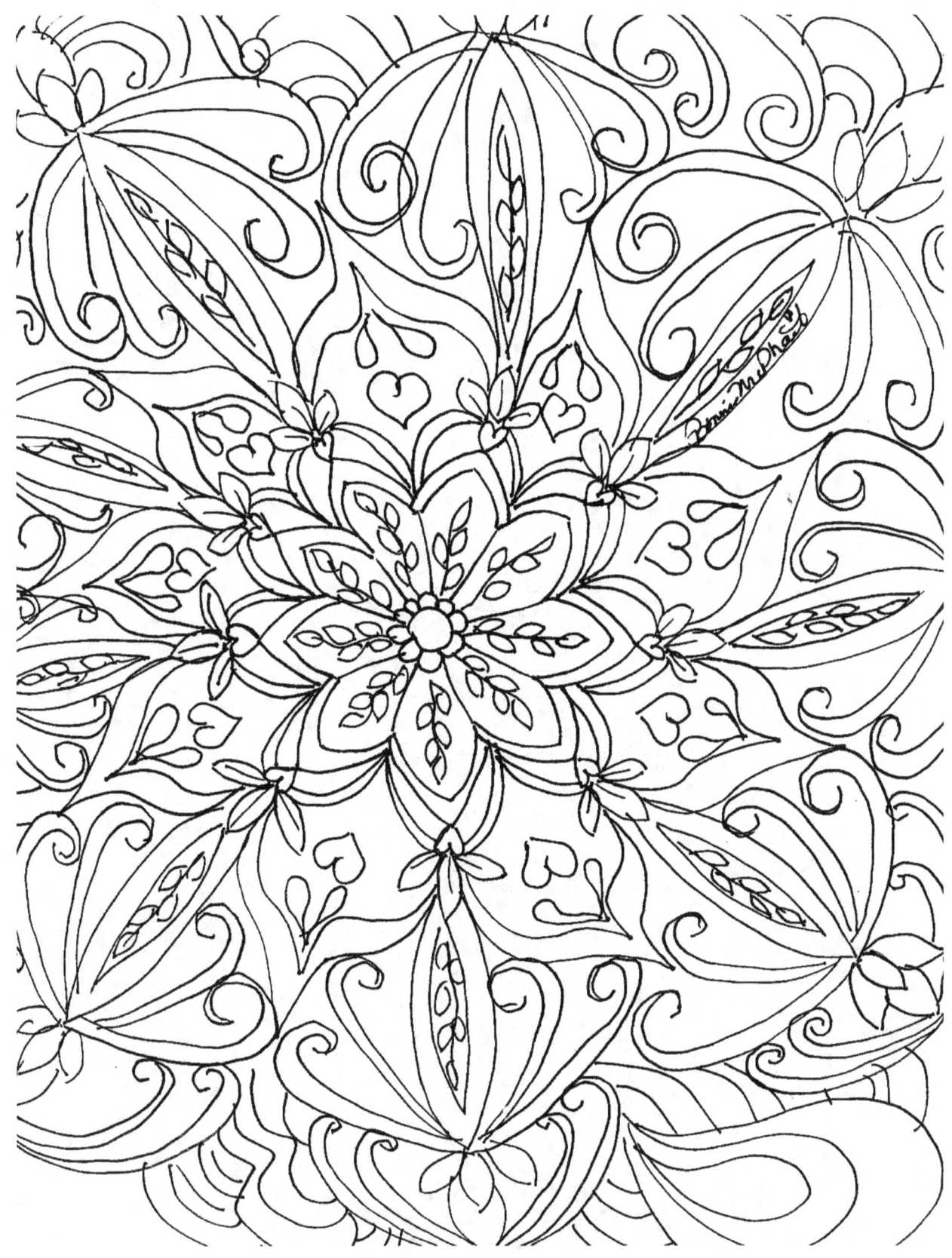

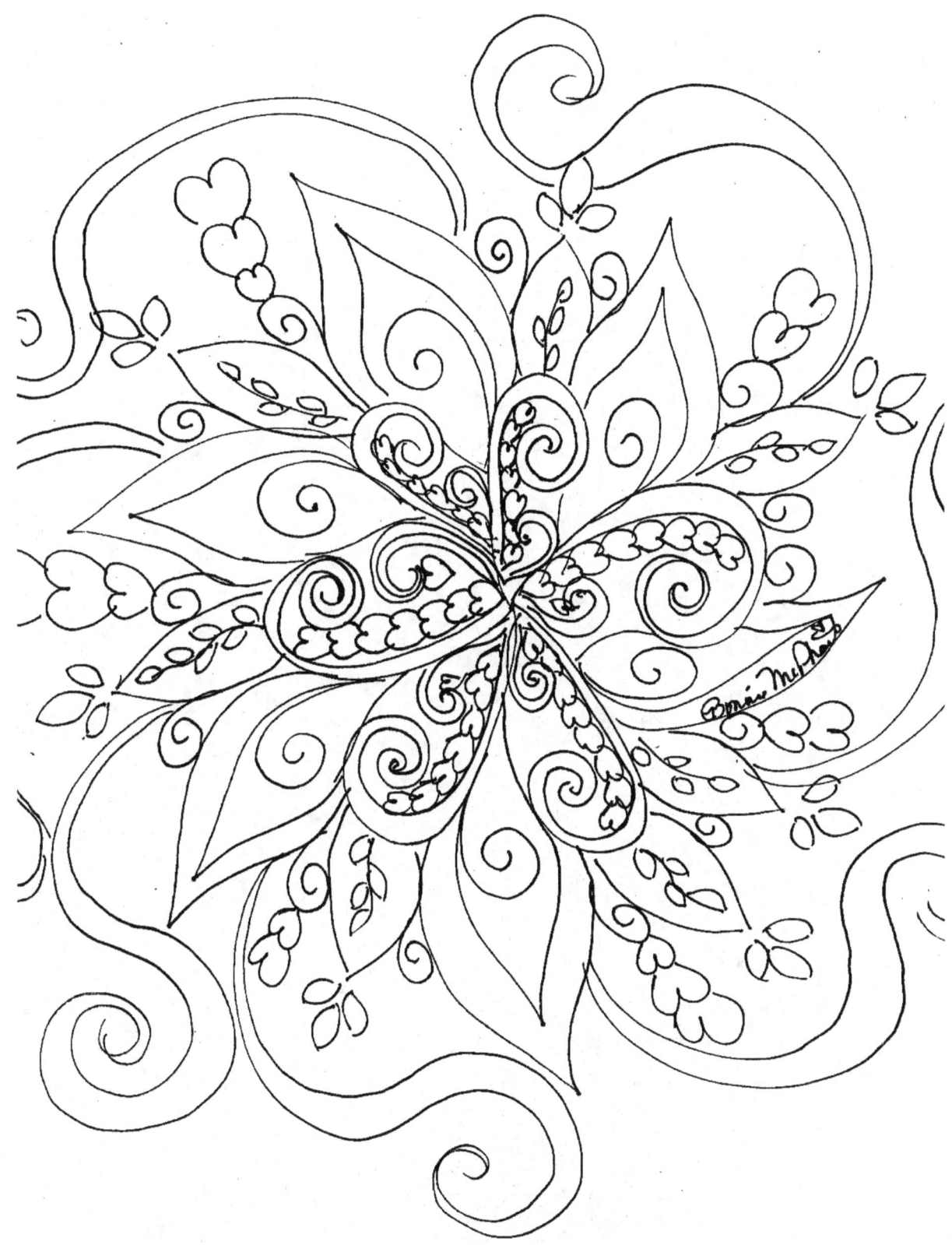

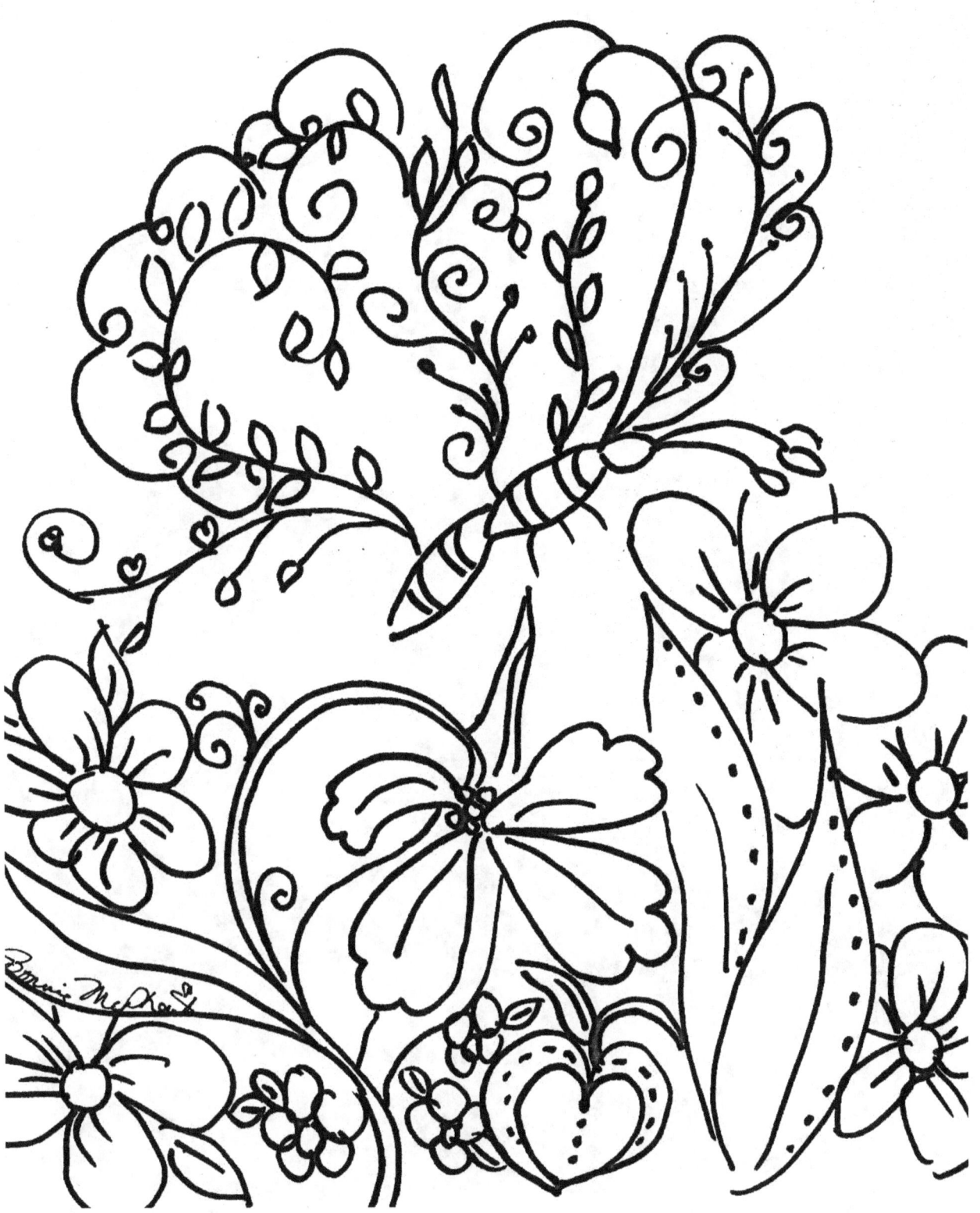

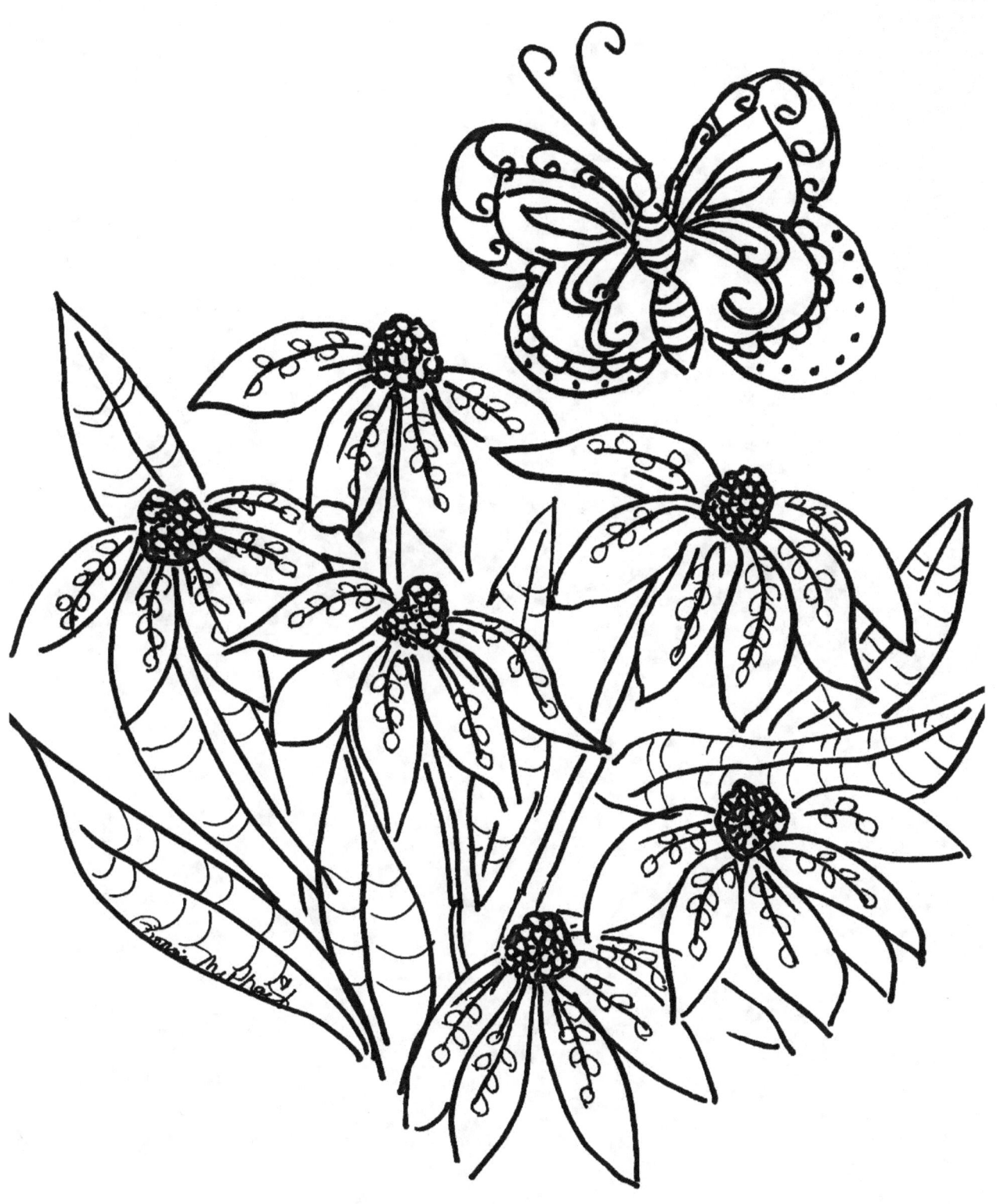

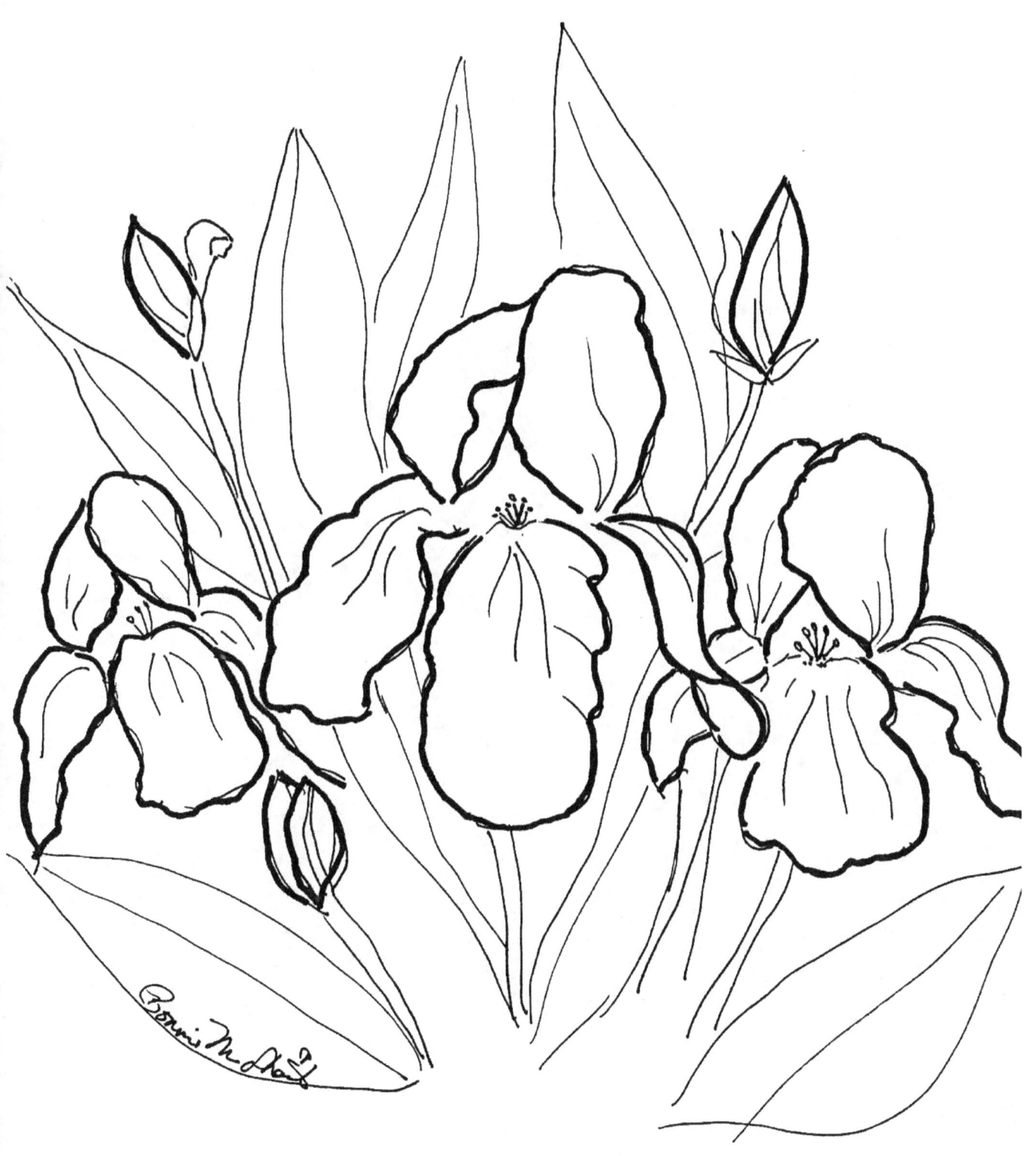

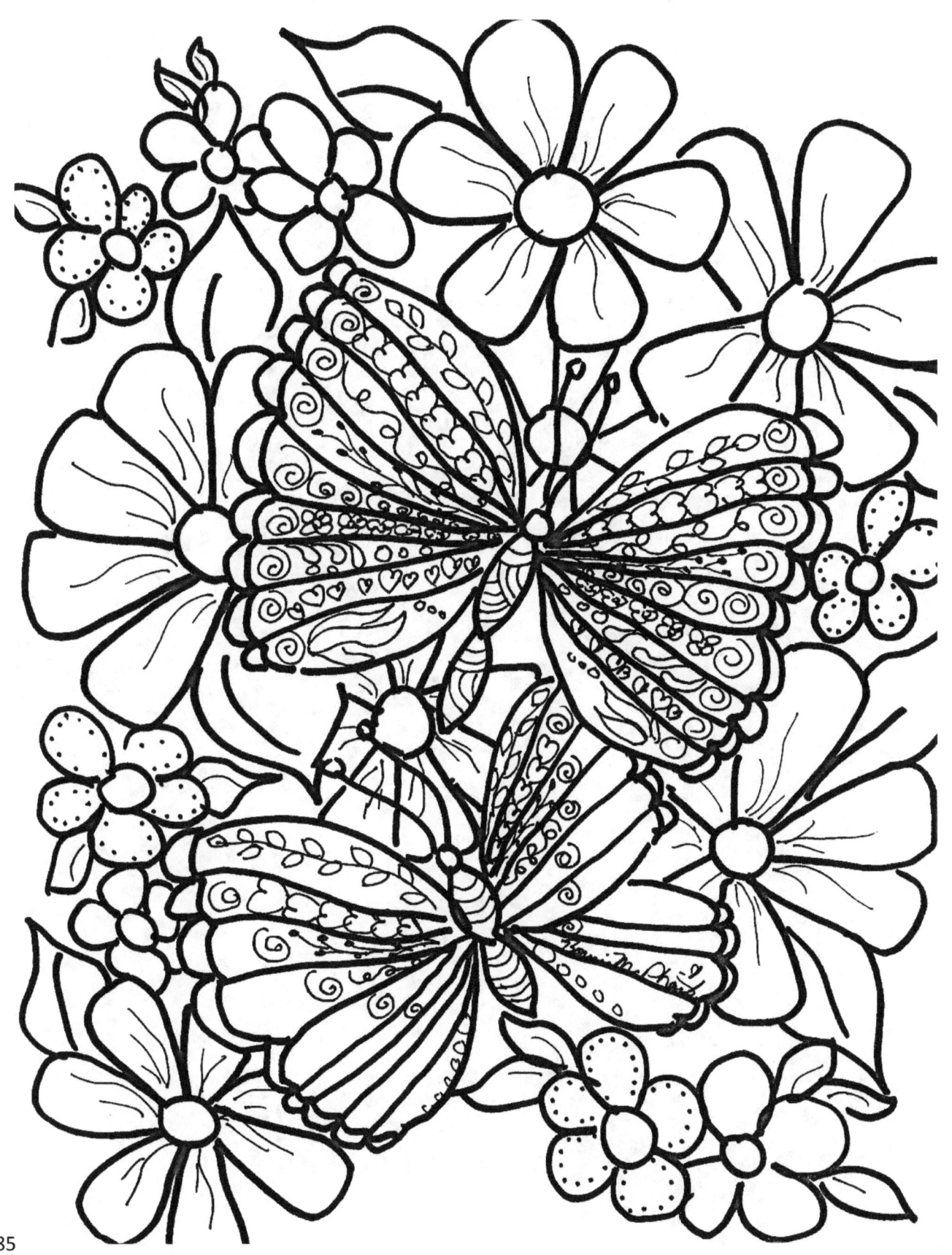

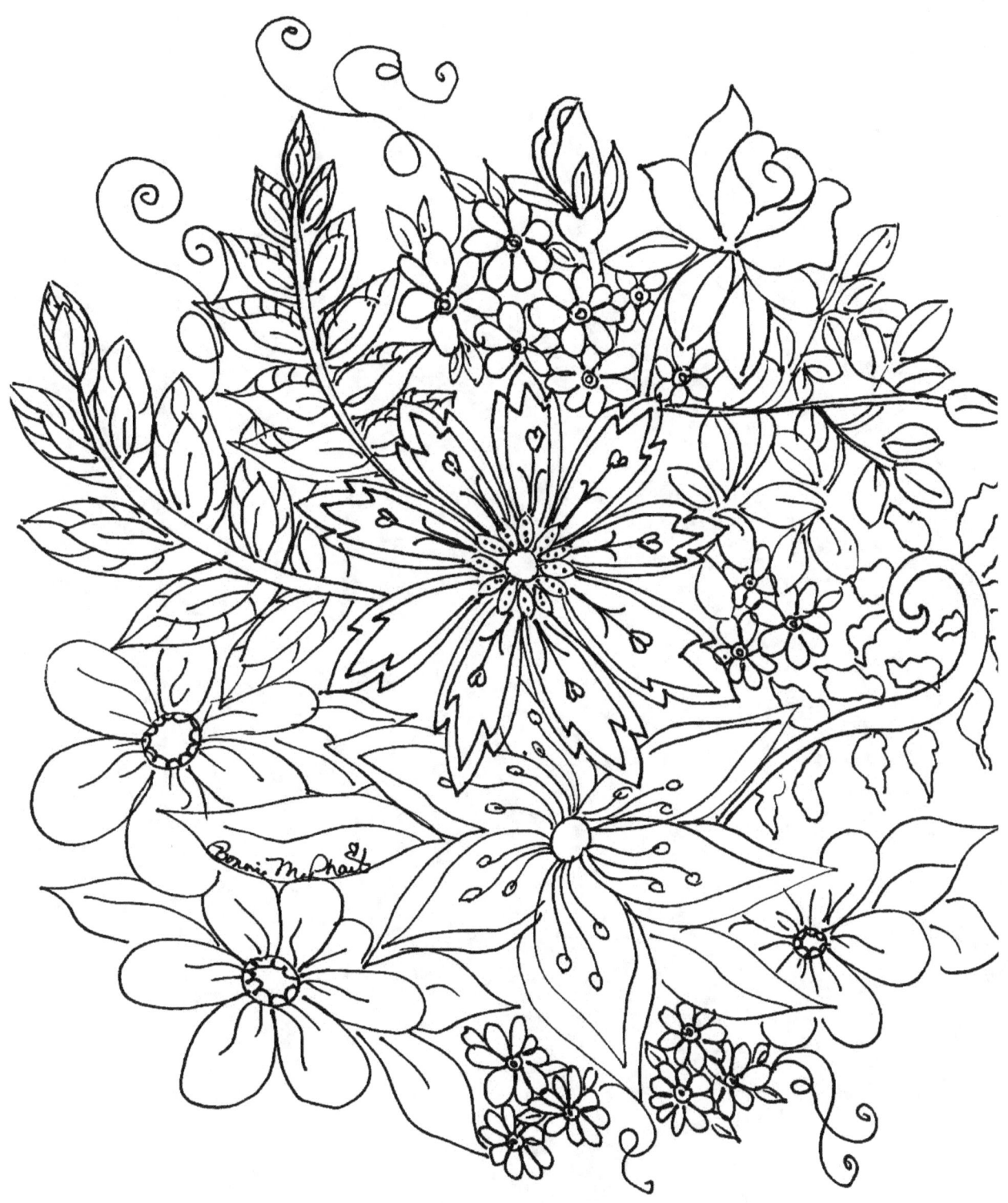

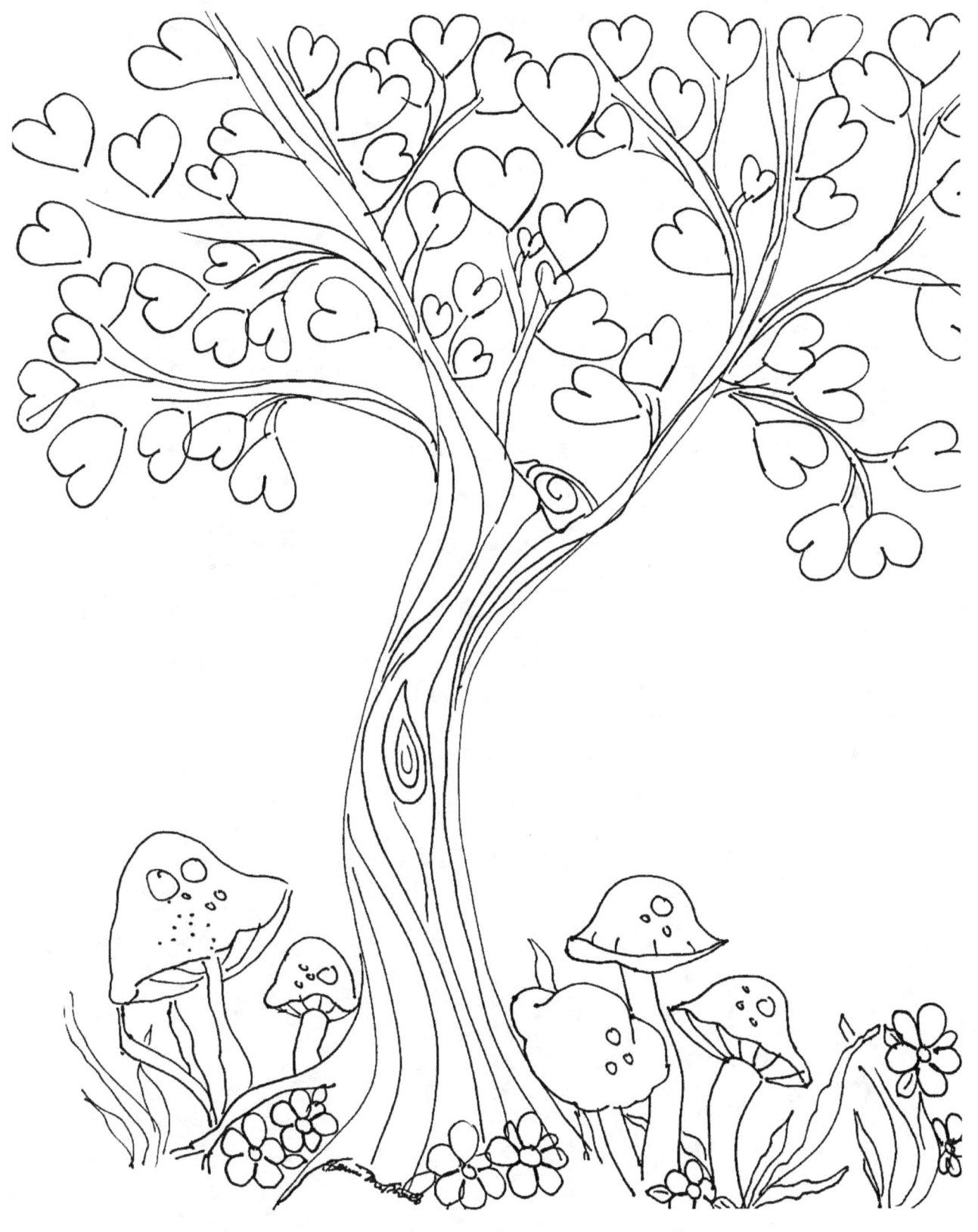

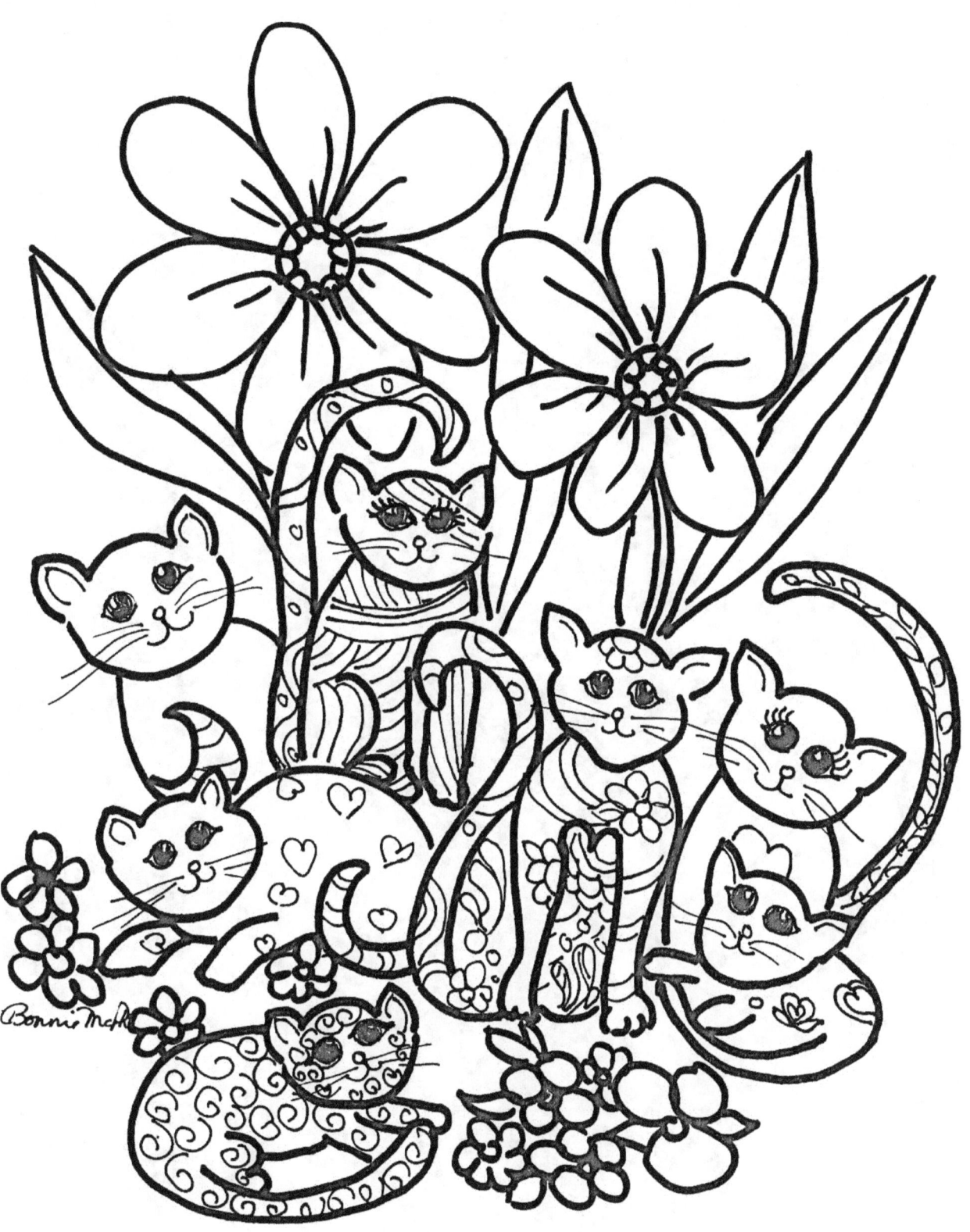

Bonnie McH

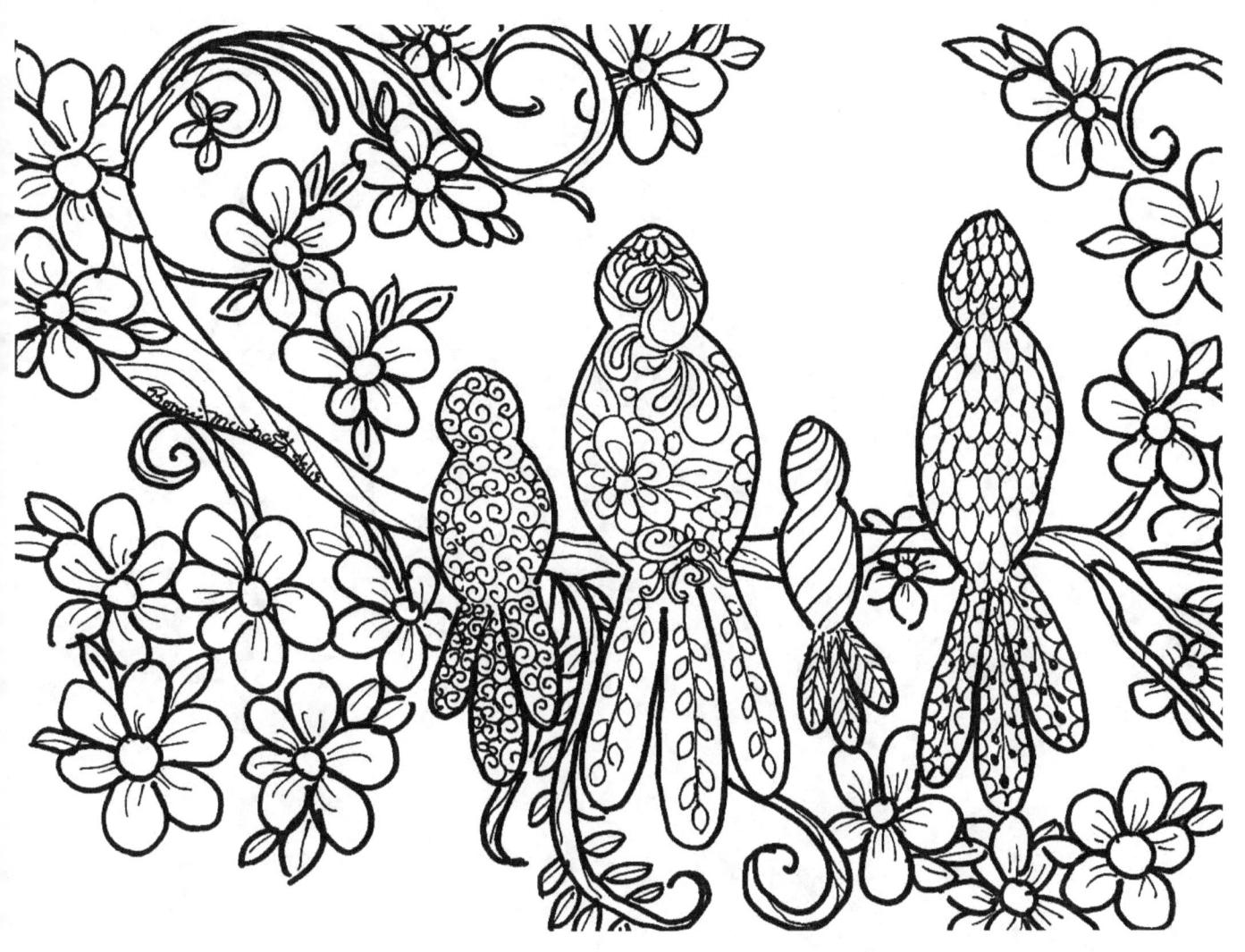

"The Lord is my shepherd. I shall not be in want. He makes me lie down in green pastures, he leads me beside quiet waters, he restores my soul. He guides me in paths of righteousness for his name's sake. Even though I walk through the valley of the shadow of death, I will fear no evil, for you are with me; your rod and your staff, they comfort me. You prepare a table before me in the presence of my enemies. You anoint my head with oil; my cup overflows. Surely goodness and love will follow me all the days of my life, and I will dwell in the house of the LORD forever." Psalm 23

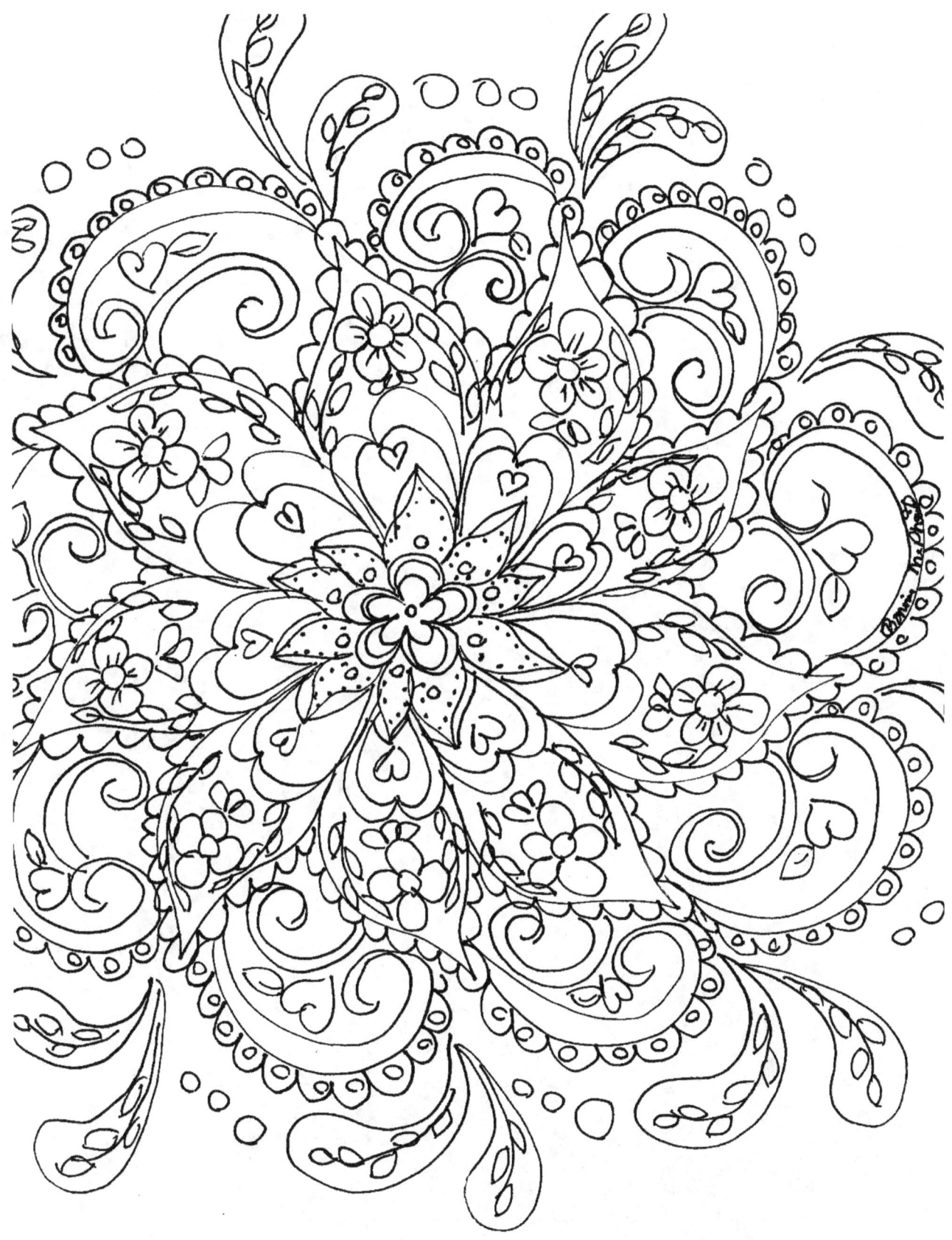

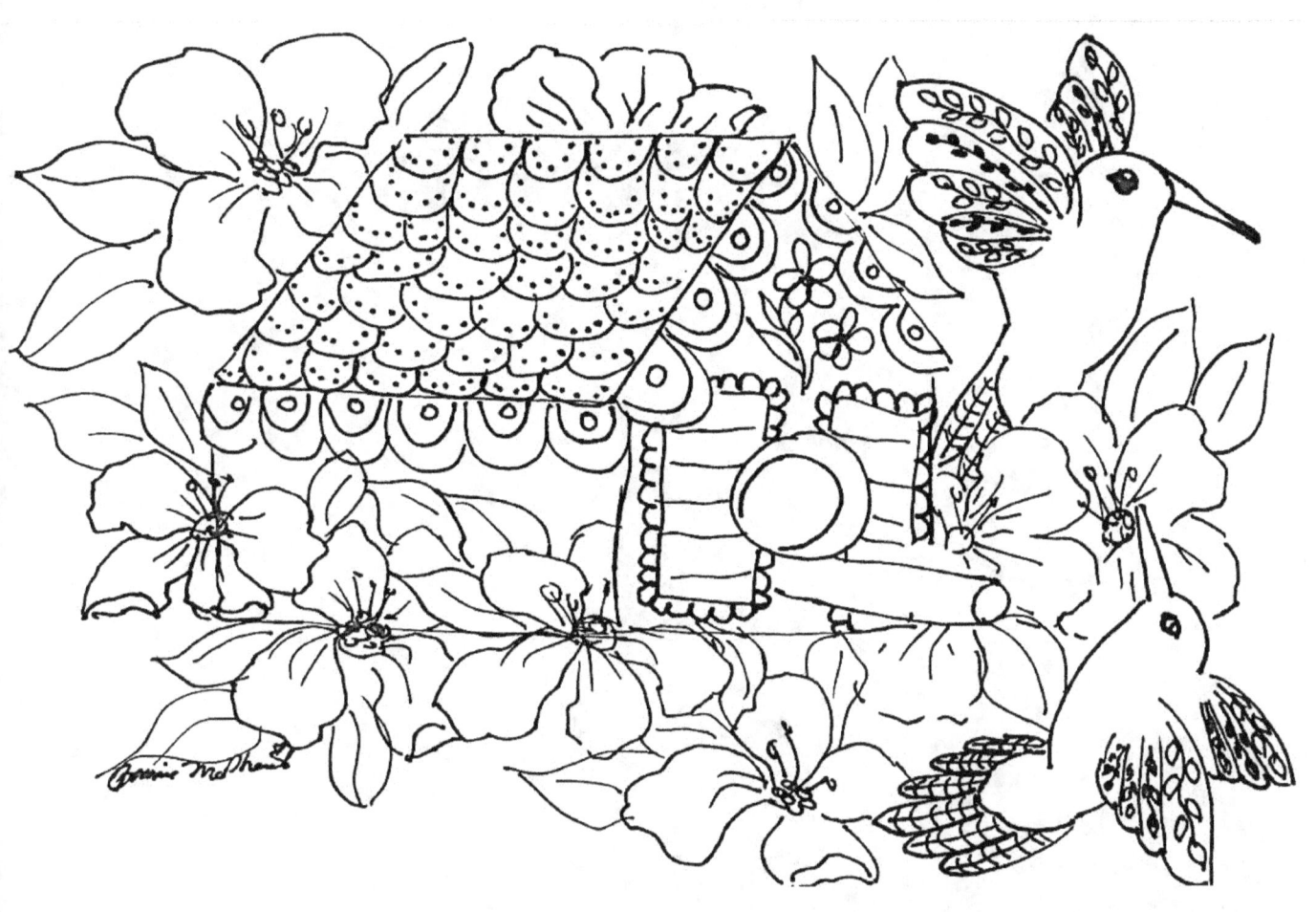

"I can do all things through Christ who strengthens me." Philippians 4:13

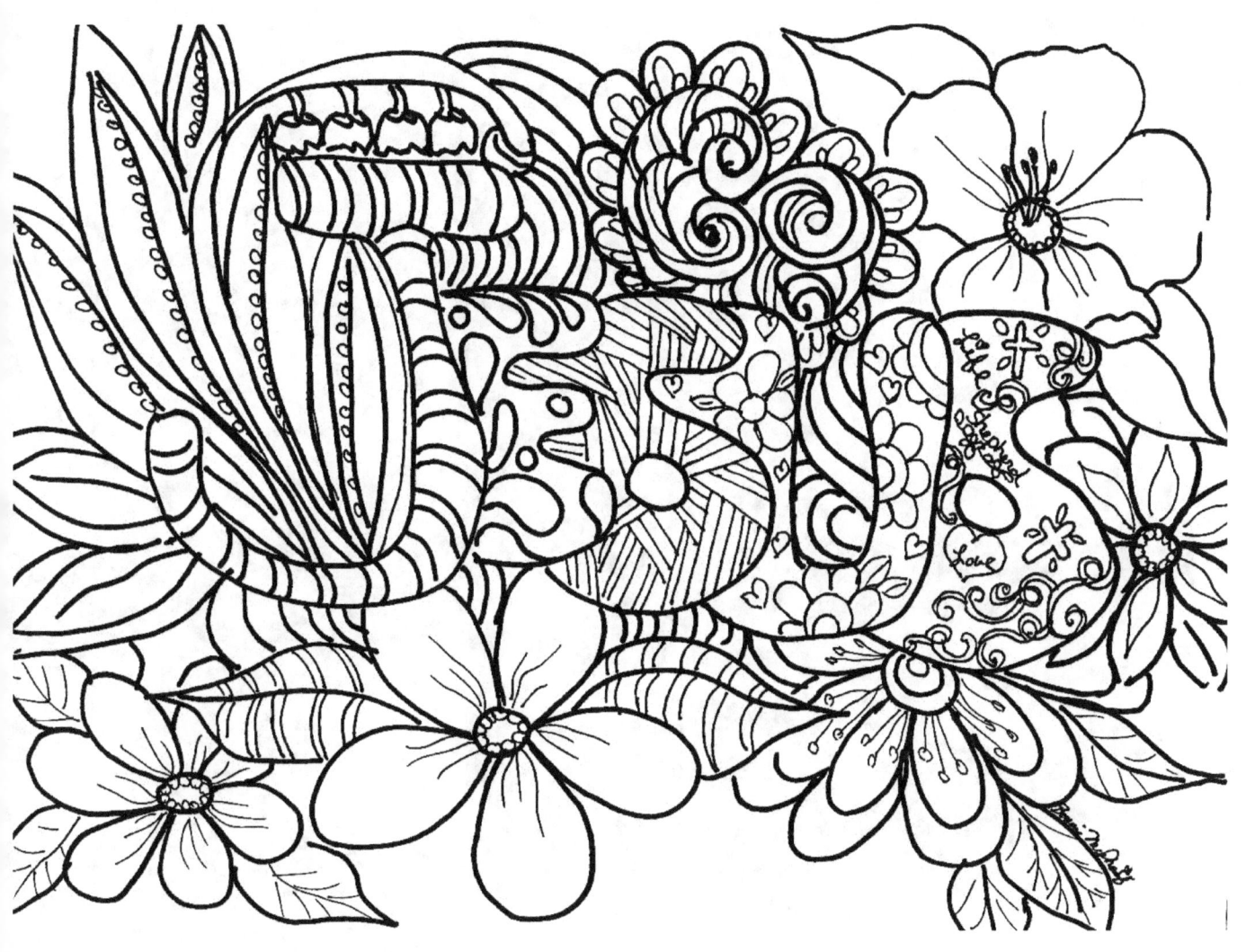

"For God so loved the world that he gave his one and only Son, that whoever believes in him shall not perish but have eternal life." John 3:16

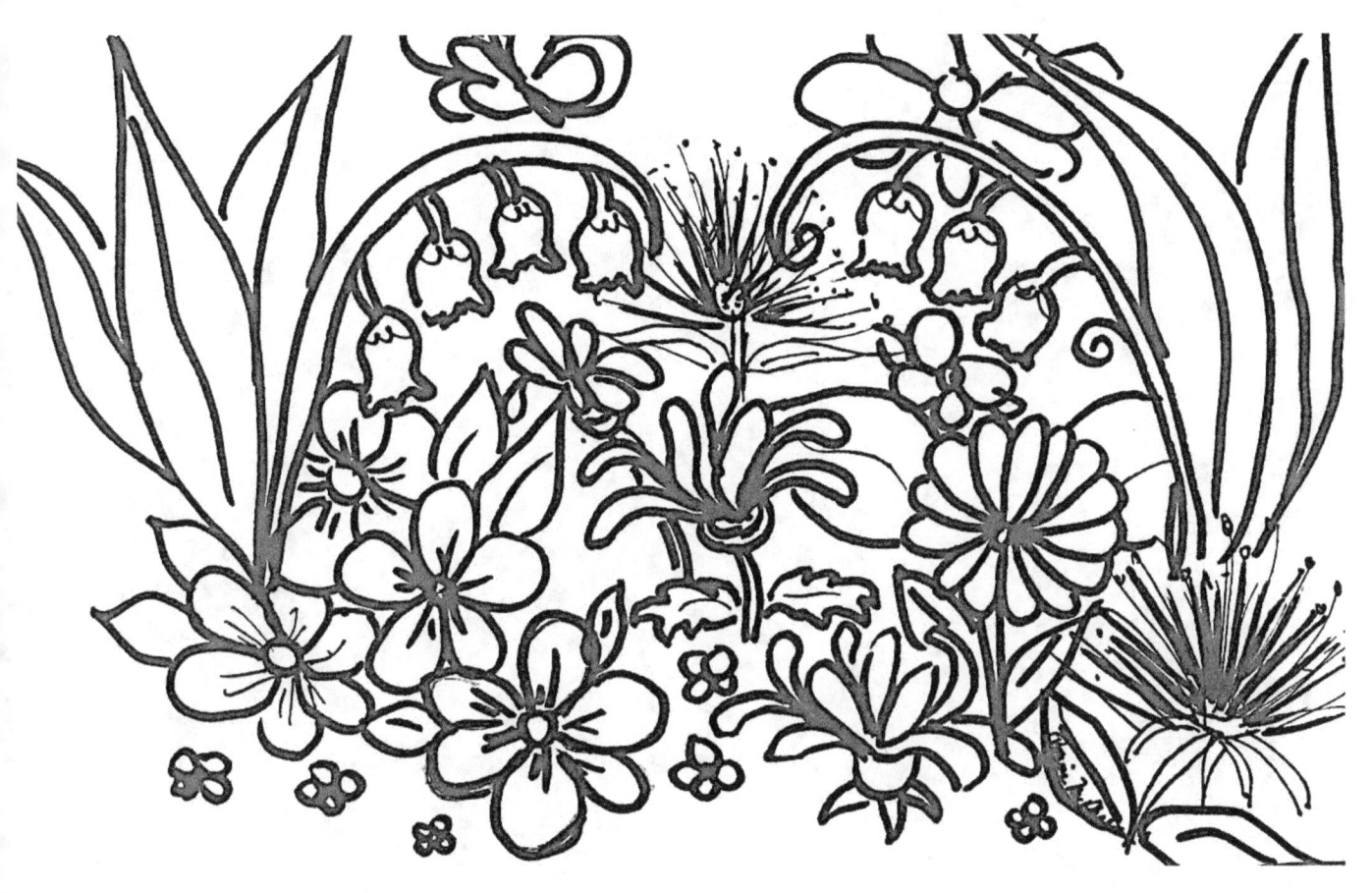

"Now I know in part, then I shall know fully, even as I am fully known. And now these three remain: faith, hope and love. But the greatest of these is love."

1 Corinthians 14:13

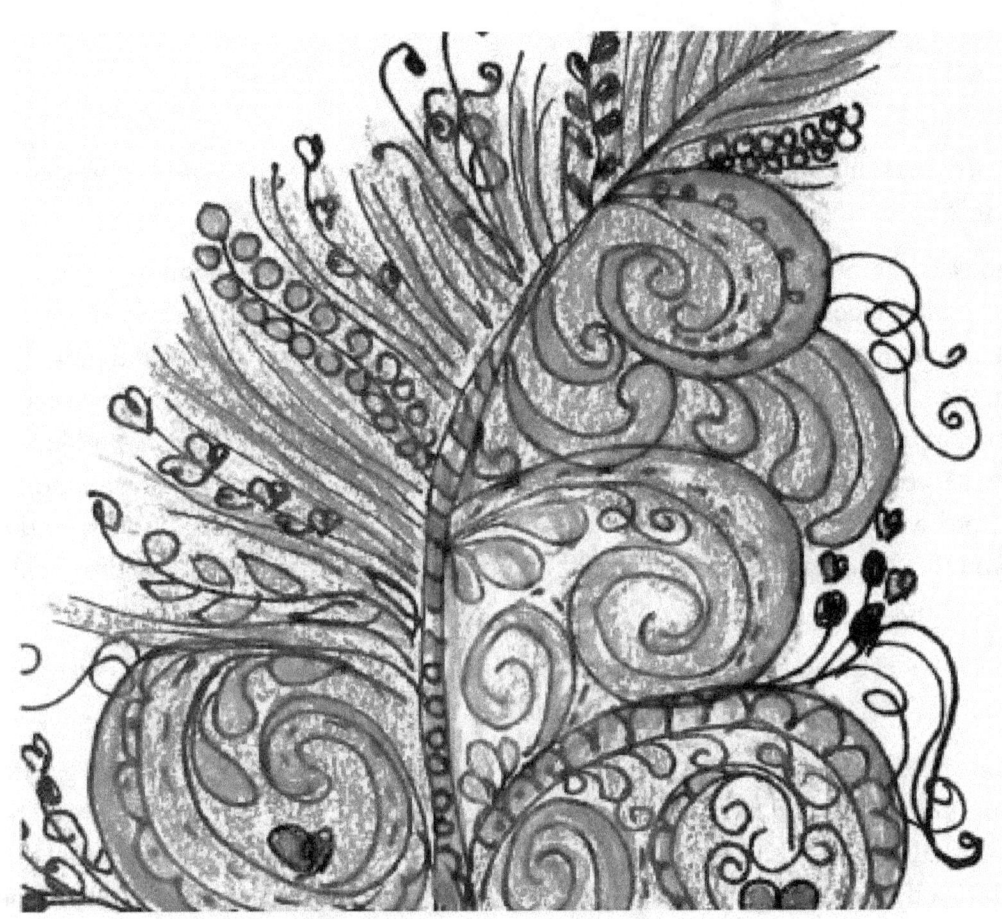

Love Comes Down
A Rich Multilayered
Spiritual Experience

Reverend Bonnie McPhail

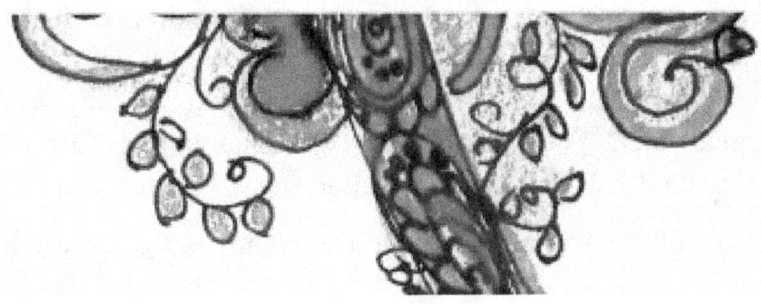

Love Comes Down

Dear Friends,

This is my personal favorite out of all hundred or more books the Lord has graced me to write. It is by far the best and most important work.

This book combines personal inspirational life stories and actual encounters with angels, there are places for you to write your thoughts and prayers and a daily devotional. This book also contains over 60 pages of original artwork for you to color and make your own, even the headers at the top of each page are designed to be colored in. The pieces are integrated throughout the book with many at the end of the book that have a blank space to write your thoughts, dreams, ideas and prayers. A keepsake to go back and see what the Lord was doing in your life of your own thoughts idea, dreams, prayers, and I promise you the Lord will speak personally and directly to you as you spend time in the pages of this book.

This book is designed not to just read but to truly be a rich, meaningful and powerful experience.

In the pages of this book you will work through one simple prayer a day along with a daily devotional that I was given directly from the angels just for you, and there will be personal journal entries along with activities including the coloring book pages that will lead you into a deep inner work so that you might experience the glories of all that God has for you.

I will guide you step by step along the way by using my own personal stories as a launch pad for you to experience your own.

I do not profess to have any ability in myself. The Lord has directed me to do this for your benefit. He loves you so very much! I am just an obedient vessel who is willing to take the time to listen and I write what I hear. So all the credit goes to my Lord and Savior Jesus where it belongs.

This book will bring enlightenment, encouragement, inspiration and make the scriptures come alive. I will teach you how to wage war in prayer and stand on the word of God and also how to "see" into the heavenlies. You are getting ready to encounter the Lord in a way like none other. You just have to be open and willing. God gives the most amazing and profound gifts and I cannot wait to share this with you!

I promise you God will speak directly to you. He has a specific and wonderfully unique plan for your life.

God loves you. He wants to speak to you. He wants to guide, direct and answer your prayers, he wants to take you right into the heavenlies and experiences the glories of heaven for yourself. He has an amazing plan for your life!

Love comes down and meets us right where we are. May he grant every heart's desire, bring you delight, and reveal amazing truths as you work through this book!

Blessings dear friends, from my heart to yours…

Pastor Bonnie

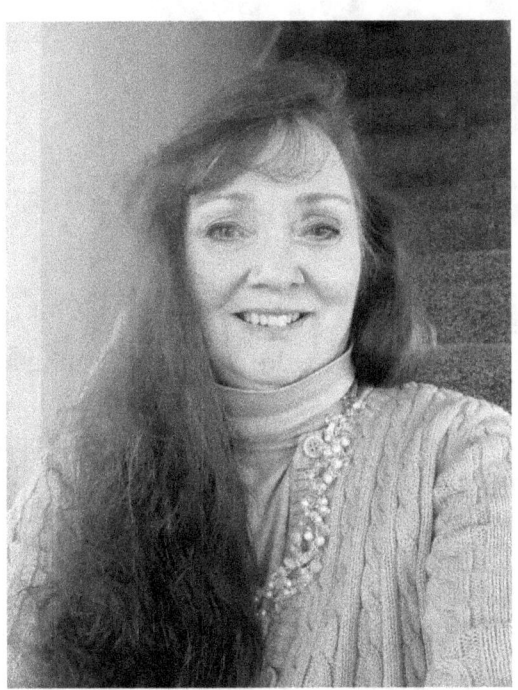

About the Author

Reverend Bonnie McPhail has a B.S. in Organizational Management and Ethics, an A.S.N. in Nursing, and certifications both in pastoral studies and life coaching. She is an ordained Assembly of God minister. Her nursing background gives her special insight into the emotional and physical needs of women, and she serves as a pastor to women when she ministers to them. Her work has been published both nationally and internationally, and she is available for conferences and workshops.

You can contact her via email if you would like to schedule a class or workshop at angelcare6@yahoo.com

"For this is how God loved the world: He gave his one and only Son, so that everyone who believes in him will not perish but have eternal life. God sent his son into the world not to judge the world, but to save the world through him." John 3:16 NLT Ask Jesus into your heart he will give you new life! He loves you!

www.ingramcontent.com/pod-product-compliance
Lightning Source LLC
Chambersburg PA
CBHW081716220526
45468CB00008B/1862